M000280863

Walking My Dog, Jane

Walking My Dog, Jane

from Valdez to Prudhoe Bay
along the Trans-Alaska Pipeline

Ned Rozell

Copyright 2020 by Ned Rozell

ISBN: 978-1-7339482-1-0

Contents

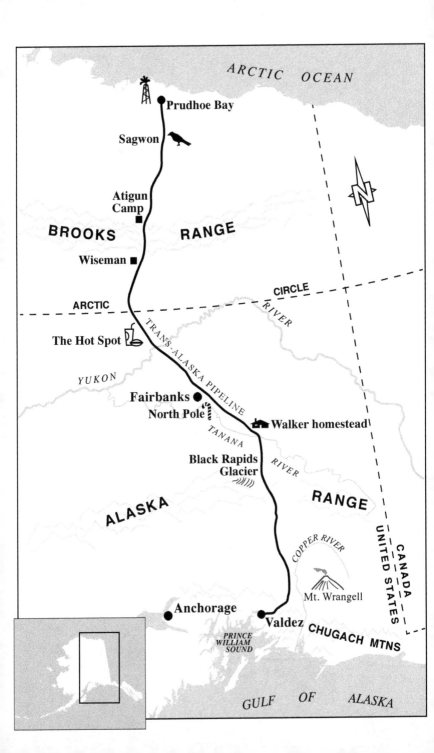

Introduction

Someone posted a sign at the Alyeska marine terminal in Valdez, where supertankers sidle up to wooden piers for oil fill-ups. The sign says:

At the terminal, walking, other than short distances from building to building, is not permitted

Nobody walks at the marine terminal. Nobody walks in Alaska's oil field, 800 miles north. Not many people walk in between, either. Alaskans drive, mostly, whether we have to go one mile or 20. We roll to work, insulated from the ground by tires and asphalt and upholstered seats. When covering longer distances, we use Cessnas or 737s. When we fly to the East Coast, we cover four time zones with our feet touching nothing but carpets and polished floors along the way.

Only losers walk. And old people, and people who have dogs. At twenty below and colder, it's a safe bet that any Alaskan on foot is walking away from a stalled car. Some teenagers walk, too, during the awkward the transition from childhood when they don't want to depend on Mom and Dad for a ride.

I was one of those teenagers, 17 years-old, six months from the start of Air Force basic training, drunk on seven beers bought with a fake ID. At a bar on the shore of an Adirondack lake, a guy I knew offered me a ride home.

"No thanks," I said. "I want to walk."

"But it's 20 miles," he said.

"I know," I said, "I'm going to walk."

I walked, heading toward home on a 60-degree spring night without a moon. As my eyes adjusted to the darkness, I scuffed the blacktop, pushing pine needles with my sneakers.

The road took me past a marina, part of a bay the shape of Florida. Boats were docked at the Tampa end. Because I was chilly and tired, I wanted to sleep. Finding a suitable boat, I looked around and saw no one watching. I unsnapped the vinyl boat cover and wormed inside.

After sleeping badly for a few hours on damp carpet that smelled of gasoline, I squirmed to the light. No one was around. The sun was filtering through the white pines, robins were singing, the beer was no longer with me. I was groggy, fully aware now that I had turned down a ride, that I now had to get home on my own. But I still liked what I was doing.

Listening to morning birds, I walked ten miles of road. The sun turned the night moisture to mist. A whitetail doe tiptoed across the asphalt, looked at me without alarm, and continued though the vapor. A few minutes later, a raccoon slunk like a cat, returning home from a night of ambushing mice and voles. Like the deer, the raccoon paused when it saw me but didn't run.

I hiked to a cross road, heavy with Sunday morning traffic. People going to church, golfers headed for the country club, shoppers rolling west to the Aviation Mall. For the first time ever, I walked backwards and extended my thumb.

A man stopped. He drove a green van. His name was Phillip. He played stand-up bass on a sternwheeler that circled the lake, had just finished his all-night shift. Phillip gave me a ride five miles to my parents' house, which was then my house. He didn't make a pass at me, a skinny boy with a girlish face, as would other drivers on later trips. He said he was happy to help.

When I appeared at the door, my mother's eyes widened. She wasn't mad. One of her greatest gifts to her children was her willingness to let us make our own mistakes.

"Where have you been?"

"I slept in a boat!"

Since sleeping in that boat, I joined the military, came to Alaska, finished my tour in Mississippi, worked at a radio shop in New York for a year, returned to Alaska on my own. College at the University of Alaska in Fairbanks was the reason I gave, the reason people accepted. But there was more. I learned in the Air Force that Alaska was a special place, a place where people didn't mind that they smelled like wood smoke, a place that seemed to fit an image I had of myself.

Over the next 10 years, tastes of real Alaska came slowly — napping on dry muskeg with a crew of 14 other men, one woman, while fighting fires in forests with no roads. Hearing a bull moose's grunt as I drifted past on the

Yukon River. Running on an old mining trail off the Yukon, stopping at the sound of a twig snap, staring into the eyes of a gray wolf.

With the real Alaska came the other real Alaska — the rumble of jets from Fairbanks International Airport, the ice-fog moonscape of 40 below, warehouse stores offering everything from tanning beds to 10-pound bricks of cheese.

Through a decade in Alaska, I've had two constants — a rented cabin two miles from the university in Fairbanks and a dog named Jane. The cabin is frame, heated by spruce, birch and aspen, sometimes willow that smells of soap. No water pipes. An outhouse. The dog is a chocolate Lab, ears of silk, obedient to the point of meekness, prone to overeating.

"She's just a dog," a friend often reminds me. I know, but I have a deep emotional attachment to this dog. The way she groans when she plops down, the way she leans into me when I knead her ears in the morning, the way she makes me laugh when she barks at hot air balloons.

Why not do something great with a great dog? Five years ago, I wanted to take Jane on a hitchhiking trip, from Fairbanks to Hudson Falls, New York. Think of the rides I would get, with a dog wearing a backpack. I chickened out a day before heading off across the continent, alone, leaving Jane with my girlfriend.

No chickening out this time. Jane didn't have enough good years left. And the path I chose across Alaska — the trans-Alaska pipeline — was perfect for a dog. Next to the pipeline is a gravel road bounded on all sides by muskeg, forest and mountain. Jane would carry a pack, but she would be free to follow her pulsating nose for an entire summer.

This trip was not just a four-month walk with the dog. Here was a chance to get to know better a land that will not allow me to return to upstate New York, the home of my mother, father, and two brothers, with a sister close by.

Why Alaska? I can't drive to catch a Yankee game from here, but I do have wilderness less than an hour in any direction. I can't buy a meal for less than five dollars, but white Christmases are a sure thing. I can't recycle a bottle, but I can get the feeling I'm the first one to do something, like standing in a remote valley, even if I'm not the first.

Here, I've bounced from newspaper receptionist to lawnmower operator to wild lands firefighter to park ranger to science writer. My current job is half-time, from one to five p.m. Monday through Friday. The schedule gives me plenty of time to squander, but there's a price: no hot shower to chase the chill after a ski, water jugs that freeze to the bed of the truck, limited reading time in the outhouse at 20 below.

I wanted a few things from this walk. I wanted to be able to look at a map of Alaska and, on a certain vertical line, have a memory for anywhere I stuck a pin. I knew a lot of rivers only as green signs at highway bridges. I wanted to drink these rivers, cook my dinner with them, cool my feet in them. I wanted to spend a whole Alaska summer outside, to be there when the robins returned north, when they mated, hatched eggs, when they stopped singing, when they left. I wanted to bake in the summer sun, to nap under spruce trees when it poured, to shiver in the mountain snows. To be part of the cycle.

I wanted the quiet times, alone with my dog. Maybe to

learn something about myself, maybe not. I wanted to see where my mind would go during a summer with no music, no TV, to see what it would be like not to drive for a few months. I wanted to carry my home across Alaska on my back.

This trip would be about time. For one summer of life, I could walk, and I'd never be late. Hours, minutes and seconds wouldn't matter. I wouldn't wear a watch; the sun circling the horizon might help, but it usually only confused the matter in Alaska's summer. It was time to shift to the lowest gear possible, and stay there for a few months.

A friend asked me if I hated humanity. Why else would someone choose to walk away from people for a whole summer? His question bothered me because it might be true. Though I really don't think the gang of us has improved this planet much since spreading ourselves over its skin, I do rather like most people, especially the people drawn to Alaska: un-shaven adventurers who follow a mysterious impulse north and find one lifetime too short to climb all these mountains; environmentalists who abandon their home states and find plenty to protect here; Army soldiers who get stationed here and never leave.

To make sure I wouldn't return as a mumbling hermit, I decided not to do the whole trip alone. Eight people would join me, for half the miles of the trip. Girlfriend, brother, brother-in-law, other friends who had the time. I knew I would meet many more people on the way.

I wanted to find out who lives here, where they came from, and why they stay in this land of mosquitoes, cold, and twenty-dollar breakfasts. Alaska has always been a place for explorers, for runners, for people looking for someplace new and different and hard: Natives crossing the Bering Land Bridge, Russians in leaky boats, gold-crazy stampeders. Soldiers and airmen, homesteaders, oil boomers, conservationists. Who's here now, at the end of the century? Why do they stay? Why do I?

My weird path had not been walked before. Who would want to walk next to a pipeline? I told a former trapper named Fred who works at a Fairbanks bicycle shop about my trip. He winced, shook his head. "For me," Fred said, "when the pipeline went in, it was the end of Alaska."

The end began in 1968, when drilling crews for two oil companies, Atlantic Richfield and Humble, tapped into an oil field never seen before on the continent. Natural gas belching from the discovery well sounded like the runway at Chicago O'Hare. When the geologists calculated the size of the massive deposit, it ranked as the largest oilfield in North America and the 18th largest in the world.

But how to get the millions of barrels of oil to refineries, the closest of which were on the West Coast? The defense contractor General Dynamics proposed a fleet of tanker submarines that would carry the oil under the pack ice of the Arctic Ocean. The discovery was less than 10 miles from the ocean, after all. Boeing engineers drew plans for a massive aircraft — powered by 12 jet engines — that would airlift the oil down south.

The oil industry executives saw another way: a giant pipe across Alaska. Environmentalists urged that, if there was to be a pipeline, it be threaded through northwest Alaska and then through Canada to avoid oil spills in the ocean. Alaska labor leaders and the oil industry countered that a pipeline though Alaska would bring an incredible amount of jobs, as would a tanker terminal in Valdez.

President Nixon agreed to the all-Alaska pipeline route, but several years passed before the pipeline became reality. In the 1970s, environmental groups sued and delayed pipeline construction until the Arab oil embargo made another source of American crude irresistible. Nixon signed the Trans-Alaska Pipeline Authorization Act in fall of 1973.

The rush was on. Thousands of migrants flew to Alaska and made the biggest paychecks of their lives stringing the pipeline across three mountain ranges, the Chugach, Alaska, and Brooks. Some of those who were against the pipeline found themselves unable to resist the big money. Today, each Alaskan receives between $800 to $1,700 a year in one lump sum from a state investment heavy with royalties from oil. The Permanent Fund, tended to by 11 Alaskans who wake at 3 a.m. to invest on East Coast time, is now worth about $24 billion. Even those who hate big oil and what it has done to Alaska find it hard to refuse the Permanent Fund dividend checks. Those who do refuse are rare enough to become the subjects of feature stories. In Alaska, oil is unavoidable.

As is the pipeline. Like all the moose, caribou and bears alive today, I entered the state when the four-foot wide, 800-mile long tube was already part of the landscape. I never saw Alaska before the late seventies, a time when the pipeline was assembled in three years, for $8 billion.

The trans-Alaska pipeline pops from the ground in Prudhoe Bay and worms its way south for 800.3 miles — about the distance from Denver to Los Angeles — to where it dives under a chain-link fence at the Alyeska Marine Terminal in Valdez. Covered with sheet metal and four inches of insulation, the Japanese-made steel pipe is visible 420 miles above the ground; the pipe is buried for the other 380 miles. Whether the pipe is conspicuous or buried under 10 feet of earth, a gravel road runs alongside it. Pipeline workers call this road "the pad."

The pad and the pipe were stretched across Alaska when in the early 1980s I was an 18-year old airman at a base 30 miles south of Fairbanks. The pad made a great trail for cross-country skiing. I had my first close encounter with a moose near the pipeline. I almost lost my pinkies to frostbite while skiing on the pad at 30 below zero. I was shooed off the pad by a helicopter pilot who thought I was a terrorist on Rossignols. In my Alaska, the pipeline was just *there*.

I don't think it's pretty. I think it's an excellent symbol of what's wrong with a species that takes more than it needs. Though it provides me with a big check each year and strengthens the state to the point that I have a job, I think Alaska would be better off without it. But the pipeline is here, I don't refuse my Permanent Fund dividend checks, and I drive. Almost all my outdoor gear — from boot soles to tent to polypropylene underwear — is made from the goop inside the pipeline. The pipeline is not offensive enough to cause me pain. And the pipeline provides a path across Alaska, one that would enable a person to cross the state at a leisurely pace in one summer, accompanied by a dog that tends to wander in front of moving cars as if she were still a puppy.

The pipeline people were not crazy about my idea. They work for Alyeska Pipeline Service Company, formed in 1970 to design, create, operate and maintain the pipeline. Alyeska is the blend of seven oil companies: British Petroleum (the main ingredient, owning 50.01 percent of Alyeska), ARCO, Exxon, Mobil, Amerada Hess, Phillips and Unocal.

Alyeska, an Aleut Native word meaning "mainland," employs about 800 people who perform various task to keep oil flowing through the pipe. Alyeska also hires security guards whose duty it is to patrol the pad by red diesel truck or helicopter. They watch the pad in order to guard the pipe, because people have tried to destroy it.

On July 29, 1977, the *Anchorage Daily News* proclaimed on its front page that the first oil had made its way through the new pipe: "Oil Reaches Valdez!" Those dropping their gaze below the banner saw another pipeline-related story about three men who'd tried to blow up the pipeline. Led by a 26-year-old man who raved about the evils of the Rockefeller family, the saboteurs attached dynamite to the pipeline about 20 miles north of Fairbanks. The damage — the loss of insulation that covers the pipe, but no rupture in the half-inch steel of the pipe wall — wasn't found until several days after the blast. The bombers, who worked on a nearby gold mine owned by a Fairbanks dentist, were convicted of malicious destruction of property.

The pipeline was again blasted in early 1978. The latter bombing, a more professional job, was performed by someone or a group still at large. He, she, or they opened a one-inch hole in the pipe that blackened the snow-covered muskeg near Steele Creek in Fairbanks with more than

670,000 gallons of crude oil. When the oil pressure subsided, Alyeska crews repaired the pipe by sheathing it with a steel sleeve. The unsolved bombing inspired Alaska Senator Ted Stevens to support a bill that made damaging the pipeline a federal crime, because the pipeline carried "vital resources for other states."

The bombers made my task a little more difficult. I sent the chief of Alyeska security a proposal in November. By January, a woman in Alyeska's corporate affairs office in Anchorage told me over the phone that I could indeed hike next to the pipeline, though I would not be allowed into the oil pumping stations for meals as I had requested. I was satisfied with that, and plunged into planning the walk. For the first time in my life, I had to think more than one week ahead. What food would I need for the entire summer? Should I carry a gun? How was I going to cross 834 rivers?

A month later, after still not receiving Alyeska's letter that would allow Jane and me to walk beside the pipeline without being hassled by security guards, I again called the woman at corporate affairs. She had bad news.

"We were in error when we gave you permission to hike the pipeline," she said, quickly firing off the reason: "There's over 200 separate land owners on the pipeline corridor, and you'll have to ask each one of them for permission."

I hung up the phone and closed my eyes. I imagined my proposal moving from desk to waste basket in a carpeted office 350 miles away. But after dreaming about the trip for months, after telling everyone I knew what I was planning for the summer, I had too much momentum to fold. I tried to contact the 200 land owners.

It was impossible. I couldn't find many of the people whose names appeared on sections of the pipeline right-of-way, 57 of them on the pipeline's path through the Fairbanks area alone. A few entities — the U.S. Bureau of Land Management, the State of Alaska, two Native corporations — owned extremely large pieces of the pipeline right-of-way. With letters and faxes and phone calls, I received permission to walk over their portions, but I never contacted a single private person to ask for permission to walk next to the pipeline near Fairbanks and Delta Junction, the only places along the route where the pipeline goes through backyards. I agreed to walk around those areas, by using nearby highways, four-wheeler trails, or any other convenient walkway.

This diversion was OK with me. The pipeline pad was an excellent path for Jane, but it was simply a means to get where I was going, a way that was slightly better than the highways. I wanted to walk across Alaska in one summer, and a manmade path was the only way to succeed. For the most untainted walk, a person would just get up in the morning and start walking: no permission obtained, no food drops planned, no attempts to predict the unpredictable. But Alaska is just too big, and Alaska summers are just too short, to set out without charting a course. I could have bushwhacked a route north to south across the state, but I couldn't envision myself busting through trees and shrubs, twisting my ankles on tussocks, and still making enough miles each day to traverse Alaska by winter. In northern Alaska, winter arrives in September, sometimes in August.

I had only two steadfast rules: I wanted to carry my pack the whole 800 miles, and I wouldn't accept rides.

A month before I started, I still did not have permission from Alyeska Pipeline Service Co., but I planned as if the walk would happen. I bought hundreds of dollars' worth of freeze-dried dinners, peanut butter, pilot bread, dried fruit and other food that didn't need refrigeration. My girlfriend planned meals for me. With saint-like patience, she and a friend scooped oatmeal, raisins, Tang crystals and other foods and dumped them into hundreds of plastic bags, which we then loaded in cardboard boxes to be dropped at checkpoints or delivered by a hiking partner.

I pestered large companies with faxes and phone calls. Some agreed to give or loan me equipment or supplies in exchange for photographs or written endorsements of their products. Eagle Pack, Inc., gave me enough high fat/protein dog food to last Jane four months. Katadyn, Inc., loaned me a water filter. Sevylor, Inc., a company based in Los Angeles, sent me two of their "Trail Boats" for crossing rivers. A local store, Computerland, loaned me a computer the size of a paperback, a Hewlett Packard HP 200 LX. A veterinarian in Fairbanks gave me a first-aid kit for Jane that included two syringes should I need to knock her out to pull porcupine quills. The local representative for Guard Alaska, a pepper spray company, gave me 12 canisters, enough for several lifetimes. I whiffed on hiking boots and rain gear, but I didn't mind buying them at a local sporting goods store.

With the supplies crowding my small cabin, I still needed to accomplish one of the hardest tasks — quitting a good job. For two years, I had worked as a science writer at the Geophysical Institute, an eight-story building at the University of Alaska Fairbanks where dozens of scientists study earthquakes, volcanoes, the aurora borealis, and other natural phenomena that add drama to life in Alaska. My 20-hour-a week job forced me to learn something new every week as I wrote a newspaper column, the Alaska Science Forum.

I held off telling my boss until two months before I planned to leave. I couldn't put it off any longer on the day when a pipeline security man gave me a gold pin of Alaska with the pipeline's path engraved in black. "You can wear that when you finish the walk," he said.

I had thrown my boss some curves before — requesting large chunks of unpaid leave to work on projects for the National Park Service — and she had given her permission. But four months was too long, I thought. I'd have to quit.

Standing at her desk, looking out the window at Birch Hill, I wound up and tossed my pitch. She surprised me by suggesting I write science and personal columns from the trail, thereby keeping my job while drawing attention to the Geophysical Institute.

At first, I was petrified at the thought of writing columns from my sleeping bag. In order to write the science column while under a roof, I spent 10 hours each week interviewing scientists or burying myself in the library; both those resources would not be available while I was walking across Alaska, even if I did occasionally find a phone.

In the weeks that followed, I decided to do all the column research before I left. I tried to write columns that related to where I would be in Alaska. When I walked through miles of gray forest with dead spruce trees in the Copper River valley, for example, I would write a column on the bark beetles that had killed the trees. My last month at work became a blur while gathering the information for 18 columns — one for each week of the hike.

With less than two weeks from my take-off date, I had most of the stuff I would need to walk cross Alaska in my backpack. But I was still missing the great enabler: Alyeska's "letter of non-objection."

I busied myself with a mountain of tasks — predicting what food I would eat on the trail, buying that food, sewing sponsor patches on a dog backpack, researching columns, calling potential sponsors, deciding which sleeping bag to start out with, making a ground cloth for my tent, buying white gas, writing columns, trying to sublet my cabin, fixing my red truck's exhaust leak so my hiking partners could use it without dying of carbon monoxide poisoning. I did all this without knowing for sure if Alyeska would give me permission.

I bombarded my Alyeska contact's voice mail, leaving him seven messages in one day. He called back that afternoon and told me I'd have my letter soon. Eleven days before I began the trip, the fax arrived.

In the four-page document, he stated my mission, one he said no future permission seeker could possibly duplicate: "for the purpose of hiking across Alaska in commemoration of the 20th anniversary of the Trans-Alaska Pipeline and the 21st anniversary of the Alaska Science Forum."

My girlfriend joked that it was 20 years since she'd graduated from high school, so the walk should also celebrate that. Another friend pointed out that a car dealership was playing up its 20th year, and perhaps I should carry its banner. A public relations person from the university wanted to tack on a sentence about the walk commemorating the 85th anniversary of my employer.

I tucked my letter of non-objection in a Ziploc, along with my letters from the Native corporations and the Joint Pipeline Office, the representative of the state and BLM. These pieces of paper went in my backpack. Together, they said I could hike across Alaska with my dog. Having permission was like passing a chemistry test after cramming, only to dump the information seconds after leaving the classroom. The real challenge — walking across the largest state in America — was just days away. With it came the unknowns of Alaska.

I pictured a lot of bear faces before the trip. The pipeline cuts through country still wilderness by many peoples' standards, mostly areas where bears outnumber people. I asked people what protection they would bring for a summer outside in Alaska. An Alaska old-timer told me in his Russian accent he would carry no bear protection at all. "You can yell at dem and dey run away," he said. Less seasoned Alaskans told me to carry everything I could, including explosives, to save Jane and me from the bears. It came down to two simple choices: I could react to the environment, or I could try to control it. I like to have control, or at least the illusion of control, so I bought a stainless 12-gauge shotgun, and my hiking partners would wear pepper spray on their hips.

For all my fretting, bears did not keep me awake in the nights before the hike. Rivers did. When I closed my eyes at night I saw churning water that took Jane away, that ripped the pack from my back. The maps showed 800 water crossings, four in the first day. These blue lines on the map were my frontier. Each river could end the trip in a few seconds. I tried to tell myself to take each stream and river as I found it, but I took them all late at night, during the last two weeks before the trip. When I was a boy, I almost drowned in a neighbor's pool after walking to the deep end and slipping down an underwater ramp. I pushed from the bottom of the pool a few times to raise my head from the water, but I got weaker with every rush to the surface. My friend's father saw me, jumped in and pulled me out. After my mother tucked me in bed that night, I dreamed of cold bubbles tickling my face, of the bitter smell of chlorine. Now, thirty years later, the dream returned, only Jane was there, clawing at me with a desperate look in her eyes.

And what about people along the pipeline? I'd met a few end-of-the-roaders, people who were here because they'd been kicked out of everywhere else. When I lived in Eagle, Alaska, one summer, a man dressed in camouflage shot a Super Cub airplane with a rifle, making good on an earlier threat. He was later to surface near Fairbanks, closing a highway for 30 hours after shooting a hole in the door of a state trooper's sedan. Even Alyeska people warned me off some sections of the pipeline: "They'll pull a gun on you" was advice I received about residents who lived near a certain mountain.

People asked me if I had trained physically for a summer's worth of backpacking. I hadn't, but I was sure I could make the trip because I'd run a bunch of marathons in Alaska and camped for weeks while fighting fires. What about Jane?

I hoped she'd have the summer of her life, but maybe hiking every day with a full pack was too much for a 10-year-old dog. I had no way to know.

In the days before the walk, my friends and family fell into two categories: they either loved the idea of walking the pipeline or they thought it was irrational, pointless, stupid. A man where I worked called it a boondoggle.

My sister Nora, who lives in New Hampshire with two young sons and a husband who is somewhat like me, just didn't get it. She wrote me a letter that made me laugh out loud in the post office. "Of course," she wrote, "Jeb can see the appeal of what you're doing, but the idea does not interest me in the least."

At that time, I was so in love with the idea of walking across Alaska I couldn't believe someone would think it was silly. I stepped back from the counter at the post office and thought of what I was really doing — walking alongside a giant pipe for a whole summer, not really getting a wilderness experience but getting all the bugs and the rain and the blisters. For a moment, I saw how absurd the idea was, how some people might not list walking along the pipeline as something they would want to do in this or any future lifetime. Then I thought of spending the summer in a hot building, looking out a window at the green hills, longing for weekends that would give me time outside. Then, as now, walking through those green hills every day made perfect sense to me, the same feeling I had when I was 17 and refused a ride home from a bar in Lake George.

1 | Valdez

Battery-operated clippers groan. Tiny blades struggle to bite chunks of hair. The hair is mine — at least, it was mine. My girlfriend, Smits, makes my head lighter by removing most of my hair. She tries to be gentle, but I wince every few seconds when the clippers pull my hair. Curls, two-inch crescents from the back of my head, fall to the ground.

She laughs as she works. John Arntz laughs too. He documents the shearing through the dusty lens of an old Nikon. John is a friend since we met at the University of Alaska 10 years ago. He drove his red Subaru wagon from Fairbanks to Valdez with us. He's here to help me begin the hike across Alaska. I'll begin walking, with Smits and Jane, tomorrow.

Smits rids me of shoulder-length hair. I know I won't miss it because I worked one summer in the Alaska woods with longish hair that became a pain. In 1990, I was a wildlands firefighter, called out for three weeks at a time to help douse the Tok River fire. After working and sweating in fine ash every day, my hair became dirty straw. It stayed like hay for as long as our crew remained on the fire line.

In the yellow light of a spring afternoon, our barber shop is framed by mountains that rise like walls, a mile into the sky. At the base of leafless alder trees, snow clings in dirty pyramids. The afternoon temperature is 52 degrees, and the air smells like a starfish. I sit on a rusted metal pole suspended like a stiff arm across a pipeline access road. My chair is part of the locked gate that prevent vehicles from driving on the pipeline pad. My hair falls, bounces off the pole, and lands on flakes of gray rock. Jane approaches, sniffs the curls and snorts, deciding they aren't edible.

Smits, Jane and I, in Smits's white Toyota Camry, and John, in the Subaru, drove to the gate so we could test the snow cover on the pipeline pad here in Valdez. Will I need snowshoes tomorrow? No. The snow is deep in places, but the April sun has done its work. Crude oil has helped, too. The heat of the buried pipeline has melted a path through the rotting snow. It is comfortable to sit on a metal gate wearing only a pile top, a long-sleeve T-shirt beneath, canvas pants with no long johns. Here, Smits decided, would be a good place to cut my hair.

Smits is my human partner for the first two days of the hike. She wasn't born as Smits. It's short for Smitty, her nickname, which she earned by being very much unlike all the Smittys I knew when I grew up. Smittys worked as mechanics, their lower lips bulging with minced tobacco, spit stains on the cement floor of the garage when they had no beer bottle to spit in, a bottle they sometimes swigged by mistake. They loved to hunt whitetail deer, sometimes with a spotlight. They never missed a New York Giants football game.

They farted in public, then said something stupid.

Delicate and proper, Smits is the anti-Smitty. I've only heard her swear once, when a caribou crossed our ski tracks while we had been hunting for them elsewhere. She's reserved enough that she will not honk her horn if she sees me running with Jane alongside the road. She explains she thinks other drivers may think she's beeping at them. She's brave enough to give up a lucrative career for the Department of Environmental Conservation to go back to school. She's disciplined enough to have saved enough from the DEC job to buy her own comfortable house. She's smarter than I'll ever be, and not just in atmospheric chemistry, the subject she's chosen to study.

Smits is 37 years old, three years older than me. While she cuts my hair, her smile shows the gap between her two front teeth. She wears a ski cap with a black-and-purple toggle, attached to top dead center by a string of purple yarn. The cap covers little of her high Lithuanian forehead, a gift from her father. Her fingers are slender, like feathers; when she chats, her hands beat the air, tiny wings. She eats breakfasts of Gouda cheese, sourdough bread, cucumber slices, sometimes an onion. With brown hair knotted in a braid and an almost oriental tilt to her eyes, Smits is mistaken for a native when she visits eastern Europe. In this land of migrants, she is a true Alaskan. Her parents lived in Salcha, near a bend in the Tanana River. Smits first breathed Alaska air at the Eielson Air Force Base clinic, 30 miles south of Fairbanks. The clinic was a shorter drive for her parents than Fairbanks Memorial Hospital. If her father had tried to make it all the way to Fairbanks, she would have been born along the Richardson Highway.

We drove the Richardson Highway down from Fairbanks yesterday, 368 miles. At Valdez, we reached the end of the highway late at night. Smits, Jane and I shared a tent floor on the sand next to Mineral Creek, where Valdez ends and the Pacific Ocean begins. John slept close by, crooked in the back of the vehicle he calls "Subaru," as if it is a person. Subaru is 14 years old. The car scared John once, as he was driving an Iowa interstate. At 60 miles an hour, the grill partly detached. Clinging by a lone screw, the grill hovered in John's view like an alien for a few seconds before disengaging. Subaru's red paint is fractured like the skin of a bird's foot. When John arranges his sleeping quarters in the back, a rectangle of sheet rock props Subaru's tail gate.

On May 4, we woke to a cloudless day. Sixty inches of rain soak Valdez each year, but today we have clear skies and exposed peaks in every direction. Playing in softball tournaments at the Gold Fields in Valdez, I've stood in the batter's box and looked beyond the center-field fence to see the white lobe of a glacier hanging from a mountainside. Here, the Chugach Mountains rise like surfacing sharks from the gray bed of the Lowe River, which empties into the ocean. In a vertical progression, river gravel yields to cottonwood trees, some weighted with bald eagle nests. As the mountains rise, cottonwoods give way to clean-scented Sitka spruce and mountain hemlock. Where the hemlocks surrender, shrubs and rocks stubble a difficult pathway to pointy black peaks. Valdez would rank as one of Alaska's most beautiful settings even without the ocean. With it, on a clear sunny day, Valdez has no match in this state, maybe on this planet.

Port Valdez is a blue thumb on the map, a calm patch of gray water sullied by the glacial silt delivered to the port by the Lowe River. Under its sleepy surface swim thousands of salmon that follow the tides. Pinks return to Port Valdez first, then silvers. Both, especially the silvers, bend the poles of shore fishermen who fret about monofilament knots as they reel, squint, and yell "Fish on!" hoping the others will retrieve their lures. On previous trips, my friend Dan Joling named me "the Michael Jordan of netminders" as I helped him get his silvers safely to the rocks of Allison Point. Our teamwork resulted in orange flesh wrapped with butter and onions, slowly steaming whitish pink in a bag of foil. Food for a king, harvested by serfs.

Antonio Valdes y Basan was a Spanish naval officer forever honored by Don Salvador Fidalgo, another Spanish naval officer who sailed as far east as he could into Prince William Sound on June 16, 1790. In a fiord surrounded by alps, Fidalgo named his discovery Puerto Valdes. Valdez is today pronounced "Val-DEEZ." That was how the first white settlers spoke the name, due either to their unfamiliarity with Spanish pronunciation or to a wave of nationalism during the Spanish-American war, which was being fought as Valdez grew into a town. As successive maps drawn by Spaniards, Brits and Americans reflected each culture's language, Puerto Valdes became Port Valdez.

Today, the town of Valdez sits on the knuckle of Port Valdez's blue thumb. Before 1964, it sat on the thumbnail, in the flood plain of the Lowe River. The town's location was chosen in 1897 by sea-weary gold seekers whom a shipping company lured to the port in search of the "all-American" route to riches. By reaching the gold fields using an Alaska trail, the shipping company promised, stampeders could avoid Canadian regulations and taxes imposed on those who reached the Yukon Territory via the Chilkoot Pass.

Joe Bourke of Brooklyn, N.Y., was one of the restless men and women who stampeded in 1898 to what was to become Valdez. He booked passage on the *Valencia*, a steamship owned by the Pacific Steam Whaling Company. With whales, and whaling profits, declining, the company executives saw a chance to earn money by sending their empty ships north with human cargo. The ships returned to Seattle heavy with salmon.

The company promised ticket-buyers that Valdez was a fully functional town, a place where a man could outfit himself for a journey to financial security. Bourke and other passengers on the *Valencia* found otherwise as they sailed into Port Valdez on March 18, 1898. Bourke, later to document much of the folly of the all-American route with his photographs, detailed the scene in his journal: "Arriving at Valdez, we found no wharf nor storehouse or any other convenience, nothing in fact but a snow bank."

The would-be gold miners tossed their goods on the snowbank and eventually set up a canvas tent city near the mouth of the Lowe River. Originally called Copper City, the town evolved to Camp Valdez, Port Valdez, Valdes, and finally Valdez. Three to four-thousand people were deposited here in spring and summer of 1898. Spruce-log cabins replaced tents, mercantile shops popped up, and eventually Valdez resembled the town promised to the early arrivals.

The all-American route to the Klondike from Valdez was a fable. The alleged trail to the gold began with a traverse of Valdez Glacier, 23 miles of ice and snow that rises from near sea level to 4,800 feet. At the summit, a descent on Klutina Glacier leads to Klutina Lake. Here, gold seekers could build boats to take them down the Klutina River, which empties into the Copper River of Alaska's interior. From the Copper, steamship companies and ill-informed newsmen reported, one could negotiate the river upstream to Mentasta Pass, from where stampeders could reach the headwaters of rivers that flowed into the Yukon River. The Yukon, everyone knew, led to the rich ground of the Klondike, near Dawson City of Canada's Yukon Territory.

The Copper River consists of thunderous, rolling mounds of brown water. The truth to the rumor of its negotiability was published in *The Klondyke News* of April 1, 1898:

"We warn our readers against any attempt to reach the Klondike country by way of the Copper River. No living man ever made the trip and the bones of many a prospector whiten the way.

"In the first place it is almost impossible to ascend the Copper River. There are trackless mountains to cross, by the side of which the Chilcoot Pass trail is quite a boulevard..."

At the time those words were published, thousands of men and women were pulling sleds up Valdez Glacier. Many completed the trip, boating down the Klutina River to where they found the infant town of Copper Center. Most gold seekers abandoned plans to go further when they saw the violent nature of the Copper River. Some stayed in Copper

Center to prospect for gold in the expansive river basin. This was the main objective for most, who assumed the streams of the Klondike probably were covered with wooden claim stakes by then. Many retreated back over Valdez Glacier and waited at Valdez for ships that would take them home. During the winter of 1898 to 1899, more than 100 people who couldn't catch a boat died from scurvy.

The all-American route traffic slowed to a trickle, but Valdez lived on. By 1907, the Valdez Trail to Fairbanks was passable by dog team and sled. By 1964, a thriving town — complete with a highway link to Fairbanks — sat near the Lowe River. This location, chosen by gold seekers in the last century, proved a fatal choice. On March 27, 1964, the second most powerful earthquake ever recorded on seismometers struck Alaska. Its epicenter, the place where two of Earth's colossal plates (the Pacific and North American) lost grip on one another, was 45 miles west of Valdez, beneath the waters of Prince William Sound.

The jolt was powerful enough to have wiped out all five boroughs of New York in seconds. A magnitude 9.2 shook the water-saturated sands beneath Valdez for four minutes, jarring the structure from the soil. Suddenly, the town's foundation acted more as a liquid than a solid, and a slice of the waterfront 4,000 feet long and 600 feet wide disappeared. Nearly 100 million yards of sand grains flowed to the sea in an underwater landslide. The displacement of water caused a *seiche*, a wave that sloshed back and forth within the mountain walls of Port Valdez like water in a bathtub. The town was struck several times by waves as high as 30 feet.

Though the earthquake's effect on Anchorage, Alaska's largest city, was the main focus of news stories, only nine people died there. In Valdez, 32 people who were on or near the ocean docks were killed. Whole families died.

After the earthquake, the Army Corps of Engineers and the U.S. Geological Survey condemned the Valdez townsite despite the fact that relatively few homes appeared to be damaged. The Alaska State Housing Authority ordered the old townsite vacated by Sept. 30, 1967.

The earthquake survivors rebuilt Valdez upon soil hemmed in by islands of bedrock. The new town, near where Mineral Creek enters Port Valdez, is four miles west of "Old Town." New Valdez has streets laid out in orderly fashion, with none of the 100-year-old buildings that lend charm to other Alaska coastal communities.

Today, an outsider has to hunt to find the stumps of dock pilings, the bare cement foundations, and the rusted pretzels of plumbing that mark the former Valdez.

March 27, 1964 was remembered by engineers who were hired to build the trans-Alaska pipeline. Along earthquake faults, the pipe sits on crossbars 40 to 60 feet apart. Where the pipe support touches a support crossbar, it rests on shoes made of Teflon, which enable the pipe to slide during an earthquake. The pipeline terminal in Valdez is anchored in bedrock, part of a rock hillside that was dug out by explosives. While all these precautions have served the pipeline well during its 20 years, another Good Friday earthquake would make a mockery of it all in seconds. You can't prepare for a 9.2.

A carved salmon the size of a killer whale welcomes

travelers to the Hook, Line and Sinker tackle shop. Next door, waitresses at the Totem Inn pour coffee into white ceramic mugs so heavy they encourage the use of two hands. Beverages with more bite are served at the Pipeline Club. To the south of the merchants is a small boat harbor, separated from Port Valdez by a finger of land that holds a fish cannery and the office of Alyeska Pipeline Service Co., the town's largest employer.

Across the blue thumb of Port Valdez, more than a dozen biscuit-shaped tanks — the storage units for North Slope crude oil — hunch on a green hillside at the Alyeska Marine Terminal. At the terminal, mile 800 of the trans-Alaska pipeline, oil reaches Valdez after a five-day trip from Pump Station 1 at Prudhoe Bay. Oil tankers with decks that could accommodate an NFL game, including the crowd, float next to the terminal. The monsters sink slowly in the water with the weight of ancient plant and animal life. From Valdez, tanker captains steer full loads through the half-mile pinch of Valdez Narrows to the Gulf of Alaska, then pilot the oil along the Pacific coast to refineries in Puget Sound and along the California coast. Eight years ago, the tanker *Exxon Valdez* failed to reach the open water of the gulf. Eight years ago, hundreds of job seekers who met the minimum qualifications of an Alaska driver's license and a beating heart earned 16 dollars an hour by toweling rocks and breathing moist diesel fumes.

I was one of those who left rubber boot prints on the suddenly disgusting beaches. In an experience I never want to repeat, we all became thousandaires. The first day of cleaning oil from rocks, I wrote in my journal:

Thursday, May 18th, 1989

I had wondered about the true story of oil spill cleanup. Legit, or bullshit??

Bullshit. I wouldn't have believed today if I hadn't have mucked through it. Today proved that a), Veco, the oil spill contractor, has no game plan for its 200 newest workers; b) the oil spill destroyed miles and miles of shoreline in one of the beautiful areas of the world, and c) there is no way, or at least Exxon knows no way, to successfully clean these beaches.

We were told to be on the foredeck of the ship at 8:30 a.m. At noon, we finally got on a smaller boat and headed out into the bay. Our supervisor had no clue as to where to take us, he chose a strip of blackened shore only because one of the girls on the crew had to take a pee.

The crude oil on the rocks wasn't slippery, but it covered everything in shiny black, right up to the high-tide mark. It smelled like a mechanic's garage. We sprayed the rocks with cold water hoses, forcing loose oil to float on the ocean. As the tide went out, the same oil we just freed from the rocks settled on lower rocks. The beach was left with some half-cleaned rocks, none totally clean, that the tide will nail again tomorrow. In pools on the shore are big, gooey patches of crude oil, brown like a chocolate milkshake.

By the end of the day my raingear and rubber boots were coated with sticky oil. Stripped them off on a barge before returning to the big ship, and was ordered to throw them in a 55-gallon drum. No one is cleaning the raingear. Helly Hansens that will be thrown out after a day's use. We're supposed to get a new set tomorrow. Unbelievable. One of the guys called this operation a clusterfuck. With us bumping into each other, directionless, it fits. Still, no one talks about quitting. Must be the scenery.

Beautiful sunset and rising moon over Eleanor Island tonight. Marred only by a black ring on the shoreline, and the presence of all these clean-up ships, and the legions Exxon has paid off, throwing cigarette butts into the bay.

A sad image today. Standing on the beach, feeling useless moving oil around with water only knowing I'd see it again tomorrow, I looked up. Two bald eagles, a mated pair, circling. Looking down on all these people in bright raingear, hearing all these diesel engines. Seemingly wanting to land but staying in the air, knowing something wrong had happened. They looped above us all day. After we finished a 14-hour shift and came back to the boat, I took a shower and went to the deck. When I looked up, the eagles were gone.

At Allison Point, a 10-mile drive around Port Valdez's thumbnail from the Totem Inn, I walk down a steep pathway to the ocean. The closest vehicle to me is an oil tanker that ingests a load of North Slope crude. Smits and John have driven to stash her car near Keystone Canyon, 15 miles away. Smits will hike to her car. Her trip with Jane and me should take two days.

Jane and I walk out on Allison Point. The Pacific Ocean smacks the rocks under the toes of my greased, hydrophobic hiking boots. I watch the oil tanker slowly get heavier. The air smells of hydrocarbons, pushed into the air by crude oil that spills into the tanker. The loaded oil comes almost directly from the pipeline. Technicians in the marine terminal's operation center touch pressure-sensitive squares on a video screen to route the pipeline's oil briefly into the biscuit tanks. From there, a valve opens to a pipeline and oil streams 250 feet downhill to the ever-present tankers. Two are here today; almost three tankers a day docked at the terminal in March 1988, when a record 88 came empty and went home full.

I once walked aboard one of these floating blimps, the *Overseas Juneau*. The captain, Earl E. Sheesley, didn't look as I imagined a tanker captain would look. He was tall, thin, dressed comfortably in sneakers, gray slacks, and a button-up shirt. If I saw him in Valdez, I would guess he was a weekend fisherman from Fairbanks or Anchorage.

At nine the night before, Sheesley had parked the *Overseas Juneau* at the terminal's floating dock. Sheesley's big brown eyes were now wide open as he stood in the wheelhouse on the bridge, the top floor of the tanker's "house," a T that sits like an apartment complex on the stern. His ship was receiving a gravity-fed injection of 101,000 gallons of crude oil per hour. It would take several hours to fill the multiple compartments of the tanker.

When full, the tanker weighed about 258 million tons. A handy part of the *Overseas Juneau's* bulk was a propeller that pressed against the deck of the bow, a 58-ton spare. Including the propeller, the ship had the equivalent in mass to 3.5 million Janes, all laden with full dog packs.

"How do you park something this heavy?"

"Very slowly," Sheesley said.

"You can't bump these things in, like you can a speed-boat. You get to bumping in with a tanker, next thing you look over and the dock's gone . . . You can get it moving easy enough. It's getting it stopped that's a real bitch. In the open sea, if I shut down the engine, we'd cruise eight to 10 miles before she'd stop."

Sheesley steered the *Overseas Juneau* with a tiny crescent of steering wheel, just 10 inches across. It looked like it belonged on a plastic Batmobile. With this, he controlled the rudders that allowed him to keep his toxic cargo within the three-quarter inch steel skin of the tanker.

Sheesley talked with the cadence of an easterner. Though his 10 years of piloting tankers had taken him primarily from the Valdez terminal to refineries in California and Washington (he estimated 165 round-trips), he lived in Portsmouth, New Hampshire, on the 17 miles of New Hampshire that touches ocean. He was a third-generation sailing man, piloting a boat his daddy and granddaddy never had an opportunity to — a vessel 883 feet long and 138 feet wide.

"This is the ultimate boating adventure," he said. Sheesley added, though, that 165 round trips sometimes turned an adventure into a job. The tankers are used like commercial airliners, pressed into almost continuous service from oil source, to refinery, to oil source. The *Overseas Juneau,* a 25-year-old, single-hulled relic, was almost ready to be moth-balled. But she had plenty of runs left, Sheesley said, and the ship was in a constant state of busy.

"There's no time nothing's going on," he said, looking down four stories at crewmen, who scurried through chores on the greenish expanse of metal deck. "These are very expensive to run. If it's not loading, discharging or moving, it's costing somebody a lot of money."

Sheesley recently piloted the *Overseas Juneau* into history. His ship was tanker No. 15,000 to get a belly full of North Slope crude at the Valdez Marine Terminal. Alyeska Pipeline Service Co. produced palm-sized stickers to mark the event. A cartoon tanker on the sticker sports the name *O/S Juneau*.

Prince William Sound, the site of the world's most famous oil spill, is easy to maneuver through, Sheesley said. Where he would float his load, to a refinery in Richmond, California, beneath the Golden Gate Bridge to San Francisco Bay, is much trickier for its curves, traffic and tight spots. But the flat world of offshore Alaska, particularly the Gulf, is responsible for weather as violent as anywhere on the globe, where storms can churn the open ocean and toss the tanker like a toy.

"You just go out there sometimes and get the shit kicked out of you," Sheesley said.

After two straight months of guiding behemoths on the Pacific, Sheesley returns to Portsmouth to spend two months off. While in the Port of Valdez for just 18 hours, Sheesley relaxed in-house. He did not go ashore, as some of his crew members did, to pick up a pizza, have a beer, or walk the sidewalks of new Valdez.

On board, Sheesley was expecting visitors besides me. One hour before the *Overseas Juneau* lumbered to sea, workers for a medical testing service would step on the ship and climb the steep stairs of the house to reach Sheesley's office. They would instruct Sheesley to inflate the mouth-piece of a portable breathalyzer, standard procedure for tanker captains only in Prince William Sound. Sheesley does not enjoy the breath test, which he sees as an overreaction to the Exxon Valdez spill.

"These people assume I'm a drunk," he said, his eyes as fierce as his nose, which curves aggressively, like an eagle's beak. "I'm guilty until proven innocent up here. It was an insult when they started doing it, and it's still an insult nine years later."

Even though I sympathized with Sheesley, if a breathalyzer prevents another oil spill, another invasion of workers who make boat anchors out of rocks in plastic bags, who cut the rope rather than pull the anchors up, I think it's just fine.

A few hours later, Sheesley passed his insulting breath test, and he and 25 crew members of the Overseas Juneau slipped into the starry night from Berth No. 3 with a full load of crude oil. In the darkness, Sheesley steered the tanker south, its bulk slicing salt water at 19 miles an hour. He would arrive in Richmond four days later.

2 | **Stepping into Alaska**

Day One

On May 4, I kneel on a flat rock. Using my hand as a ladle, I scoop salt water and bring it to my mouth. The Pacific as Port Valdez pools on my tongue, making me think of Maine. I swallow.

Subaru returns. Jane runs to greet it as I follow, climbing away from the ocean. John smiles beneath his nuclear pink baseball hat, which advertises "Montana" in cursive blue font. Smits pulls her blue backpack out of Subaru, and I grab mine. I will carry an external frame backpack across Alaska. Smits hunted around town to buy me the frame last year when I needed it on deadline. She carried the pack frame to me deep in an interior Alaska valley. With Smits's help, I used the frame to haul home 300 pounds of moose roasts, steaks, stew meat, and burger. For my birthday, she purchased a nylon pack to go on the sturdy frame.

"Got everything?" Smits asks.

"I think so."

I've stuffed the backpack with what I think I need to traverse Alaska. The lighter items go low, the heavy high and close to my back. Just above my waist hangs my sleeping bag. Above my sleeping bag are permission letters in a Ziploc, palmtop computer, bag of clothes, rain coat, rain pants, two lengths of nylon rope, first aid kit, sun screen, insect repellent, toothbrush, film, nylon pack cover, batteries, shotgun slugs, compass, pages 23 and 24 of the pipeline atlas, journal, two pens, camera, water bottle, camp stove, cookware, fuel bottle, water filter, breakfast bag (oatmeal, butter and brown sugar), snack bag (Clif bars, gorp, bags of nuts), dinner bag (freeze-dried dinners, cheese, pepperoni, chocolate), tent, three-quarter length sleeping pad, one-half length sleeping pad (for Jane), pile jacket, two-person tent, Trail Boat, plastic paddles, plastic carabiner, metal carabiner, insulated plastic mug, sneakers, zipper thermometer. The pack weighs 67 pounds. So does Jane.

Suddenly seven feet tall instead of the usual five-eight, I carry the pack to the eastern fence of the Alyeska Marine Terminal, to pipeline mile 800. The pipeline here runs under the chain-link fence and into the east metering building, where technicians shunt oil to the huge tanks or directly to waiting tankers.

Snow brushing our ankles, Smits, Jane and I step away from the fence, the first step into the unknown.

John snaps our picture and asks a question. "Where's CNN's camera crew?"

The journey begins with a climb up a hillside, popsicle green with the first shoots of spring above the buried pipeline. Ten, twenty, one-hundred steps down. Four million to go.

John leaves us after about a mile. He'll join me later in the trip. He wanted to do the whole trip with me, but I wasn't sure I would still like him after four months together, and I wanted some alone time. Among my friends, John was one of the few free to spend a summer walking, because he didn't have a job. He didn't want one, either. A recent law school graduate at South Dakota State, John's immediate plans are to absorb Alaska.

John works carpentry jobs on a freelance basis, doing good work, learning, and breaking the verbal contract when he feels the need. He avoids paying rent, preferring to barter. He paints cabins, installs oil heaters, replaces a few shingles. He gets shelter. At times, he squats, setting up a tent in a stand of birch. He squats with care, for he has overstayed his welcome at a few places, prompting friends to ask him to vacate their acreage.

One of the reasons I like John is that he sometimes puts himself in a hole just for the challenge of climbing out. I remember him buying imported cheeses and snacks for a ski trip to a remote cabin when his savings account balance was thirteen dollars.

His honesty is another reason. He often sparks confrontations, during which he stares through you with striking blue eyes.

"That wasn't a very good column," he sometimes tells me after reading the Alaska Science Forum in the Sunday paper. He is not afraid to challenge what you say. He seems to like it, whether the setting is a tort class in Vermillion, South Dakota, or streamside in the Chugach Mountains.

Now, he hikes away, back to Subaru, then on to Fairbanks. We will share the tent for many nights in the near future.

Just three miles into the hike, at pipeline mile 797, I chamber a slug because Jane has stopped moving. She fixes on a wall of alders to our left.

A black bear runs from our approach, just 20 yards in front of Jane. The bear quickly rolls into dark hemlock forest. We walk by slowly, thinking of bear eyes following us. We safely pass. Smits says what I'm thinking about the ink-black creature that just galloped away.

"They sure are beautiful — from a distance."

The bears are just stirring after five months of hibernation; inactive since September or October. They just pushed their way out of dens, having avoided the winter with adaptations that would kill a human being. Bears avoid peeing and defecating all winter. Instead, their kidneys route urine into the bloodstream, and their livers convert the urine to amino acids. Though bears sleep for almost the entire time they hibernate, they occasionally lift their heads or get up to circle like a dog before plopping back down. During the deepest states of hibernation, black bears' body temperatures drop from normal (about the same as a human's 98.6 degrees) to 85 degrees. In this fat-conserving state, a bear's heart will beat just one time every 10 seconds. Upon pushing themselves (and perhaps a few cubs) from the den, black bears walk about on sensitive feet, breath fresh air, and find a place to nap. Upon waking, they look for water, last year's berries, and new stalks of greenery. Here, the warmed ground covering the pipeline is the salad bar that opens earliest.

A day later, our second bear is sampling tender shoots of fireweed. He, too, is a black ball, but a much smaller one at one-quarter mile away. The bear is on our path. The black sphere, distinctive because it is magnitudes darker than any other natural object except the raven, grows larger as we walk toward it. It also moves toward us, unaware. We talk loudly, wave, emit polypropylene odor into our tailwind. Still, it moves closer. At 300 yards, I yell. "Hey!"

The sound waves carrying my voice take a few seconds to hit the bear. Its head springs up as if a bee has stung its bottom. I imagine it squinting as it looks our way. It sees us and crashes into the woods, toward the big mountains. We walk by slowly, afraid of a bear that is probably still running. Fear makes me finger the safety of the shotgun as we walk by. Smits holds her pepper spray at the ready. Jane is oblivious but obedient, not straying to the trees into which the bear disappeared.

We pass through the danger zone, still breathing. Two days, two bear encounters. I estimate there are 123 days to go until I reach Prudhoe Bay. I don't want to live forever, but I don't want to die at the teeth of a carnivore. The shotgun makes me feel a bit safer, but for most of the time it'll be a seven-pound stick.

Bears aren't the only exotic creatures in Valdez. Smits and I are surprised by a squadron of hummingbirds when we pitch our tent on the smooth gravel pipeline pad. Red torpedoes the size of thumbs buzz the woods around us. They occasionally hover in front of our faces, maybe puzzled by humans who are not in, or close to, a truck. On the hummingbird's zippy journeys in the undergrowth of the hemlock forest, they spout a four-note call that can only be duplicated on kazoo.

Day 3

It's time to face the Big Alone, and I don't quite know how to take it. Smits will return to Fairbanks today, where her unfinished thesis awaits. A few days ago, I thought this was the perfect scenario — my friends see me and Jane off, we travel into the horizon to face Alaska like Peter Jenkins and his dog Cooper, like Steinbeck and Charley, like William Least Heat-Moon and his truck, Ghost Dancing.

Apprehension gnaws a hole in my stomach as Smits packs her things and prepares to hike to her car. I try to place the feeling and think back to a time when my father and I got separated when we explored a cave. I shined my flashlight on shiny black walls and called his name, but I heard only echoes. I was petrified, because I was going to die in a cave. Worse, I was going to die by myself.

Now, Smits rolls up her Thermarest and stuffs her sleeping bag, which will not be next to mine tonight. I won't see her for the next two months, the time I guess it'll take Jane and me to walk home to Fairbanks.

It's been more than two years since Smits and I became a couple. In that time, we've chosen not to move in with one another, to keep our own spaces while sharing the others' often. Most times, I stay at her house; it's less cluttered than my cabin. But we both have our own spaces to fall back on, and we both need them. Smits says living together without being married is the worst of both worlds, in which you experience the drudgery of marriage without the commitment.

Today, I want a commitment. I want something besides my own fears as I walk up into Keystone Canyon and face Alaska by myself. I want a guarantee that everything will be OK, that bears won't visit in the night, that Jane won't jump on a porcupine. I feel like I did when, at 18, I stood in the hot, humid air in San Antonio as an Air Force recruit, suddenly loving my parents when I couldn't wait to get away from them days before. It was a time when basic trainees, realizing how truly isolated we all really are, proposed to their girlfriends. The bittersweet pang of loneliness, hitting as it sometimes does, like a cast-iron frying pan to the head.

Smits decides to walk with me to the base of Keystone Canyon. From there, I'll hike up a steep slope and into a place where Jane will be the only creature to talk to. This is what I wanted, to see where a little solitude would take me. But now I'm afraid of it.

It's hard to swallow as Smits and I walk to the base of the hill. Our path, framed by alders, leads to the top of Keystone Canyon. Beneath a ramp of tight-fisted wildflower buds and grass lies the pipeline.

Smits and I don't talk, but I know what I want to say. More than anyone else, Smits has made the start of the trip flow smoothly: measuring out cups and cups and cups of oatmeal and raisins, helping me plan, repeating the five most beautiful words in the world: "You have lots of time."

We reach the launch pad, the bottom of the hill. Here, I'll go my way while she goes hers. I put down my backpack and turn to face Smits. My eyes start watering when I look at hers, gray and familiar. She says the words I wanted to say, words we've never exchanged.

"I love you."

"I love you too."

Then, I lose it. I start crying like a three-year old, the pile material on Smits' little shoulders absorbing my tears and snot. I bawl like I haven't in years, again since the days of basic training when it was a pillow that muffled my sobs.

Smits pats my back as she would a baby. Her eyes are wet, too, but I seem to be the one blubbering. After a few minutes, we separate. I get to the task of buckling Jane in her pack, of checking my own load, which is lighter than yesterday because I gave Smits the Trail Boat and exchanged my hardcover journal for one that fits in my palm.

Finally, I shoulder my pack, pick up my shotgun, and step away from Smits. She comes close for one last kiss, and then I walk away.

"Take care of yourself," she says.

I'm so choked up I can't even answer. I start walking up the hill, Jane following, her bear bell jingling. A robin sings the same song robins always do.

Every time I look back, I see Smits there, where we parted. Dried tears on my face have given way to sweat. After a half-hour, Jane and I finally reach the east rim of Keystone Canyon. I look back down to see Smits, still standing there, though now a stick figure. As I take off my pack to rest, I see her moving, her distant outline like an ant, back to the woods and the path that leads to her car. When she leaves my field of view, I feel that pang again. Before I know it, my eyes are full of salt water. I blink, tears roll down my face. I'm alone, like I wanted to be, with a whole summer ahead. And I am, as my

Dad would say, scared shitless.

3 | Thompson Pass

Day Four

In the morning, under a dripping tarp, loneliness has been pushed aside. Adventure has crowded it out, coating the sharp pangs with the excitement of discovery. The view ahead keeps my mind occupied, a pleasant distraction from myself. As I'm soon to find out, the trail ahead holds a lot less of the Big Alone than I think it will.

The pipeline's path rises in front of Jane and me at the base of Thompson Pass, one of the larger obstacles of the trip, a steep ramp that rises 2,000 feet. As we walk along the pad, a rumble grows louder behind us. A black and gray pickup truck approaches. I call Jane. We step off the pad, onto the grass covering the pipeline. The driver doesn't pass. He stops and waves me to his window.

"You that guy that's hiking the pipeline?"

Mike Maze lives at the base of Thompson Pass. The pipeline pad is his driveway. He was driving home when he saw Jane and me ahead, so he pursued. Maze lives in an A-frame he built himself. The A-frame is mated to a small trailer, which doubles as both kitchen and refrigerator during winter.

His quiet outpost, 23 road miles from Valdez, consists of four hand-crafted buildings: the two-story A-frame, a shop that contains a humming generator, a bunk house he is renting to two rock climbers from Colorado, and a log home under construction by a pleasantly loud creek. All the buildings are hidden from the pipeline pad and each other by beefy Sitka spruce —blue-black bark, little green spears for leaves, upper branches drooping with long, tan cones. We don't have trees like this in Fairbanks, where winters are cold and — more limiting as far as the trees are concerned — summers are bone dry.

Here in the rain belt of Southcentral and Southeast Alaska, Sitka spruce, western hemlock and yellow cedar can grow as tall as trees of the Pacific Northwest. But there ends the illusion of lush forest in Alaska. A mongrel woodlet in Connecticut holds twice as many tree species as grow in Alaska. Away from Alaska's southern coast, as you travel farther inland, rainforest trees are replaced by spruce (white and the spindly-but-tough black), a few anemic larch, and hardwoods that would make an easterner laugh if you suggested them as firewood. The first choice of most Alaska wood burners is paper birch, a weed species in more temperate places, but here the densest fiber when compared to aspen, balsam poplar, cottonwood, and the spruces. Alaska trees have their charm — especially pipe-cleaner black spruce that cling to north-facing slopes — but they don't impress the tourists.

Maze, a Valdez baker at the moment, is in his early 40s, I guess. He has a full beard, a gold loop in his left ear lobe, and a deep baritone made for reading books aloud. He exhales a Marlboro cloud and tells me he heard about me on the radio, when a Valdez station aired a story about the trip. He himself was interviewed one summer ago, by a reporter for the Anchorage Daily News. His celebrity was unwanted, but the pipeline was disturbing his peace, and by complaining he regained the silence of the narrow valley at the base of Thompson Pass.

On a night one year ago, he awoke to a slow, rhythmic thumping. At first he thought someone was bumping about the pad with heavy equipment, but when he pulled on his boots and stepped outside, he saw nothing unusual. He heard and felt a shudder, like "a lot of tiny earthquakes." The source of the shaking wasn't the Pacific plate slipping past the North American plate. It was the pipeline.

The vibrations continued, knocking a heavy picture off the south wall of Maze's A-frame. Enough. He called the Alyeska Operations Command Center at the marine terminal. In the command center, Alyeska employees control the flow of oil from Prudhoe Bay to Valdez. If the line were to rupture, the people in the center could close any of 151 valves to stop the flow of oil. These men and women work amid a cluster of computer screens that tell them in colorful graphs and tables how much oil is flowing through the pipe, and at what pressure.

The pipeline problem in Maze's neighborhood was due to the 2,000-foot drop from the top of Thompson Pass to Maze's driveway. A reduction in the oil flowing through the pipeline created "slack," areas where oil didn't take up the full volume of the pipe. As oil tumbled down Thompson Pass, lighter crude components such as ethane and methane would boil off, only to violently reliquify in the pipe at the bottom of the pass. The explosive chemical reaction made Maze wonder if even half-inch steel could withstand such tremor.

"To create a seismic boom that could knock pictures off my wall this far away, imagine the stress on the pipeline," he says.

The Alyeska workers at the marine terminal stopped the booms temporarily by partially closing valves inside the terminal to create back pressure on the pipeline. They eventually installed new valves at pipeline mile 800 to perform the same function. Maze says the problem is much better than it was, but he still feels a pipeline-induced earthquake now and again. "They don't have it quite dialed in yet," he says.

Maze is a pioneer of sorts, the first person to live in this pipeline subdivision. He now shares his pipeline-pad driveway with four other settlers. It is quiet, remote, and dramatic, with a rampart of mountains rising immediately to the west, the Lowe River fanning to the east. Though he works in Valdez, this is Maze's place.

"I'd much rather be here. No building codes, no covenants. I can piss off the front porch and shoot my guns when I want to . . . There's no curtains on my windows."

A large picture window is the transparent south wall of his A-frame. The mural view features spruce forest dwarfed by the shoulders of mile-high Chugach peaks. A yellow Bay City crane sits idly on conveyor-belt shoes. Maze used it to lift the three ridge poles of the new cabin, which is finished but for glass and doors. The logs that make up his walls and roof are of impressive girth when viewed through the eyes of someone from farther north in Alaska. Crane trees, scribed and fit together with such precision the cabin would be as insect proof as mosquito netting if it had doors and windows.

Maze is here at the beginning of time as it applies to the Lowe River valley and the presence of white settlers. He was the first to live in this subdivision, and he still has the freedom to do what he wants here. The highway, and then the pipeline, opened the area much like the railroads did in the West, allowing Maze to clear his piece of the Frontier. Of course, others followed. And others will follow them. Looking around, thinking of the town I grew up in, I wonder if Maze will be able to pee off his porch in 50 years. I hope so, but maybe not. Time is changing Alaska, because Alaskans want what all settlers want, space and comfort.

I tell Maze of my plans to hike the highway to avoid the steep ramp of the pass. He urges me to try the pipeline pad.

"You can make it up that hill. I have. You can do that easy."

I thank Maze. He pulls his truck into reverse, performs a V, then hangs a right at pipeline valve number 121.

Thompson Pass rises to the sky in front of us. The pass, named for Frank Thomson, a Pennsylvania congressman, is one of my major obstacles of the summer. At some point a mapmaker misspelled Thomson's name for posterity, but every person who drives to Valdez remembers the pass. Twenty-eight-hundred feet above the salt water of Port Valdez, Thompson Pass is a place of glaciers and steep mountaintops covered with snow. It is too high for trees but an excellent site for alpine wildflowers and ground squirrels and dogs that like to chase them.

Driving through the pass is never boring. State plows at the nearby highway station carve paths through snow that could cover a tour bus. The pass receives an average of 50 feet of snow each winter; 60 inches have fallen in one day. The moist air from the Pacific responsible for all that snow often cloaks the pass in fog. Drivers float through a moonscape of black road and white snowbank, with no promise of help should their car malfunction. Cresting the pass, drivers see poles shaped like the number 7 extending over their heads. The poles glow amber in car headlights, the only visible sensation when the road is swallowed by mist. Driving through the foggy pass with only the glowing reflectors to guide you is like piloting the *Enterprise* through the stars.

Though only two miles in length, the pipeline's ascent of Thompson Pass was one of the most challenging sections of the 800-mile route for pipeline engineers and laborers. Workers first had to blast through solid rock to make a trench for the pipeline. To hold the pipe in place on the 55-degree slope, sections of pipe were winched by steel cable from cement blocks anchored at the top of the pass. Because it was too steep for welders to stand, they worked in harnesses, roped like mountain climbers. They compared the job to washing windows on the Empire State building.

At yesterday's perch on the rim of Keystone Canyon, I saw the pipeline's path to Thompson Pass. From a distance of four miles, the pipeline pad looked like a line on a wall. To reach the pass, the buried pipeline intersects three ridges.

As it climbs the lowest ridge, the pad is a ramp of dead grass. The middle ridge, above treeline, is a wall of solid gray rock. The third tier, covered with snow in early May, looks like the 90-meter ski jump at Lake Placid.

Jane and I walk to where the underground pipeline crosses the highway and hinges upward to the pass. I tighten my boot laces and kiss Jane on the head. We toe into the grass section and climb slowly to the first bench.

Jane and I ascend to the rocky section, where the pipeline is covered by brittle shale. We are suddenly above the level suitable for trees; even the willow (33 species in Alaska, but none big) have surrendered.

To free my hands, I tie my shotgun to the pack; I now look like a lowercase t. A black electrical wire runs up the slope. I grab it and, hand over hand, reel myself up the hill. The shale is a pile of marbles; as I climb, a mini-avalanche rolls toward Jane. She jumps to avoid it, but gets clipped by a fist-size rock that makes her yelp.

That's it. I'm not going to brain my dog just to get up a hill. We abort the mission.

Back at the first bench, I see a pathway that was pushed eastward through the alders by a bulldozer. I follow it. Jane follows me. We slog the road, which is a stream in places. Little ponds appear. Two drake mallards with dark green heads float silently together, no doubt having just arrived after a commute from Nebraska, Oklahoma, maybe New Orleans. A postage stamp. Jane doesn't see them. I don't point them out to her because I prefer them as still life.

To get up higher, I cross a snowfield. For some reason,

this particular snowfield holds my weight as if I am a water-bug relying on surface tension. Jane and I soft-step across the crust. We then pick a pleasurable path of exposed alpine tundra. Jane finds Doggy Heaven; she grids the tundra in an attempt to catch every squeaking ground squirrel. I hold my breath as she sprints over steep rock formations. She is a mountain goat wearing a backpack with a bear bell. The bell is constantly ringing.

Puffing, we climb 1,500 feet together to reach Thompson Pass, the lowest navigable route through the Chugach Mountains. With a clear, panoramic view of polished chrome Chugach peaks, I look past the brown blur of Jane to the valley. I now have an airplane's view of where Jane and I started the day, six hours and two miles ago. We are nested in the Chugach Mountains, 2,812 feet above the salt water of Port Valdez.

No tent tonight in Thompson Pass. Jane and I have climbed above the bugs. The warmth, too. It's near freezing as I cook dinner. Our kitchen table is a rock scarred with corduroy lines by a retreating glacier. While eating spoonfuls of sweet-and-sour pork with rice that crunches, I am warmed by almost every piece of clothing in the pack: underwear, long johns, nylon pants, rain pants. Gloves, mittens over gloves. Two light polypropylene shirts, one heavy one. A pile jacket. A wool hat. A raincoat, hood up. Thompson Pass is clear; the heat of the day shimmers away.

One last stroll before hitting the sleeping bag, to experience again the first real reward of the hike: the pleasure of looking back, miles back, to the stand of cottonwood where

Jane and I camped the night before. A satisfied feeling, that these little legs carried us that far, that it took all day, that we have all summer to feel this again and again.

4 Golf Under the Volcanoes

Day 16

"It's easy to lose your ball on this hole," Doug Vollman says. "The muskeg just sucks it up."

Doug has invited me to play golf with him on his five-acre homesite. I accept, and we use our hands to part the brush, looking for my second shot from the tee. It went long.

"This is actually the best time of year to play," Doug says, bending, "because there's no leaves."

He sees white among the bushes. "Here it is! A Titleist 3, right?"

We resume play, both gripping seven irons that were leaning in the arctic entryway of his cabin, which sits in the Copper River Basin. A pan of lowlands the size of Yosemite Park, the basin is rimmed by the Chugach Mountains to the south, the Alaska Range to the north, the Talkeetna Mountains to the west, and the Wrangell Mountains to the east. The majestic Copper River drains the basin, carrying water and mountains of sediment south to the Gulf of Alaska.

Two miles west of the Copper River, Doug has constructed a rustic, impressive, nine-hole golf course. Spruce sticks the thickness of pool cues serve as pins, marking each of the nine holes. To make his pins more visible, Doug has capped each with a fluorescent orange dog bootie, made of fuzzy pile, worn to transparency by the feet of his 12 sled dogs. Putting greens are a lumpy combination of wet moss and wood chips. In the center of the course, beneath a few spruce trees, is a faded green Ford Torino station wagon. The wagon has no wheels. Its rear axle has been scavenged.

"You get a free drop if you hit it in the station wagon," Doug says.

"Is there a hole in which the station wagon is a factor?"

"It depends on how bad your aim is."

I met Doug Vollman one week ago. He was working as a bartender at Tsaina Lodge, about 60 miles south of here on the Richardson Highway. Doug and his wife recently moved from Valdez to this isolated subdivision, just two miles by dog sled from the Copper River, one mile from the Richardson Highway. They made the move not because of job opportunity, or any other reason related to economics.

"It's where we want to live," Doug had said at Tsaina Lodge. His words came back to me as Jane and I walked the Richardson Highway to bypass private property along the pipeline. It was midnightish, but beautiful—clear and cool. To our right, suddenly, were the Wrangell Mountains, snow-white peaks nosing upward. The highest, Mount Blackburn, pokes three miles into the atmosphere.

Mounts Drum, Sanford, Wrangell and Blackburn all stood at blue-white attention in the subarctic twilight.

Wrangell, an active volcano, held its sulfurous breath, though the locals say its puffs are visible in winter.

To avoid private property adjacent to the pipeline and the rumored inhospitality of those who live on the flanks of Willow Mountain ("Those people will point a gun at you," a pipeline official had told me), Jane and I walked the shoulder of the Richardson Highway. Because we walked faster than usual trying to get away from the cars and broken glass on the roadside, we covered 16 miles, a new distance record. Just as we were about to hike back to the pipeline along an access road, I remembered that Doug had said he lived at a certain milepost on the Richardson Highway. I set my backpack down, pulled out my notebook, and found we were within a mile of his home.

As Jane and I walked a dirt road off the highway, a headlight appeared. It was Doug, driving a four-wheeler that puffed blue smoke into cold night air.

"Let me take your pack," he said. "You can get on the back, too."

I had carried my pack every inch from Valdez; I wanted to carry it across Alaska. I felt a bit silly about my reluctance to give it up, but Doug nodded when I only gave him Jane's load.

Doug slung Jane's pack behind his seat and throttled on through a neighborhood without lawns, each house with its own distinct style: a plywood rental, a house adorned with license plates and other signage (including a pilfered Alyeska no-trespassing sign), a western-style ranch complete with horses. Ten families live in the subdivision; all have acquired homesites.

Though the Homesite Program, created by the Alaska State Legislature in 1977, Alaskans were able to claim up to five acres for the costs of surveying the plot and a $10 application fee. To make sure the homesite applicants were serious about hacking a home from the forest, the state also required participants to "prove up," to construct a permanent, single-family dwelling on the site within five years and to live there for 35 months within seven years of the application. The Homesite Program is currently in a state of slumber. State land managers are too busy with other tasks to select lands and administer the program.

"One of the problems is that they don't generate any revenue," state resource manager Dick Mylius said of the homesites. "The public wants to keep the costs of government down. We get more inquiries from people who want to buy land now than we do from people who want homesites or homesteads."

Except when Oprah's on. A recent Oprah Winfrey show on homesteading in Alaska had Mylius and other state employees fielding dozens of calls from those outside Alaska who dreamed of a home in the Alaska bush. Before explaining that homesite and homesteads are virtually unavailable, Mylius and others disarmed the callers by mentioning the first qualification for homesteads and homesites — state residency.

Jane and I walked through pink twilight. Though nearly midnight, it was light enough to read a book outside on May 18th. The closer we got to Doug's homesite, the more the road deteriorated. From hard-packed soil, we turned south to a blackened clearing that smelled bitter, of freshly minced willows. The road was now a bog of black peat that looked like a rototilled garden. Only the most functional of four-wheel drives had left tracks through the spring quagmire. It was hard to walk without losing my boots to the muck. I worried about Jane being impaled on a willow dagger. As Doug rolled into the port of his driveway, Jane and I followed, reaching his haven of dry soil.

Jane's tiptoe into the yard caused 12 sled dogs, chained to spruce trees on both sides of the driveway, to erupt in choppy barks.

"You can camp anywhere," Doug said, "but I'd suggest on the other side of the house, where the dogs can't see Jane."

For the tent site, I chose the fairway of hole No. 1. A square of plywood nailed to a spruce tree tells golfers that hole No. 1 is 75 yards, par 3, handicap 6. With tent standing and sleeping bag unstuffed and slowly inflating, I sat on the stump of a tree that was removed to allow for the flight of golf balls. I boiled water for a late freeze-dried dinner. An hour later, inside the tent, Jane and I fell asleep to the song of a few hundred wood frogs, howling huskies, and the spooky whistle of the common snipe.

With Jane sniffing around the course, Doug and I are now on the eighth of nine holes. Due to the shallow groundwater table, many of these holes indicate success with a splash. The ground makes squishing noises.

Doug lofts his second shot toward hole No. 8. The ball flies with a promising arc toward the bootied spruce stick.

It falls directly in the cup, its landing padded by leaves and mulch. I shake my head.

"I don't believe you just did that."

"When you play as often as I do, you're bound to do that a few times," he says. Golfers have nailed four holes-in-one on the course; Doug has three of them. He's a young 40, with a trim, symmetrical beard and brown hair that tumbles over his right eye; he frequently skirts the hair aside with his hand. Today, he wears jeans, a navy-blue sweatshirt, and a blue baseball cap with the name of his favorite team, the Seattle Mariners.

My final putt rolls over moss and sinks to the bottom of hole No. 9. Though I've been whipped, Doug compliments me for parring two holes. He, his wife, and a friend constructed the course during the last year-and-a-half. The field of play covers several acres, including a fairway that was once part of the Eagle Trail, a route from Valdez to the Yukon River where a telegraph line was strung in the early 1900s.

The surrounding forest contains many standing dead — the legacy of the bark beetle. Doug removed many of the trees to make his golf course. He's passionate about golf, about sports in general. Baseball is a favorite topic. "I don't think you can be considered a superstar unless you score 100 runs a season and drive in 100 runs," he says. "Lou Gehrig did it 14 times."

After our morning round of golf, chores call. Doug pulls two rectangular gaskets from a plastic bag, then busies his hands in the guts of his pickup truck. With the gaskets, he hopes to plug whatever gap is causing his truck to stain the driveway.

I use the day as a break from hiking, a day of gear mending and body maintenance for me and Jane. Jane stretches in the sun, which continues to bleach her fur from chocolate to strawberry blond. My hiking partner lies on the grass with a groan and, satisfied I'm not going anywhere, naps in the sun.

I stitch the leading corners of her doggy backpack. Her abrasive journeys through the bushes in search of hare and grouse are pulling the seams apart. I do the best I can with dental floss and duct tape. After finishing, I dab wax on my hiking boots, set them in the sun, and drape my damp clothes over the tent. I wear my river-crossing sneakers, happy to be out of the hiking boots for a day. My ankles, stiff every morning from the previous day's hike, flex without pain today.

Jane starts to snore; I kneel down to pet her warm fur. She snoozes from honest days of exercise. It makes me happy to watch her sleep.

Doug Vollman and Marnie Graham have lived at this homesite for the past three years. They didn't prove up: they purchased the land from the man who did. Their house consists of three parts, from two eras. Two milled lumber sections, the color of a faded canary, were the work of the original landowner. Doug and Marnie also inherited the Ford Torino hazard, several 1970s-era snow machine exoskeletons, and assorted other hunks of metal and wood, some of which they're still discovering in walks around the property. To the canary house, Doug and Marnie added a handsome 20-foot-square log room, which projects north, toward the swampy subdivision road.

Inside the house, the log section is bright, a quality Doug credits to Marnie's patient work with triceps and sandpaper.

Marnie, 10 years younger than her husband, has clear blue eyes and a smile that stays even when her face muscles relax. She laughs frequently, a genuine laugh. She seems taller than she is, four-foot-eleven and one-half-inch.

The door to the cabin is left open. It's a warm day today, but it wasn't six months ago. In winter, the Copper River Basin — expansive flats between everwhite mountains — holds some of the coldest air in Alaska. The peaks hem in the frigid molecules, which slumber under a layer of warmer air. Only winds, which mix cold with warm, can break a cold snap. Sometimes the winds stay away for weeks.

The couple stays warm with a drip oil heater and a woodstove. When nature calls, they follow the urge outside. An outhouse, otherwise serviceable, has a door attached by only the top hinge. A plywood pendulum. Doug could repair the door rather quickly, but he hasn't. It works as is, and he'd rather spend those minutes running his dogs in winter, or building steps for the cabin in summer.

The subdivision has electricity, which sometimes powers a television set. Doug tuned it to "The Price is Right" this morning while he cooked two helpings of fried eggs, coffee, and toast. When he talked to me, his eyes rarely strayed from Bob Barker.

Doug and Marnie treat me to a couple meals. The second is a dinner of steak, baked potatoes, cucumbers, tomatoes, and baked beans. In the cozy log section of their home, Doug and Marnie tell me how they got here.

Six years ago, Marnie was working at the library in Valdez; Doug had returned to town after spending a few months chasing halibut on the ocean. A mutual friend introduced them, Doug started calling. He made Marnie smile.

After they married, they decided Valdez, Alaska's seventh most populated city with 4,400 people, was too crowded.

"At the time, I was moving to Valdez because I thought it was the most beautiful place on Earth, and that's where I wanted to live," Marnie says. "Doug was just ready to leave because he had just worked the oil spill and he was burned out."

"I was having to travel to fish because the fisheries weren't doing too good for me in the sound," Doug says. "I was on my way out, she was on her way in. Somehow we stayed in Valdez about four years."

"Before he convinced me, and I saw through the whole experience myself that that wasn't the life I wanted to live."

They chose a remote subdivision at the end of a quicksand road. Why?

"I'd like to learn how to live a little bit differently," Marnie says. "I like living up here because I'm not exposed to so much materialism. I don't have signs telling me to buy something every day. Just now, if we were to drive down to Valdez, in one day I could spend easily two weeks' worth of money that I would spend up here. And you're not even trying. You're just going out to dinner or buying a birthday card instead of making one."

"It's easier to simplify your life up here," Doug nods. "We have less distractions. The closest restaurant — I guess we could go to the Grizzly [pizza restaurant] to eat, about a mile away, but there's not the temptation to just go out and spend. It takes an effort sometimes just to get out of the driveway."

Doug no longer removes pulp from the juicer at Tsaina Lodge to earn money. He just got summer work with the Alaska Department of Fish and Game. He'll be counting king salmon that return from the Pacific to the Copper, then hang a left at the Klutina River. Marnie is working seasonally for Wrangell St. Elias National Park and Preserve. Today was her first day. Doug's pickup survived the mud bog as he drove to nearby Copper Center to retrieve her in time for dinner.

Their recent job changes remind me of a friend who came to Alaska searching for something other than the constancy of a secure job. His last job, picking mushrooms, lasted only a month but was exactly what he wanted. He sleeps on my couch occasionally, or camps in the yard. He makes enough money to last a few months, then tries another job, having faith that something else will come along when needed. Something always does. Just like Doug and Marnie, what really matters to him is that he enjoys what he's doing, and that he enjoys where he's doing it.

"I can't think of any other place that I'd want to be right now," Doug says. "And now, with the job situation falling into place, as long as we enjoy our jobs we'll probably have them. Plus, it'll allow me to develop a good dog team that will somehow pay for themselves. In my dreams, at least."

The cabin is a familiar style, the Alaska Work-in-Progress: a bale of hay serves as a step. Inside, a plywood floor, a gravity-feed water system. Sitting in a corner, an acoustic guitar.

"Hopefully, at some point, living here as opposed to in one of the cities in Alaska will allow us to become more creative," Doug says. "We pretend to play music at times, and I've done a bit of writing for the newspapers down in Valdez. Marnie does some sewing, and she's knitted and done other things."

"It's definitely not for everybody," Marnie adds. "Last summer I had friends come and visit, and they got caught with lots of free time, lots of sitting time, quiet time, thinking time. They don't know what to do with themselves. It really makes them nervous and antsy."

Marnie gets me thinking about quiet time, something I've had in abundance during the walk. Though silence is a gift that's often easy to find in Alaska, it usually hits you unexpectedly, like a pocket of cool air on a hot day. You either sit back and savor it for its contrast with normal life, or you make some noise to fill the void. At home, I usually play music when the quiet gets me too introspective. Out here, I'll sing or talk to Jane, but must of the time I leave the hush alone.

Eleven p.m. The light's still with us, so it's time to get back to the pipeline. Doug has told me about a shortcut, a path through the woods that he uses as mushing trail in winter. I grab Jane's pack. When she hears the bear bell, she walks the other way, not thrilled with this new ritual of carrying her own food. I coax her with a dog biscuit. As she pulverizes the biscuit, I saddle her with her pack and click the plastic snaps snugly to her belly and chest. I heft my own pack, now a bit heavier than my dog, and fasten the waist belt. Grunting at the weight, I pick up my shotgun, which was leaning against Doug and Marnie's house.

As we leave, Doug repeats a suggestion he first made when we met at Tsaina Lodge. Anybody could walk the pipeline, he says. Why not *golf* the pipeline, hitting a ball from Valdez to Prudhoe Bay?

"You're sure you won't take that seven iron?"

5 | Copper Center

Day 17

An orange sign clamped to the pipeline tells me that Jane and I have walked 100 miles. On May 21, one-eighth of our journey is complete. We have hiked to, through, and away from the Chugach Mountains. In 16 days, we have tasted salt water at Port Valdez, ice water in 2,812-foot Thompson Pass, and bitter brown water from a wood frog breeding pond near Pump Station 12.

I filter water where I find it. Jane laps puddles and creeks as she stands in them. Sometimes she dips her tongue like a pink ladle while in pursuit of a snowshoe hare.

Alyeska Pipeline Service Co. engineers once counted the number of waterways the pipeline intersects in its path across Alaska. They came up with 834 — 34 major rivers, such as the Yukon, and 800 streams. Most of the streams I've been able to walk across without topping my hiking boots.

Stopping to pump water is my favorite part of the day. Sitting streamside, listening to water born of winter snows tumbling over rocks, my slow-motion journey rolls to a halt. My shoulders out from under the backpack, I feel feathery, free. Jane, seeing me pull out the water filter, makes one to three revolutions above a nap site, then plops down with a satisfied groan.

I filter the water mainly to avoid Giardia lamblia, an organism that could stop the walk in one dreadful afternoon. Giardia live in beavers, muskrats, dogs and people who have swallowed one or more cysts, invisible little eggs that attach to the wall of the large intestine, multiply like crazy, then block uptake of liquids. I got Giardia once just by licking my lips to taste the spray of an Alaska river. It wiped me out for a week, sucking away all the energy that was left after my sprints to the outhouse. Before this trip, when I wrote the Katadyn company asking for a water filter, I told them it was the most important thing I would carry.

Because the human body's cells work better when they're saturated, I force down gallons of Alaska every day. When people don't drink enough in the outdoors, they get cold easier, they get tired easier, they feel like crap and they don't know why.

I drink one quart for breakfast tea, two quarts back-to-back before I begin hiking, several more bottles during the day, and one quart for my nightly tea. It makes me stop to pee several times each mile. When I'm drinking enough, Alaska water looks the same on the way out as on the way in.

Quiet moments by the water, when I drink and Jane snoozes, have been the best times out here. I think of where the water comes from—a silent November snowfall in the mountains, water that had fallen elsewhere on the planet at another time. This water, like all the water on Earth today, has been recycled by the sun countless times. Snow and rainfall percolate through the ground, or are absorbed by plants or animals, which give water back to the atmosphere when they breathe. The water vapor finds its way back to clouds, and the cycle repeats itself. Earth's water has changed forms since the beginning. These clear streams in the Chugach were once Pacific Ocean, recharged by rain and glacial melt. A water molecule in this stream could have part of a snowflake on Mount Fuji a few years back. Through ice ages and warming periods, the same particle may have trapped as a solid for centuries as glaciers covered North America, then freed to once again flow to the sea. A few molecules of this water may have quenched the thirst of a Tyrannosaurus Rex, who a few hours later made an impressive contribution to the hydrologic cycle.

Whatever its past, I know this water's future; it's on its way to the Copper River. The Copper is not one of the 834 rivers and streams the pipeline crosses. The pipeline elbows northwest at Copper Center, a community of 500 at the junction of the Klutina and Copper rivers. Near Copper Center, the Copper River is a two-mile walk from the pipeline pad. I decide I need to dip my feet in the roiling brown river, to see where all this mountain water is going.

Jane and I walk down an incline. We step into spring. Where deciduous trees were bare one-half mile ago, we're surrounded by aspens topped fuzzy, neon green. A million solar panels slowly unfold.

Walking into the valley where the Klutina River races

toward the Copper, I see a sign: *Keep Out*. I think of my shotgun. The stainless-steel barrel makes the gun impossible to hide. Even though some people call this the Last Frontier, a shotgun-toting backpacker still merits a good hard look from the locals. The first local to glance my way is a man on a three-wheeler. He rolls to a stop and starts a conversation with the question he most wants to ask.

"What're you up to?"

I tell him what I'm doing. Jane, wearing her backpack, is instant confirmation. The man nods, then takes a short swig of Miller High Life in a can.

"Gun to keep the bears off?"

"Yup."

"Use it yet?"

"Nope. So far, so good."

"Looks like you're carrying about 57 pounds."

"Yeah, probably right around there."

"That's a pretty good pack."

"I like it so far. I hauled a moose out with the frame last year."

"No, I mean you're carrying quite a load."

He carries a Ziploc of bloody burger behind him, on the seat of his Honda Big Red. His four-wheeler has a gas tank that looked as if a softball bounced off it.

"Meat's rancid," he says. "Too much garlic. I'm taking it for a ride to the river. Get rid of it. Oh, I'm Mike by the way. Mike Phillips."

I shake his hand while telling him my name.

Mike looks as if he has missed a night's sleep. He wears a flannel shirt and jeans over a boyish, thin frame. I can tell by his breath that this beer is not his first of the day. He says he has done quite a bit of work on the pipeline, but this summer he'll pilot his boat, the R-J, in Bristol Bay. Fishing for salmon, drift netting. Damn tough work.

"How old are you?" he asks.

"Thirty-four."

"Cool," he says. "You picked a good time to do this. Seize the day. Enjoy this trip while you can."

I guess Mike is about 45.

"Can you tell me the shortest way to the Copper River?" I ask.

"Hop on back, I'll give you a ride."

"I'd rather walk, thanks."

"OK. I don't want to mess up your system."

He tells me the best roads through Copper Center to reach the Copper River. He speeds off, dragging a cloud of dust.

I hesitate, finding Jane's leash and ejecting shotgun shells so I can carry my shotgun with an open chamber.

By the time I've walked 100 feet, Mike Phillips drives up to me again. He has disposed of the meat. I wave. He stops. I double check my route. He patiently repeats directions, then extends an invitation.

"If you want to come back this way, you can set up your tent in my yard. There's a trampoline on the lawn. If you want to, set your tent up right on top of the trampoline. Best view in town. Just go up the hill until you can't go any farther."

He motors toward home. Jane and I begin our diversion to where all the water is going.

The paved streets of a town feel different under my boots than the gravel of the pipeline pad. My feet strike the pavement at the same angle with each step. It's more tiring than gravel, but it's also familiar and comfortable. Walking into town, I would be more comfortable without the shotgun. Jane, leaning on her leash, pulls me across a bridge that spans 20 yards of roiling gray river. The Klutina. It was here that the gold seekers from Valdez dragged their whipsawed spruce boats ashore 100 years ago. I look at the Klutina's tumbling whitecaps and random boulders and think of wood smashing on rocks. Luther Guiteau, a French cook from Freeport, Illinois, kept a diary of his travels in 1898. He described his trip from Valdez, including a run down the rapids of the lower Klutina:

It was a terrible, swift and thrilling ride. When we pulled out from shore at the head of the Rapids, we could hear all kinds of remarks from the twenty or thirty people who stood there to bid us goodbye. One fellow said, "We'll never see those suckers again."

Guiteau and his boat partner, Philo Snow, successfully shot the rapids in homemade bateaus — flat-bottomed boats with boards forming Vs at bow and stern — thanks to a steam-fired saw mill that a few entrepreneurs from San Jose sledded over Valdez Glacier.

Those who made it down the Klutina found a tent city set up on a sandbar where the Klutina meets the Copper River. One of the early arrivals at the site, a Norwegian named Mr. Holman, laid out a townsite, named it Copper Center, and set up tents that became a post office, hotel and store. Mr. Holman created the first town in Alaska's interior.

Jane wears her leash, but Lucky doesn't. Lucky is a black-and-white husky who bolts from a roadside trailer to sniff Jane's privates and bounce along with us. I know the dog's name is Lucky because Lucky's master is calling him from the doorway of the Copper Center Bar. Lucky doesn't respond. He joins us as we move past two long-haired men standing by their motorcycles outside the Copper Center Bar, which looks like a red shoe box.

"Don't shoot," a blond man says through yellow teeth as he raises his hands in mock-surrender.

"Don't worry. Uh, can you tell me where the Copper Center Lodge is?"

"Keep walking the way you are and you're gonna run into it."

The Copper Center Lodge was known as the Blix Roadhouse 100 years ago. It's a tight, symmetrical log structure, two stories tall, with a tin roof. I clip Jane's leash to a birch tree next to a smaller log building that now houses the George I. Ashby Memorial Museum. I'd like to go in, see some of the possessions of the men who were here a century ago, but the museum is closed. Lucky, sensing the fun is over, turns and trots back toward the bar.

I walk into the lodge. The air is too warm. Four blond women busy themselves preparing the dining room. One looks at me, squints, then smiles.

"Paul, when did you get back? Nice to see you again."

I apologize for not being Paul. The woman says I look just like a Copper Center boy who went off to join the service.

I tell her I'm looking for a nice path to the Copper River, and I wonder if she can tell me the history of the area. She points the way to the river and hands me an information sheet: "The history of Copper Center Lodge is rooted in the Gold Rush of 1897-1898 when 4,000 men crossed the Valdez to Klutina glaciers on the way to the Klondike." A one-sentence history for a place that peaked a century ago. This place reminds me of my favorite place in the world, seven acres in the foothills of the Adirondack Mountains. In an old hay field, my father built a cabin about 20 years ago. Copper Center tickles the memory of upstate New York because, just like that old hay field that's slowly being invaded by shagbark hickories and sumac, this town has less going on now than it did a century ago. Despite this being a beautiful area, the people haven't come. Places like this defy logic — billions of people live on this planet, enough to justify the whole world looking like downtown Tokyo, but there are some corners that won't get touched in the near future. Maybe 40 below and a lack of nearby jobs has something to do with Copper Center's obscurity.

I return to Jane. She vaults. I unclip her, pick up the shotgun, and we scale a gravel mound that protects the lodge from the floodwaters that sometimes rise from where the Klutina thrusts itself into the Copper just 50 yards behind the lodge.

A rutted four-wheel-drive trail leads to the Copper River. Jane trots past grounded icebergs shaped like cumulous clouds. Taller than Jane, the hunks of ice weigh as much as a pickup truck. The icebergs are leftovers from the Copper River spring breakup, when a thick crust of ice decayed in the sun and was taken by the river. The river shrunk to expose a shoreline of rocks the size and shape of shot-puts.

Jane takes large bites of the Copper River, which is frothy and brown. The Copper carries soil from streams behind the Wrangells, powdered rock from the mountains. Though it shares its color with the Yukon, the Copper River squeezes through more narrow channels and has many times the punch.

The river cools the spaces between my toes, and I pump a quart of Copper River into my water bottle. I drink the nectar of the Wrangell Mountains while looking at Mount Drum, a white dome rising from the flatness of the basin. It's the same view men and women too far from home had a century before. They looked at the white mountain with apprehension, wanting to go beyond but hearing few stories of those who had succeeded.

It's time to find a trampoline to sleep on. Jane and I walk back through Copper Center, into the setting sun. Lucky doesn't show. The motorcycles are no longer parked in front of the Copper Center Bar. The door to the bar is open, though. I feel eyes upon us. As we pass the bar, someone cranks the stereo. "Freedom's just another word for nothin' left to lose," howls Janis Joplin. The volume drops to inaudible.

Mike Phillips' hands are smudged rusty brown. In his palms, he cups crescents of asbestos, the rear brake pads from his wife Lanette's minivan. With him in the garage is his son. Dan, 14, is as tall as his father. Like many boys who live in remote areas, Dan isn't shy. He doesn't avert his eyes when shaking a stranger's hand.

Mike stretches a spring with the tip of needlenose pliers, finishing the brake job. "Let's get cleaned up, Dan. Then we'll show Ned to the tramp."

I lift my pack and Jane's to the bed of Mike's pick-up truck. He drives us 200 feet up a hill, to the broad aspen plateau upon which he built his home. It's easy to tell this is his dream home, something he put a lot of thought into before building. The house is sturdy, with wooden steps that feel like cement. Wood siding that doesn't compete with the aspens. Picture windows facing east, toward a calendar view of the always-white Wrangell Mountains. Mount Drum tugs a cigar of cloud to the north. Its foothills have ridges as sharp as knife edges. To the left, Mount Wrangell, the volcano, lies like a body under a white sheet. Between the Phillips house and big mountains is a broad, flat, mosaic of dark and light green — the Copper River basin.

The Klutina, flowing from the mountains to the west, curves around the bench of aspen that surrounds the Phillips home. The river's static is louder than passing cars on the Richardson Highway, one-half mile off, in the direction of Mount Drum.

On the lawn sits the trampoline, a 15-foot-diameter elastic disc. I opt to camp on Kentucky bluegrass instead, because my tent needs to be staked to stand. My loss. Or maybe not. The lush green makes a sleeping pad optional.

Tiny palms of aspen leaves no longer catch the sun's rays. Dusk has fallen, and Mike strikes a wooden match. He bends and lights newspaper under kindling in a fire pit near the trampoline. Soon, flames lick beams the size of railroad ties. Mike sits on his picnic table, Miller in hand. He is joined by his wife, Lanette, a youthful brunette with white hairs framing her face as if she were walking outside at 30 below. Ten-year-old daughter Colleen uses her mom's legs as a back rest. Young Dan fiddles with the fire. Mitzie, a rodent-size Llasho Apso puppy with a bow in her hair, yips and launches herself at Jane. Sensing a pending Labrador explosion, I gather Mitzie in my lap.

As we talk while staring at flames, a pick-up truck so new it looks plastic rolls up the driveway. Out steps a man who smiles and nods.

He is tanned to redness, wearing a sleeveless black T-shirt with a white Nike swoop over his heart. His mane of curly brown hair sits atop a broad forehead, and his black beard and moustache hold clumps of white. He shakes my hand, says his name is Mark Gager, and listens to my recent history.

Mark is a storyteller. Hearing about me and Jane makes him remember back 20 years, when he and Phillips worked as pipeliners. It was a time that changed Alaska in ways they couldn't realize.

Mark talks fast and his laugh makes me laugh. He's from the south side of Chicago, and it's easy to picture him shirtless in the bleachers at Wrigley Field. When he talks, I notice he's missing his right ear.

Mike is smiling, sitting back because he knows a good story is coming. I pull out my little tape recorder and ask Mark if he minds. He doesn't.

Mark traveled north in 1974, looking for adventure, then a job.

"Me and my friend had our car ripped off in the Yukon,

and we didn't have any money and we're thinking, 'God, what are we going to do?' And we thought well, they're building this pipeline up there in Valdez, and all those people are going to go to work on the pipeline, and we can slip into the jobs that they quit. That was our plan."

"You had a car stolen in the Yukon?"

"At Dawson. Discovery Days, when they celebrate the Gold Rush. Yeah, it was just a drunken bash. We couldn't get our car started for a couple days, and we finally got it going. We thought we'd better get out of town while it's running. I didn't want to turn it off again. So I parked it, locked it, and left the vent window open so I could get back in, and we came back and it wasn't there. Found it in a ditch about 50 miles out of town."

"What about all your gear?" Mike asks, thin legs crossed at the knee, his body relaxed.

"It was in the ditch. We had a kitty, a money kitty, a little can on the dashboard. We had like 50 bucks in the kitty on the dashboard and it was still there. I had a gun that I smuggled into Canada, it was under the seat. That's what I was worried about, that they were gonna kill somebody with the gun I smuggled into Canada."

Both Mike and Mark settled the Copper River valley in 1974, when the pipeline ignited a boom.

"Temporarily," Mark laughs. "We came out here temporarily. At least I did."

"Was there a drastic change after the pipe went through?"

"I think it was a big change for the community," Lanette says, leaning into Mike. "We had just gotten here, so we didn't really notice, but I remember people talking about how it never went back to the way it was."

"A lot of yellow pickups," Mike says, uncoiling. "A lot of yellow pickups."

"I remember at the school they had like 50 kids in each class," Lanette says.

"Land prices kinda got crazy here too," Mark adds.

"Yellow pickups?"

"Alyeska pickups, they were yellow then. How did that work, Mark? Fifty below, in front of the Hub, and little yellow pickup trucks sitting all over there idling —"

"In front of every bar."

"In front of every bar, every night. Gun fights. How many gun fights can you think of? I can think of three."

"The only one I remember is the one where I took the gun away from Bob." Mark laughs. "I couldn't get it away from him, so I fired it off in the parking lot. He was gonna go blow Barry away." More laughs.

"The bars were full every night," Mark says, sitting on a sawhorse, a chopping block for his footrest. "There was Glennallen [pipeline construction] Camp up the road and Tonsina Camp down here. Close to Tonsina Camp was Tonsina Lodge. Bob and Margaret, the owners there, used to cash pipeliners' paychecks on Friday. And there was a race of these guys coming down to Tonsina Lodge because Bob and Margaret would cash $1,000 paychecks. All they would keep were the cents, whatever the change was in the check, and they'd just give you the greenbacks. May cost you a penny, may cost you 99 cents to get your check cashed. And then everybody went around and spent it at the bar and Bob and Margaret got the money right back.

"Little Margaret — remember Mike, when somebody tried to rob her? Little Margaret, a little 80-year-old lady, would drive to Glennallen to the bank and pick up $100,000 in cash and drive back down to Tonsina Lodge. In her little red 1972 Dodge Duster. Well, somebody caught on to this."

"A hundred-thousand in 1975 dollars," Mike says.

"Yeah," Mark says, "So that's like probably a quarter million now. And she drives down to Tonsina Lodge from the bank, and somebody tried to rob her. And they couldn't catch her. She just put the pedal to the metal and outran 'em."

"What were the camps like?"

"There's still one in Valdez," Mark says. "If you want to walk back to Valdez and see them. You go to the airport and there's an original pipeline camp there."

"Close to a thousand men in each one," Mike says.

"Pump 12 had 230 men and nine women. We had 25 percent of the women there, Mike and I did," Mark laughs. "We both had our girlfriends working there too."

"The rooms were like sheer snot," Mike adds. "Paisley carpeting on the floor. I was at Valdez man-camp last winter and I took a knife and I cut a square out of the cloth and I sent it to my brother to remind him of the good old days … You could hear everything through the walls — snoring, arguing, a poker game, whatever went on. They were like cardboard walls. No — cardboard would have been better. No privacy at all, especially if you had a roommate. It was harsh. You were working 24 hours a day, basically.

"You've got to understand, when you're in a camp, they own you. If you've got slack time there, you've just about got to get paid for it to make it worth your while because you're there."

"The first couple of nights in a camp, you say 'God, these are nice accommodations,'" Mark says. "Like in the pump stations today, you've got cable TV. You've got a workout room that rivals any health club. But it gets to the point where that's an artificial environment. Especially up north, at Prudhoe. In the wintertime, you do nothing outside, recreationally. I got a hard time recreating at 50 below."

"I have a hard time recreating after working 12 hours a day," Mike says. "I get tired. And they own the other 12 because you've got basically enough time to get back to camp, have a meal, and get maybe an hour or two of your own space, and that's it."

"What was the wage 20 years ago?"

"Ten bucks."

"Actually, '76 was the most money I ever made," Mark says. "Mike and I have been through this. Made enough in six weeks to buy a brand-new, four-wheel-drive pickup truck. Then, I didn't know which end of the shovel to push the dirt with. Now, I'm supposed to know a little bit, and it takes me about 20 weeks to buy a four-wheel drive pickup truck."

"Just about anybody that wanted a job, got a job," Mike says. "People chose not to deal with it too. Things were crazy. There was a lot of fast, easy, money made. Valdez was even crazier than here. That place was nuts. There were women of the night and anything else you wanted at the bar."

"How did it compare with Valdez after the spill?"

"That's a different era, '89 and '76. It was wild after the spill, but it wasn't *as* wild. The spill was a flash in the pan compared to the pipeline. But it still was crazy. Mark worked down there."

"Yeah, I got a job as a diver. Didn't even know how, but they hired me anyway. A couple days later I'm in a wetsuit diving under the *Exxon Valdez,* where it was hung up there on Bligh Reef. We were just inspecting it. The guy who knew what he was doing took me under it. The thing was rocking, making a lot of noise. *Rrrrrrhhhhhtt.* It was real noisy under there. And he was swimming under it. I wouldn't go under it. I kept like a six-foot clearance between me and the bottom. I didn't know how much that thing was gonna rock. Talk about being squished like a mosquito. Fifty bucks an hour, guaranteed."

The railroad ties in the fireplace are now glowing white briquettes. They collapse at the touch of a stick. Coolness surrounds us like fluid. Mike clamps his hand on Dan's knee.

"It's getting close to my bedtime, bud. What do you say we all go up and show Ned the helipad?"

Dan concurs. He and I and Jane jump into the bed of Mike's truck. Mike and Mark step into the cab. We motor to the Richardson Highway, cross the Klutina River bridge, then chug up a steep road through woods that smell of spruce. Dan and I pin our backs to the cab window because the moving air is too chilly to take. I hug Jane to my chest to keep me warm and to keep her from jumping out of the truck.

The "helipad" is a table of sand several hundred feet above the Phillips' home. Mike kills the engine. We all exit the truck. Jane is the only creature not smitten with the view. I throw a spruce stick toward the bushes. She bounds.

Up here, we have a 180-degree vista. The Wrangells are powder blue. To the south is the bumpy white belt of the Chugach Mountains. I feel a sense of accomplishment — Jane and I walked through those mountains. A waxing moon, one day from being full, hangs above the Chugach. Looking down, I see through the spruce trees what looks like a strand of barbed wire — the pipeline. From here, I remember a poet who described the pipeline as a glistening thread of spider web stretched across Alaska. The author wanted to show both the beauty of technology and the pipeline's insignificance on a landscape so vast, but from here the beauty isn't working. The sharp line cut through aspen and spruce hillsides doesn't fit with these mountains, with the moon, with the flatlands that drain into the magnificent Copper. The pipe is an example of man accomplishing the bizarre to fuel a lifestyle that further threatens Alaska all the time. Oil flowing through that strand of barbed wire will be burned in an inefficient Chrysler in Toledo and made into a plastic milk jug that will sit in a Boise landfill for hundreds of years without decomposing. The pipe doesn't look like a spider web from here. It looks like order among beautiful disorder.

We corral Jane, busy wrecking a stick, and ride the brakes back down to the Phillips house. As I crawl into the tent, Mike asks me if I want him to wake me for coffee in the morning. I do.

I stay an extra day with the Phillips family. My third installment of columns is due, and I need to write them. The picnic table makes an excellent desk. Jane seems to enjoy the off day. She stretches out on the lawn, occasionally rolling on her back to moan at the pleasure of tummy rubs.

Later that night, after eating cheeseburgers in 70-degree heat that has us all moving in slow motion, Mike and I linger at the picnic table.

Mike sits on his picnic table, watching the fire. He's a fisherman 100 miles from the ocean, closer to a volcano than to salt water. His home here is an island, privately owned land amid hundreds of square miles belonging to a Native corporation, which is in turn surrounded by state and federal lands. When he looks out to the Wrangells, he sees the largest national park in the United States. Mike has told me that his island of aspen is where he hides from the world, retreats to projects like brake repair that keep him humble. His time here is his own.

Mike's a type I've seen often in Alaska, someone who doesn't want other people doing too much for him. Stubborn and resourceful, someone who learns how to do a lot of things by himself with whatever materials may be at hand. In a storm at sea, I'd trust him to find a port.

We both watch the moon, now full, climbing up naked stems of aspen. Mike points his beer can toward the floating white circle.

"See that full moon? Think of us the next time you see it. The next time you sleep under a full moon, think of us, sweating blood in Bristol Bay."

6 | **Alaska Roadhouse**

Day 26

Since crossing the highway bridge over the Gulkana River a few days ago, Jane and I have been walking uphill. We're making the subtle climb to the Alaska Range, a fold of snow-covered mountains curving from Canada to the Alaska Peninsula. Mt. McKinley, a molar among canines, juts 20,320 feet on the western end of the range. On our end, the east, the Alaska Range relaxes. Pipeline engineers chose a path through Isabel Pass, a broad table in the mountains, 3,420 feet above sea level.

We have walked out of the warmth of the Copper River Valley. The tailwind Jane and I have enjoyed is still there, but now, on May 29, the wind has enough bite that I pull on a wool hat when we stop at night. As we step toward the Alaska Range, the pipeline zigzags in a fashion that would make the pad an irritating drive at 30 miles per hour. It's a pleasant walk, though. At walking speed, I don't notice the pipe's twists and turns, a design that allows the steel pipeline to expand

and contract with Alaska's drastic changes of temperature.

Though the Alaska Range is clear, threatening clouds lurk behind us, and they're gaining. Now overhead, now blocking blue sky. After two weeks of sleeping without a rain fly, we are due. Thunder claps through the valley. I wonder if my stainless-steel shotgun is a lightning rod in my right hand.

More immediate problems appear from the woods. A cow moose and her two calves step out from the alders, 100 yards ahead. The calves are newborn, gangly and orange, eyes like coal on a snowman.

"Hold up, Jane."

The mother has seen us. That's bad. I'd rather see a bear this close than a cow moose with twins. She'll defend her babies with seven-hundred pounds of maternal energy. Jane has been charged in my backyard in Fairbanks by a mother moose. Jane didn't get stomped, but only because the cow missed, its hooves pounding the ground instead. Jane, then a pup, learned a good lesson as she slunk back to the cabin that day. She wants nothing to do with big animals.

I slowly back up; Jane does an about-face and follows.

Hair on the cow's neck is standing, like an aggressive dog's. As I walk backwards, I chamber a noisemaker shell. The metal clunking of the shotgun's action seems to do the trick — the cow turns and leads her babies back into the brush. Heart pounding, I decide this is a good time for a break.

Poor mother moose. While the bull moose donates nothing but sperm to the next generation (a biologist once called bulls "serial monogamists," a definition that made me laugh until I realized it also described me), mama moose face the yearly trauma of watching their babies die. Wildlife biologists think a moose population is healthy if four calves out of 10 make it to their first birthday. A newborn moose calf can't outrun a bear until it's about five weeks old, making late May a good time to be a black bear or grizzly. With hooves and fury, mother moose are excellent defenders of their young, but bears still find a way to nail a wandering twin or a single calf that doesn't stay close to its mother.

When we start walking again, I notice the earth's warmth is fleeing. My thermometer read 65 in the morning. Now, with Jane nested in soft moss as I make camp at nine, it's 43. I've camped close to the Richardson Highway because I need a phone. My columns are due, and pumping the water filter is now like bench pressing 200 pounds. I can't move the handle anymore. I've tried taking it apart, washing it, boiling it. It still takes more muscle than I have. I need cleaning instructions for the Katadyn Pocket Filter. I need to call the company.

That night, the rain comes. I've suspended a tarp over my screen tent. The tarp is loud with water droplets smacking blue plastic. The rain is heavy enough that I worry about leaks, about a wet sleeping bag.

In the morning, my rain worries are over. Two inches of snow sag the tarp. A cozy snail, I burrow in my sleeping bag. Jane rests her brown head on the ridge of sleeping bag covering my knee.

Hunger pulls me from the tent. The cold makes me hyper, as if I just drank a few cups of coffee. I deflate the tent, then shake and fold the wet tarp. Knowing Meiers Lake Roadhouse is just a mile away, I slip two energy bars in my raincoat pocket. To retrieve breakfast for Jane, I lower the food bag from between two trees. She gobbles the nuggets like a shark attacking a carcass; I don't think she breathes when she eats. After 30 seconds, she finishes. I put her pack in the food bag, cinch the top, and hoist it once again out of other mammals' reach. I'll leave the stuff here rather than carrying everything to the roadhouse.

Jane and I walk out to the Richardson Highway. Collared and leashed, she is my willing captive. We walk on shiny pavement through snowflakes the size of nickels. Down the highway, a lake appears. At its southern edge is Meiers Lake Roadhouse.

I clip Jane to the roadhouse porch that projects toward the highway. I turn a faulty doorknob several revolutions before the gears catch. A bell rings when I close the door. To my immediate left is an old-fashioned cash register, no electricity required. Three people sit in a bar next door. I join them.

"Hi," I say, wrapped in black raingear, mittens and wool hat. "Can somebody tell me if there's anywhere I can get my dog out of the snow?"

A man with an overflowing waist and glasses that give him the look of an owl wipes his hands on a stained apron.

"No," he says, shaking jowls east and west. "Can't bring it inside. It's against the health regulations."

I see a plastic kennel and dog toys on the floor, but I don't point out the contradiction. I walk back outside and splay Jane's foam mat on the ground next to the porch. The fur on her head is wet, clumping together like duck feathers. Her sad little girl eyes are too much for me. I take her with me into an arctic entryway where there's a pay phone. With Jane at my feet, I dial the 800 number for Katadyn water filter company. A guy named Ed tells me he has been enjoying my columns and that I can clean the filter by scouring the ceramic surface with sandpaper.

While I talk to Ed, Jane tugs the leash. A poodle the size of a loaf of bread prances into the entryway. Little-dog barks shatter the air. A stern-faced man with a baseball cap apparently made from the skin of a dairy cow follows the dog in.

"Put that dog in your car!" he growls. He steps past me and into the roadhouse, glaring at Jane. I hang up the phone, and take Jane back out to the porch. I stake my buddy out in the snow. "Sorry, Bones. I'll try to make this quick."

Back inside, I meet the man who snarled at me. Galen Atwater is the owner of Meiers Lake Roadhouse. Robin McCormick is the cook. Sitting at the bar are Ray, an old-timer in a red felt hat, and Connie and Bob, a couple from Anchorage up to check out land they just purchased at Hogan Hill, where I saw caribou legs left by hunters and gnawed by bears a few miles back.

I tell Atwater that Jane and I are hiking across Alaska, that I don't have a car to put my dog in, that I am writing weekly columns for the Fairbanks newspaper. With apologetic brows, Atwater asks me questions about the trip as I hang my damp raincoat on the back of a chair. I order a breakfast from McCormick. Atwater grabs my sopping mittens and wedges them into a crack in wood paneling near an oil heater. Jane still can't come in.

Atwater's speech has a Kennebunkport edge. He came to Alaska from Maine in 1955, for "a betta life. Tired of workin two jobs, not having enough money to pay the bills in Florider and Maine. My wife had been here before, told me great stories about it that were all true. Utopia."

"What was it like then?"

"Pretty slim. There were no jobs. I had a job. I was selling appliances for Bigelow's Vacuum Sales and Service, 326 Fifth Avenue in Anchorage. And I did well at that and then I bought Mendeltna Lodge at the KOA Campground there on Mile 153 of the Glenn. Lost everything I had. Then I joined the carpenter's local and got it back. But it was pretty slim. If my neighbor, my very best friend, would come home with a shopping bag, we would all run over to his house and see what was in the bag, and probably share it. If we came home with a bag, here comes his family. And that's the way it was. There were no service groups. The Salvation Army was here, but hell, I didn't know anything about the Salvation Army. I never thought to go ask them for a pound of butter or a loaf of bread. We cut Christmas trees, anything to make a buck. It was pretty slim then."

The warmth of the lodge massages my skull. Frank Sinatra sings "When I was 17" as McCormick places a plate on the bar in front of me. I bite into runny eggs.

Mickey Mouse, the poodle, is 15 pounds of white curls. He walks toward me, the bar his polished sidewalk.

"Mickey and I came out the same year, in 1928, so I named the dog Mickey Mouse," Atwater says. "But I changed it to Mickey Mooch, because he's such a bum. He mooches off'n everybody. All the time. He sits and stares with those big, round, brown eyes. See him do it? That's food he's thinking about — nothing else. No love, no nothing, just food. Right? Food. Heh-ha."

I think of Jane, outside absorbing wet snowflakes. I should be out there with her, but I need to fax two columns to Fairbanks. I tell McCormick I need a phone to send my columns.

"How?"

I pull out my palmtop computer.

"Wow. That thing's tiny."

McCormick finds me a phone line to fax the columns with. I drape wires over the bar and spill data over the phone line to Fairbanks to beat my deadline. With a fax modem card, thin as a Graham cracker and half the size of one, I can fax from anywhere I find a female phone jack. Thus far, phones have not been hard to find on the pipeline corridor.

I look out the window again. The snow, one degree from being rain, drops at 33 feet per second. Despite my sympathy for Jane, my dry feet are in no hurry to leave the warm, smoky bar.

Atwater urges me into a dining room and shows me a picture of the original Meiers Lake Roadhouse, a few log cabins surrounded by wall tents and hay bales. The Fairbanks-to-Valdez trail, a muddy rut in the center of the photograph, evolved into Alaska Route 4, the Richardson Highway, in 1923.

The log roadhouse was built 93 years ago by C. J. Meiers. In an area where a gas pump stands today, Meiers provided a different type of fuel.

"Meiers was working with Paxson," Atwater says. "They

were partners. When they needed a place every 20 miles to take care of the horses freighting from Valdez to Fairbanks, he moved down here and started raising hay and he built the lodge. One year, he sold $1,500 worth of hay. And this is like 1908, 1909. He was just tickled to death. That's a lot of money in those days."

A few of the Meiers' buildings remain. Atwater pulls me to a window and points out a relic privy.

"That's about 1908, see it, that little building with the white door? And when you go use that outhouse you leave the door open and you can see the world going by, so we call it the little theater. Heh-ha."

Atwater lives with his wife at Paxson Lake, about 15 miles north. Here, he says he found refuge from the encroachment of Anchorage, Alaska's largest city, upon Eagle River, 10 miles north. Time has changed Atwater's Alaska, but here, just like in Copper Center, he's found a place where time should remain frozen for awhile.

"I moved to Eagle River in 1955. And when McDonalds went up and so forth, I sought more peaceful grounds. Had to get the heck away from the traffic, and the people, and the murdering, and everything else that occurs. Eagle River's nothing more than a part of Anchorage anymore. It's just as problematical as Anchorage is."

Atwater pauses for a second, then looks at my tape recorder.

"Dealing with my dog and the swans out on the lake and the otter, and even the grizzlies — we respect their ground and stay away from it and they don't bother us. But it's much nicer dealing with the animals than it is the people."

A dog musher I know once stayed at Meiers Lake Roadhouse during a winter race through the Copper River Basin. He described Atwater as a grump and remembered having to ask more than once that the water be turned on so he could water his dogs. When Atwater turned on the plumbing, all the water was cold.

"What's it like in winter here?"

"Quiet and peaceful. We're open in winter but we don't do much business. I was in the North Slope restaurant in Eagle River not too long ago, having coffee with my old buddies. One of them asked me how business was. I says, 'Well, not too bad day before yesterday. We sold a Coca Cola. But yesterday we didn't sell anything.' It costs me sixty dollars to open the front door. But, it costs me sixty if I don't open the front door. The generators and the heat go on and on and on. We are contributing greatly to service oil's future."

"You've seen Alaska before and after oil. Which version do you like better?"

"As far as I'm concerned oil's the greatest thing ever happened to the state. Absolutely. No question. Anyone that doesn't agree with that has some kind of a mental problem. When you see the benevolence bestowed on the Alaska community by the oil companies, how could you not be in agreement with that? The education things they've done. Look at the money we receive, the Permanent Fund check. One-thousand, twelve-hundred every year. I'm 69 years old in August, and I get $250 a month for the rest of my life, unless they change the law. [Atwater receives the Longevity Bonus, where every Alaska resident over the age of 65 gets a monthly check just for living here.] That's all oil. What would the infrastructure be? If you think it all wouldn't go to hell in a hand cart if the oil companies closed down, you're wrong."

He looks at me sharply, as if to accuse me of thinking it all wouldn't go to hell in a hand cart if the oil companies closed down.

"There's no way what we've built with the oil money could survive without it," he continues. "And a lot of our legislators who want to tax, tax, tax the hell out of the oil companies should realize that. There's gonna be a point where they're gonna back off and say 'good-bye friends.' And here we are stuck with all these fancy things we've started, and can't maintain."

A driver, tired from the road, enters the roadhouse.

"Is there a bathroom I can use?" he asks timidly, the voice of a man who is not going to purchase anything.

"No, it's out of order," McCormick says.

It's funny. I just used the bathroom a few minutes ago and the toilet was working fine. I wonder how I might have been received if I hadn't told these guys I was writing weekly columns. It's not unusual to see unusual people in Alaska, like the Japanese climber who summited Mt. McKinley alone in winter and pulled a cart from Anchorage to Prudhoe Bay. Another guy walked along the railroad track all the way from Anchorage to Fairbanks. Nuts are scrambling over Alaska every year. I'm different though, just because I carry a little computer and a tape recorder. I don't wonder where I'd be without them, without money. I think I'd be out there with Jane, getting wet.

Before I leave, I order a cheeseburger. Atwater fixes it

himself, then hands me the plate.

He blackened the buns on the grill, then spread butter over the charcoal. I crunch it down because I paid for the calories. As the buns turn to carbon particles in my mouth, I wonder if C. J. Meiers's wife would have thrown them to the birds and started over again.

7 | **Sixty-Eight Cans of Pop**

Day 27

As it runs above treeline near Paxson Lodge, the pipeline's horizontal cross-beams remind me of billboards. Twenty years ago, workers wrote on the gray sections with a "heat stick," a marker of liquid lead. Welders used heat sticks to label sections of pipe with measurements and other instructions. Here, pipeliners wrote messages about their rides out of Alaska.

> *TO GET WARM, THINK UNITED AIR*
> *Wein and United to 80 degrees*
> *NORTHWEST ORIENT*

At pipeline mile 634, a more personal scrawl, in cursive: *Jim Epperhart, Morehead, Kentucky.*

After 20 years, could Jim Epperhart still live in

Morehead? A telephone operator told me the number for a James Epperhart in Morehead, Kentucky. Morehead is in the northern clump of Daniel Boone National Forest, home to about 12,000 people and Morehead State University.

When I call, a few months after the hike, a boy answers. "He isn't here right now." No, wait. Jim Epperhart is just coming through the door. His son Matthew, 14, hands him the phone.

"Uh, hello Mr. Epperhart. Did you work on the trans-Alaska pipeline?"

"Yessir I did. Why?"

Now 49, Epperhart earned $10 and $18.55 per hour respectively as a pipeline welder's helper and journeyman in late 1975 and early 1976. He left his mark on several hunks of pipeline support beam, scribbles that have survived for 7,600 days, more than a third of his life.

Epperhart, then 27, was a 798er, a member of Pipeliners Local 798 out of Tulsa, Oklahoma. The 798ers were mostly southern boys who considered themselves the best pipe welders on the planet. Alyeska agreed, and the 798ers made each of the more than 100,000 welds it took to make the pipeline an 800-mile tube.

"Seven-ninety-eight is still the only pipeline local in the world," Epperhart says. "To be a welder, every job you go on you got to take a welding test and they got to x-ray it, and they got to cut scraps out of it. These guys are the best in the world. If you couldn't pass the test down here they wouldn't even send you up there."

Now a trucker who tows house trailers, Epperhart spent nine months helping build the pipeline in the Alaska

Range. He had been in Alaska once before the pipeline days: as a young draftee, he'd looked out an oval window at the Chugach Mountains surrounding Anchorage. Then his plane had continued on to Vietnam.

During pipeline construction, Epperhart worked mostly on vertical-support-member crews, teams that installed the posts upon which the pipeline sits.

"VSMs, you might drive 500 in one day and the next day it might take you all day just to drive in one. Some you pounded in, just like a big hammer hitting a nail. Some of them you drilled out. Some of them we went down one-hundred-thirty-two feet. You bring that ice out and it's just like looking through the windshield of your car. That's how clear it was."

"Was there a real push to get the pipeline done quickly?"

"Alyeska was flying over in helicopters continuously. For each worker, seemed like to me, they had two inspectors. The job was done right, but they was in a big hurry to get it done. If you had an oil spill or something, it was all dug up and pulled out and clean dirt put back in."

Epperhart penned his name throughout the Alaska Range, from Isabel Pass to Donnelly Dome. Some days, he thought he would leave a frozen finger or two.

"December and January, you earned your money, really you did. When the wind was blowing and it was cold. Sixty, seventy below zero and the wind blowing fifty miles an hour, it was hard work. Only time we didn't go out was during a whiteout. Most of the time then, you couldn't even get from your trailer to the mess hall."

Pipeline workers hung their hard hats at 20 camps set

up along the pipeline route. Epperhart lived in Delta Camp, located in Delta Junction, and Isabel Camp, at the foot of Gulkana Glacier in the Alaska Range. As many as 1,652 workers lived in Isabel Camp at one time, second only to a camp near Valdez. Epperhart says he can still taste the atmosphere.

"The food was great. We had steak, lobster one night. Then the next night you'd have salmon, shrimp. New York steaks, T-bones. Or if you didn't like that they had hot dogs, hamburgers, onion rings, French fries. You get up in the morning, they'd fix you eggs, steak, or anything you wanted. Pancakes, waffles, cereal. Then they'd have a table fixed with sandwiches. You could go in there, get any kind of sandwich you could imagine. They already had them made, you just pick out what you want. They had sardines, they had snack packs, pudding packs, potato chips, donuts, polish sausage, boiled eggs. Anything you wanted to pick up, it was all free."

"Did you gain any weight?"

"I gained 40 pounds.

"In '75, when I first went up there, they were giving you all the pop you could drink. In '75, I think they was 10,000 people there, working from Valdez to Prudhoe Bay. They said each person had to be drinking at least 68 cans of pop a day."

"Six-to-eight?"

"Sixty-eight. A lot of people was taking it and selling it to supermarkets. But the company changed that. In '76, you didn't get pop that way. It was still free in the mess hall, but you just couldn't go and get cases of pop."

Humans weren't the only species filling their bellies with oil's bounty. Epperhart has a scrap book to prove it.

"I've got pictures of bear in the bus eating steaks, sitting in cranes, sitting up on side booms. Wolves, badgers, owls landing on your arm. Beavers. Had eagles walking the road waddling because they ate so many salmon."

Epperhart worked in Alaska with a dozen guys who lived within 50 miles of Morehead, but he was still five time zones from his wife, Sue, and his five-year old, Melissa. Before the pipeline, Epperhart brought his family along on most jobs. But Alaska was just too far. Spouses, children, and pets weren't allowed in the camps anyway.

"That was a hassle back then, too — the phones. Used to have one free call; you had five minutes. But the only time you could get it be about twelve o'clock at night. I had to call my wife at five o'clock in the morning, her time. Then I started calling at other times. My phone bill back then was two or three hundred dollars a month. Back in '75 that was unreal."

Epperhart says he believed he was a temporary hand working on a temporary project, but the lifespan of the pipeline has been dramatically lengthened by new oil discoveries and advances in methods to suck crude oil from the earth.

"It just tickles me to death that you're still making money off it."

Including the tanker terminal in Valdez and the 12 pump stations, the pipeline cost more than $8 billion to build. As of November 1998, the state of Alaska had made $49 billion from the pipeline in royalties, property and production taxes, and court settlements against the oil companies. The oil companies won't say how much they've made from the pipeline, but Chuck Logsdon, a petroleum economist for the state department of revenue, estimated the oil industry has earned at least $60 billion from the pipeline. Richard Fineberg, an oil industry researcher, thinks the figure is more like $113 billion. By his calculations, the pipeline has earned the oil industry $10,000 for every minute oil has flowed through the pipe. And the big money eventually trickles into every Alaskan's pocket. Just a few months after passing Jim Epperhart's signature, I received my thirteenth Alaska Permanent Fund dividend check, this one for $1,300.

Alaska voters created the Permanent Fund — basically a public savings account into which a good hunk of the state's oil revenue is deposited — by approving an amendment to the state constitution in 1976. The Permanent Fund, at $24 billion in 1998, would rank in the top five percent in terms of net income if it were a Fortune 500 company. When the fund was established, the state formed a corporation and hired a team of men and women to invest Alaska's money on Wall Street. In 1996, income from fund investments topped state oil revenues.

Dividends from the fund's earnings are given to every Alaskan who has been here more than a year who fills out the dividend application. I worked near Eagle, Alaska with a park ranger from New York who called the dividends "Alaska welfare checks." The program, along with a lack of state income tax, has probably lured its share of people to the state. In 1998, the fund paid $863 million in $1,500 checks to each Alaskan who had been here a year. The application is due by March 31. Not many people miss that deadline.

I certainly don't. Getting the dividend every year is like working on the oil spill cleanup — a big check for doing nothing other than not making a fuss about all this steel apparatus snaking through the wilderness and tankers cruising on Prince William Sound, occasionally springing a leak and killing some otters. I've bought into the system because it's the path of least resistance. And because I'm getting paid.

8 | Black Rapids Glacier

Day 35

Sipping tea, I look out to the Delta River, boiling gray. On the other side of the river are haystack mounds of black gravel, the tallest reaching 200 feet — the moraine of Black Rapids Glacier, created when the glacier melted back into the Alaska Range.

Black Rapids Glacier, a vein of ice two miles wide and extending into the mountains the distance of a running marathon, reaches from the Delta River deep into the Alaska Range. There, it scratches the backs of mounts Hayes, Deborah, Moffit, and Shand, thirteen-thousand footers that people in Fairbanks point to and say "Alaska Range."

Were it located in a state without 100,000 glaciers, Black Rapids would have its own visitor center with binoculars mounted on iron frames. Black Rapids T-shirts, coffee mugs, foam hats. Interpretive rangers with badges. Videos at the half-hour.

Instead, the Richardson Highway across from the glacier

is quiet asphalt, except for the crumbling remains of Black Rapids Lodge and a highway pull-off with a wooden sign. The sign explains Black Rapids' brush with fame, when it was known as "The Galloping Glacier."

It was December, 1936. The Fairbanks-to-Valdez trail was now the Richardson Highway, named 13 years earlier to honor road commissioner Wilds P. Richardson. High winds polished the snowbanks along the Delta River as the Alaska Range's winter mood turned grumpy. That winter, the owners of Black Rapids Lodge, along with motorists touring the highway, heard thunder across the valley. Icebergs the size of houses fell to the muskeg from the face of Black Rapids Glacier. For a glacier to calve — to lose an immense chunk of itself while advancing or retreating — was not unusual. But Black Rapids was pushing itself with alarming speed toward the Delta River, in the direction of the highway and Black Rapids Lodge.

When they heard of the glacier's unusual advance, geologists scrambled to the Alaska Range. Ernest Patty, down from Fairbanks, clocked the glacier at 220 feet per day. On Dec. 3, 1936, he marked the glacier's leading edge, a mile-wide wall of ice with gaps glowing blue. For three months, he traveled south to look at the marker. By March, Black Rapids had crept four miles toward the highway.

After disturbing the dreams of the Black Rapids Lodge manager for a quarter of a year, the glacier stopped for reasons unknown. The lodge was spared the embarrassing fate of being run over by a glacier.

In the sixty years since, the glacier has slowly retreated to the mountains, enriching the Delta River as it melted.

Also in those six decades, the bulk of the glacier in the Alaska Range has been gaining magnificent weight in the form of fresh snow and ice. Glaciologists say the increasing bulk of the glacier might be one of the forces that triggers the next surge of Black Rapids. Will Harrison and Keith Echelmeyer, two glacier studiers who work at the Geophysical Institute in Fairbanks, have drilled through Black Rapids using hot water and rock-coring drills in an attempt to find out what makes Black Rapids and similar glaciers get up and go. The secret may lie in the water and silt beneath the glacier, which may combine to provide a lubricant for millions of pounds of ice. But the mystery remains, at least for now.

Like an animal's tracks in the snow, the glacier's moraine tells the story of what happened before Black Rapids' 20th century gallop. A century before Columbus, Black Rapids Glacier spilled far enough into the valley that it dammed the Delta River. The river became a lake, one that eventually seeped northward as the air became warmer and Black Rapids Glacier retreated, allowing the water to pass.

After the discovery of oil at Prudhoe Bay in 1968, the absurd idea of a pipeline across the state became less so. Because a pipeline that might be suddenly buried under 2,000 feet of ice would be difficult to maintain, in the early 1970s scientists studied the glacier with renewed purpose. They determined that the proposed pipeline, the highway, and the decomposing roadhouse were in little danger. To err on the side of caution, engineers routed the pipeline east from the point where Black Rapids Glacier may someday stick out its snowy tongue in defiance. The buried pipe runs under the highway and cuts behind the old lodge, gaining an extra eighth-mile from the glacier. You never know.

Day 38

Donnelly Dome is a lonely mountain shaped like a volcano on a landscape that flattens out north of the Alaska Range. Seeing the dome makes me yell so loud that Jane stops in her tracks.

I remember driving down to Valdez more than a month ago. Smits, John, and I stopped at the dome. Jane shot out of the car and bounced after sticks I flung toward the mountain. Now, we have made it back, entirely by foot power. Our path, even though it parallels one I've driven many times, is different. Though we walk very close to the highway at times, the pipeline pad is a world in slow motion. This is life in low gear, Alaska at two miles per hour; wake when I wake, no shock of electronic beeps or tiny hammers striking metal. Hike until midnight, dropping pack when a nice spot presents itself, or when I'm tired, or when the mountains hide the sun.

The sun doesn't hide much at all now. June is here. It's the carefree time in Alaska. Time can be wasted. Laggers are not punished with disappearing daylight, with frostbitten feet. In summer, it's good to dally. Daylight so plentiful you can't use it all. Winter can't even be imagined. Now is Alaska's nod to the sun, and the outdoors vibrates with life — mosquitoes buzzing, buds poised to burst into leaves, songbirds crooning in all but the latest hours.

The sun has given life to one of Alaska's more interesting creatures, also one of its smallest. The wood frog is the only amphibian to hop this far north and make a go of it.

Rana sylvatica ranges as far south as Georgia, but the Alaska version is special for its ability to tolerate cold. Brian Barnes, a zoophysiologist at the University of Alaska Fairbanks, let me tag along one autumn while he tracked some of the palm-sized frogs. Following the radio signals of tiny transmitters that were superglued on the frog's backs, Barnes and his students marked the spots where the frogs dug into the forest litter to wait out the winter. When the frogs settled, Barnes and the students placed beside the frogs a tiny device that measured the temperature at frog level. Even with a foot of snow that fell later, the frogs were exposed to temperatures well below freezing. They reacted by turning into little green ice cubes. Solid eyes, rock-hard legs, hearts that stop beating. They do this every year in the deep freeze of an Alaska winter. But the frogs don't die.

They survive by becoming sweet. The creeping cold of fall sends a message to their tiny livers, which start converting glycogen to sugary glucose. All their systems are then flooded with glucose, which helps cells resist drying when osmotic forces try to pull liquid across cell membranes and out into the cold. In the spring, wood frogs thaw. They twitch, then crawl. After their bodies become more liquid than solid, they hop away from their nests, froggy as can be, in search of a mate.

The staccato croaks of the wood frog signal our exit from the Alaska Range, into the warmer lowlands of the Interior. The Interior is a chunk of Alaska the size of Iowa, hemmed in by the Alaska Range to the south and the Brooks Ranges to the north. After 11 years here, to me it feels like home.

9 | Kind of Like You

Day 42

After a night camping in spruce woods near the Delta River, Jane and I wake dusted with sand. The wind carried gray silt from the bed of the river, through the mesh walls of the tent. I feel a layer of grit on my face. Jane shakes hers off. Craving French toast, I hike into the town of Delta Junction.

After Jane and I emerge from the woods, a brown Ford pickup rolls to block our path. A message sticks to the bumper: "EAT MOOSE: 12,000 WOLVES CAN'T BE WRONG." A man with dirty jeans, a black jacket, and a black T-shirt steps out. A little boy watches from inside the cab.

"I've been looking for you guys," the man says, flashing a grin that exposes gums as well as teeth. "Been reading about you in the paper. I'd like to take your picture, if you don't mind. My name's Jeff Schultz."

Jeff greets me with a burled hand, the grip of a man who swings a claw hammer seven hours a day. He is a framing contractor, a man who makes the skeletons of houses.

"I live right near where the pipeline crosses the road south of town," he says, checking his camera for film.

"Were you sawing wood the other day?"

"Yeah, that was me."

"We passed you."

"Should have stopped in."

"I would've, but your no-trespassing signs kind of scared me off."

"Man, I should've put out a sign for you . . . I've been following your trip. Is there anything I can help you with? Anything you need?"

"Well, I'm just going over to the White Raven to catch breakfast. Do you know where I can buy a paper to read while I eat?"

"I'll get you one. Just head over there and I'll bring it to you. Before that, let me get Jane and your picture."

Schultz points, shoots, then jumps in his truck and heads for the Food Cache. I hustle Jane across four lanes of asphalt and fix a nest for her in the grass median in front of the White Raven, the closest restaurant to where we camped. It's the only Delta Junction restaurant open on a Saturday morning. As I leave my Labrador, my pack, and my shotgun in the grass, the brown Ford rolls into the parking lot.

Schultz steps out, grinning. He hands me a plastic grocery bag. In it are today's *Fairbanks Daily News-Miner*, two packs of M&Ms, one Skor candy bar, one Payday, Jerky Treats (for Jane), and a pump bottle of Deep Woods Off.

I gather my new supplies, then take Schultz's photo. He says he'll find me tomorrow on the pipeline to bring me the Sunday Paper. "I'll use my three-wheeler. Need to see that country anyways."

Though more forward than most, Jeff Schultz has been like many of the people of Delta Junction who have read the newspaper columns of the journey. Entering Fort Greely, an Army base, Jane and I were welcomed to post by a cardboard sign covered in plastic: *WELCOME TO FORT GREELY NED AND JANE! FROM THE FOX FAMILY.* Another family, the Bonsers from Eielson Air Force Base near Fairbanks, pulled over their van to say hi, as have half a dozen other people. It feels a bit like being famous. I sign autographs, watch Jane's tail wag as she's petted, pose for photographs. It's fun, something I'll probably never experience again.

Back away from the crowds, Jane and I take a break by a small pond where I pump some water. After drinking a quart and pumping one for later, I lay on a pile of round rocks, watching connected pairs of dragonflies fly. I soon hear the scuffling of gravel to my left. I turned my head to see a bull moose standing 15 feet away.

He's full grown, taller than me. A dark chocolate coat stretched over muscular shoulders and hams. His antlers, covered with velvet and in an early stage of development, are already, in mid-June, as wide as my shotgun. In the fall he'll strip his antlers of velvet by destroying small trees. He's a trophy, a dominant male, a bull that will outjoust other males to assemble a harem of cows.

I sit up, awed by this monstrous animal standing just a few steps away. I wonder if I should grab my camera. The bull watches me with impassive brown eyes.

Suddenly, the hair between his shoulder blades rises.

His nose begins twitching like an accordion. Seven-hundred pounds of hoofed creature is making a decision: "Should I run? Should I stomp this human?" Instead of the camera, I decide I should grab the shotgun. My body disagrees. I'm frozen.

Jane, eyes opening from a snooze, sees the bull. The hair on her back stands. She barks the mean bark. The bull moose pivots, then leaps. The moose's rump melts into the brush. In 15 seconds, he goes from awesome to invisible. Even his sound disappears as he somehow runs silently through the woods. I lean back on the gravel, light-headed. Jane steps over and starts licking my face. I hug her neck, grab her pack, and dig out a package of Jerky Treats, the gift from Jeff Schultz. She eats every one.

Night 42

A breeze dries my feet after a soaking in the Tanana River, one of the longest waterways in Alaska. The river flows 530 miles, from eastern Alaska to the Yukon River. The Tanana, an Athabaskan word for "Mountain River," drains the highlands near the Canadian border and widens to a quarter mile of gentle brown water here at the junction with the Delta River.

I lead Jane to the river under the pipeline, which is suspended 1,300 feet across the river along a network of steel cables stretched tighter than bow strings. Jane's feet disappear as she walks in the shallows to chomp water almost the color of her coat. I sip a quart of filtered Tanana and lean against a rock, watching and listening.

Sixteen Canada geese pop into the sky over a grove of

balsam poplar on the far side of the river. They honk away from the sun, scattered ovals against blue sky that eventually form a V. The V points upriver, toward Canada. Swallows, migrants living in the crossmembers that support the pipeline, play tag amid their summer home. Their chatter sounds like someone chewing rubber bands.

A log floats by, twirling like a compass dial. Soon the floating wood will jerk northward as the Delta River meets the Tanana. Here, the Tanana hangs a sharp right around a rock bluff to join the Delta, which gives up its name on marrying the bigger river. The spinning log, possibly from a sandy shoreline near the Indian village of Northway, or the town of Tok, may eventually float past Fairbanks, where the Tanana bows west. If it continues unsnagged, the log will meander south again, to the town of Nenana. Then north, past Manley Hot Springs, to the village of Tanana. Past Tanana, the log will become a Yukon River log. Then, if not snagged or lassoed by villagers for firewood, after 500 more miles, the log will belong to the Bering Sea.

I too seek salt water, on a vastly different path. Following an artery of goop across Alaska. Forty-one safe nights passed. How many ahead? How many sunny evenings on the Tanana this summer? Just one.

Day 43

As promised, Jeff Schultz finds us again. His transportation down the pipeline pad is a Honda three-wheeler with custom repairs: a duct tape seat cover; a plastic front fender stitched with metal wire like Frankenstein's forehead. Schultz steps off the three-wheeler, then sheds his white helmet and a military field jacket, olive drab. He wears rubber boots that reach to his knees, a blue T-shirt, and a leather belt heavy with handgun bullets that hang, single-file, from hip to hip.

He hands me the Sunday paper. In the lower right corner of the front page is a box with a map and a photo of Jane and me under the pipeline in Fairbanks. "Keep Track of Ned and Jane," a banner reads. A red arrow on the map points to Delta Junction, just over a quarter of the distance to Prudhoe Bay.

From a backpack that rides over his front tire, Schultz pulls a plastic bag. Jane quickly devours meat scraps, leftovers from Schultz's dinner last night. He also brought a gallon of water in a plastic milk jug. I'm thankful because I couldn't find water this morning. I immediately dig for my cook pots and start breakfast water boiling. Schultz decides to stay with me as I cook breakfast next to the pipeline at 1 p.m. While I ignite Coleman fuel, Schultz pulls a flask of whiskey from his jacket. He cuts the Seagrams with an erupting bottle of Seven-Up. I make a mug of herbal tea.

The sun bakes us on the white gravel of the pipeline pad. Jane snoozes on puffs of last year's grass. Today is Father's Day. Schultz received two gifts from his wife, Diane, and his sons Jacob, 3, and Colton, 1. One present was a framed picture of Tank, a 16-year-old pit bull-great Dane mix, camouflaged in the dry bed of the Delta River. Tank was recently stomped and killed by a moose. "He was a good old boy," Schultz says, looking at the ground. "Just about every picture we have of the kids and the family, he's in it."

Schultz's second Father's Day gift was the freedom to do whatever he wanted with his time today. He wanted to join us. I'm honored.

"When you and Jane started telling your story out of Valdez, since we had the property on the pipeline, we just kinda been looking forward to meeting you," Schultz says, flashing a smile. "My wife's really into reading your articles. She'd give her left nut — if she had one — to be here right now.

"I think you're kind of like me or I'm kind of like you," Schultz says. "I like adventure. Your trip is something I'd like to do. I can't believe it wasn't done before. Because you think, 'What's left to do that someone else hasn't done?' And you think about it and it seems like everybody's done everything. I was impressed with you for being able to do this walk.

"There was a time in my life where I was able to do that stuff too — I've traveled all over the country and cowboyed and all kinds of shit. In my family, people look at me like I'm the adventurer or whatever. And I like that in a person."

Schultz is 40 years old. Alaska reeled him in when he was a 12-year-old boy, on vacation with his parents from Cedar Falls, Iowa. "We come up in '69 . . . and man, I just got hooked, hard, on Alaska. Being from Iowa, growing up in a corn state where you never saw a mountain and the rivers are all brown."

He was 15 when he and brother Craig began a segmented journey to the Last Frontier. "We hitchhiked up in '72 to try to get jobs on the pipeline. We kinda looked like you, backpack and stuff."

The brothers went to Alyeska's office in Anchorage. Not only were the pair obviously teen-agers, they weren't state residents. "They just laughed at us." So, the brothers thumbed back to Cedar City.

"Took us three months to hitchhike up and hitchhike

back," Schultz says, sitting on a balloon tire without worrying about dirtying his Carhartts. "That was a hell of a trip. Probably the best thing I've ever done in my life. Missed a bunch of school. Had to do some fast talking to get back into high school. We told 'em we probably learned more in that three months hitchhiking to Alaska than you could have ever taught us in school. They pretty much took that, and let us back in school."

Like moths to a porch light, the Schultz brothers kept returning. They both moved back in 1982, and settled in different towns. Schultz moved up with a new wife and son to Houston, Alaska, a highway town 60 miles north of Anchorage. While in Houston, he purchased his Delta Junction pipeline property from "a guy who needed extra money. He was into a little nose candy... Anyway, I made a pretty good deal with him, bought the property on the pipeline. Then I ended up moving to Oregon a year later, basically chasing my son and his mother. And ended up spending several years down there.

"In '89, I brought my wife up and she liked the place, so I went back to Oregon and we got the rest of our stuff and we ended up moving up for good in '95. We been here ever since. This time I'm staying for sure."

Schultz is a nomad, picking up jobs all over the state on the merit of past carpentry work. His last job was framing the Princess Tours hotel in Denali Park after the former one burned, a sort of Exxon Valdez for carpenters. He will soon start work in North Pole. Though he has roamed much of the state, one of his constants has been the silver tube a few feet above our heads.

"The Alaska pipeline has been a big thing in my life since it started. I hitchhiked here to get on it — it was a major goal to work on the pipeline. Then I bought property on the pipeline. I hunt on the pipeline all the time. I'm always using it. I buzz all over it with the three-wheeler. To me, it's like my own personal path to get where I want to go."

I finish eating, wash my pan, and pack my newspaper. Schultz kicks his three-wheeler to life. Even though we use different methods of travel, I think he is a lot like me. We're both taking the risk of spending the rest of our short lives in Alaska, gambling that being here is what will make us happy. I'm glad to take this chance. Time here is time well spent, and the more I do, the more there is to do. I think Schultz feels the same way, though his relatives in Cedar Falls probably don't understand. Neither do my relatives.

He shakes my hand.

"Have a hell of a trip."

His face lights with a final smile. Then Schultz explores the unseen country to the north. On his own personal path.

10 | Last of the Homesteaders

Day 44

As Jane and I walk a sandy road that leads away from the pipeline, a white Subaru wagon meets us. Inside are a couple in their 60s, my parents' age, and four girls from toddler to teen. The people within are the people I've been looking for. A newspaper reporter told me to stop in on the Walker family if I wanted to see a real Alaska homestead.

"We heard you might be stopping by," the woman says through her open driver's window. Her tone is motherly, caring.

"We'd be happy to have you — the girls would like to meet your dog. You better take a ride, though. Our place is a mile back."

Because I wanted to see what it would be like to spend a summer entirely on foot, I have not ridden in a vehicle in 43 days. But today I have a headache. The girls open a back door; Jane hops in as if it were my truck. I follow her lead, shoving my pack inside. To make room for a dog, two backpacks, a shotgun, and me, two of the girls jump in the back seat to join the other two. They are a gaggle of cousins, granddaughters of Jeanette and Robert Walker.

Jeanette makes a U-turn and we head east on a road Robert Walker cut with a bulldozer 20 years ago. The sandy cut banks and open woods remind me of Mississippi pine forest near the Gulf of Mexico. But the sand here is loess, fine silt carried from the flats of the Tanana River by ancient winds. Twelve thousand years ago, when the American lion stalked the grasslands of interior Alaska, these hills were sand dunes. From forests to the east, tree seeds surfed on the breeze. A few seeds found mineral nests in the silt, germinated, grew to adulthood, and dropped their own seeds. With a pace too gradual for humans to comprehend, boreal forest settled the uplands of the Tanana River valley.

Jeanette drives us to the Walkers' house, at the end of their dirt road. The home, with an attached garage, is sided with plywood. The trimmed grass of a lawn opens to lime-green flatness of a hay field that extends toward the peaks of the Alaska Range.

My eyes are drawn to the big sky, a rarity in the pipeline's path through the forested Interior. Most of the Interior is not planted in brome hay.

I take a rest on the grass, next to a picnic table. Jane can't relax; large birds strut on the lawn, vulnerable. Jane's head is locked on a pair of turkeys, bodies black as ravens. They bob their fleshy heads nervously at the brown visitor. Jane readies to advance on the creatures, which are taller than she.

"Bones... don't." She looks at me with pleading eyes, wondering why I stifle her instinct now, when her quarry is so catchable. Her abstinence becomes more of a challenge as a Canada goose, with a black head and white patch on its cheek, waddles by. True torture begins as the goose's goslings — fluffy yellow, the size of grouse — follow the granddaughters on a romp around the lawn. Jane's nostrils move as if they are a separate organism, preparing to crawl off her face. Gelatinous spears of drool form at her jowls.

"No, no, no ... Good girl." It wouldn't be good manners for Jane to slaughter a family pet on the lawn. She shows remarkable restraint as her eyes follow the clumsy shuffle of the goslings. These images will probably be fodder for one of Jane's epileptic dreams in the tent, during which she barks with closed mouth and kicks at me with twitching limbs.

Fairly convinced Jane will not commit homicide, I climb to the bench of a picnic table, one of three on the lawn, and sit across from Robert Walker. Jeanette brings us glasses of lemonade. The bittersweet mixture is a tonic for my aching head, which might have been caused by a shortage of water.

As Robert talks, he pauses as an F-15 fighter from a base near Fairbanks screams through blue sky, at perhaps 6,000 feet.

"We hear lots of airplanes," Robert says. "That's most of the noises we hear. Some of those fighters from Eielson, they used to buzz us here some. But then lately, they go around but they don't come in close."

Robert Walker squints into the sun, making a face that reminds me of Popeye. He wears navy blue coveralls, white socks, dusty loafers. Centered on his chin is a dimple that could hold a BB. Looking toward the mountains, Robert tells me of the path that led him, a pregnant wife and an infant daughter to the unknown of Alaska 38 years and two days ago.

Robert grew up on a 50-acre farm in southcentral Pennsylvania, within the triangle made by the towns of Three Springs, Saltillo, and Broad Top City. As a young man, he subscribed to *Alaska Life* and read anything he could find about homesteading the Last Frontier. His dream was to come to Alaska, start his own farm, and be a minister of the Brethren in Christ Church. The Brethren in Christ believed in God's power to forgive, and they strived for nonconformity in actions and dress. Though not as extreme as the Amish (who shun motorized vehicles, electricity, and other things modern), the Brethren in Christ did adhere to a strict dress code. Men wore shirts buttoned tight to the neck; women wore lace caps and dresses, similar to Amish women, because a Bible passage states that a woman should wear a covering on her head anytime she prays. And she should always be ready to pray.

At 17, Jeanette went against her Catholic father's wishes and joined the Brethren in Christ, whom she believed to be one of the few groups of people that followed their faith every day of the week. She suffered for her decision.

"Living in Philadelphia, I was a spectacle," she says. "My father would not sit with me on the trolley car or the bus; he was ashamed of me."

Still, she stuck with her faith because she felt the Lord had rewarded her so often, such as the time when she wanted to go to college but her father had only enough money to support her brother's education. Just as Jeanette resigned herself to life without becoming a teacher, her brother won a full scholarship to the University of Pennsylvania.

"His way was paid and the Lord opened it up so I could go to school," Jeanette says. She enrolled at Messiah College in Grantham, Penn.

Robert, a self-described "country hick," was studying to be a minister at the same school. There, he met Jeanette, a city girl from Philadelphia. She was different from other girls; Robert saw a toughness behind the pretty face. They had a common goal — though Jeanette's family lived in Philadelphia, she preferred open spaces. He dreamed of a place so open the moose outnumbered people.

In 1959, Robert, 27, and Jeanette, 24, married, then left Pennsylvania for Alaska. Robert drove a 20-year-old International truck with a bed large enough to carry a washing machine, furniture, dozens of cases of canned food, and a Jeep. Behind the International, they pulled a 30-foot house trailer. On the trip, Jeanette held a nine-month-old daughter on her lap. Because they didn't want to worry their parents, Jeanette and Robert didn't tell their parents that she was six months pregnant with their second child.

As they crept north on the Alaska Highway, the Walkers waved politely to other drivers who pointed to flat tires on the rear of the International. The unpaved highway had eaten all their spares; the dual tires on the rear axle were now singles.

Having read that the Tanana River valley was the warmest place in Alaska to farm and that more land was available there than the Matanuska Valley in southcentral Alaska, the Walkers drove first to Fairbanks. They stopped at the local office of the U.S. Department of the Interior. An agent told them to find a spot that appealed to them; the man would then tell them if it was federal land open for homesteading, the only option for the Walkers.

"There's no way in the world we could have ever come up here and bought land," Robert says. "We were too poor."

In search of a home, the Walkers drove up the Elliott Highway, a road that reaches north from Fairbanks. There, Robert saw the reality of northern Alaska.

"The farther I went up the highway, the shorter the trees got," he says. "And after a while, they were so short I told Jeanette, 'There's no way in the world anybody could ever build a cabin out of these things.'"

They found a wide spot in the gravel road, turned around, and tried the highway south to Nenana. Something the Walkers could not define didn't feel right about the land on the shoulders of the highway. They backtracked east down the Richardson until they came to Shaw Creek, 20 miles north of Delta Junction. There, the highway department had bulldozed a turn-around spot that seemed made for their trailer. They looked at their map and saw that it was public land that had not yet been staked. This was the spot.

"Looks like she's getting comfortable," Robert says, watching Jane spin a few tight circles. As is becoming her habit, she plops down and curls into a ball of chocolate fur. When we walk together along the pipeline, Jane zig-zags along the scent trails of snowshoe hares and grouse, covering twice the distance I do. When I stop, she snoozes as if she's competing in the Iditarod, a 1,000-mile sled dog race from Anchorage to Nome. A minute after dropping at my feet, Jane begins snoring. Robert continues his tale.

His and Jeanette's first farming attempt involved chickens. To house their flock, they built a log chicken house. With almost no money left after the trip north, Robert was forced to improvise on roofing materials. He peeled bark from paper birch trees and used it for shingles.

"It turned the rain fine," he says, squinting at the memory. "But you know how birch bark burns."

On a 40-below night in January when a spark escaped the wood stove in the chicken house, it began burning. Robert and Jeanette shoveled snow on the flames, but they could not save the chickens.

The Walkers' Alaska education continued as the weeks went by. They noticed fatal flaws in their choice of homesteading land. Because their land was on the north side of a hill, they did not see the sun from November until February. What appeared to be Pennsylvania-type meadows — damp lowlands with few trees — were not. After they hired a man with a Caterpillar D7 to strip a few acres for planting, the Walkers learned about permafrost, and what happens when you remove the layer of tundra plants that insulates frozen soil from warm air.

"We picked a place in the flats there and cleared it," Walker says. "The land looked really nice. The dirt's black, it gives you the illusion of it being rich . . . It dried off on top, and I took my Jeep in there. And I nearly lost the thing. I never went in — even on foot — after that. Now if you drive by it, it's a nice little pond. A couple acres where the water sits."

Robert turns his head toward the house, calculating with his eyes closed. After a few seconds of pondering, he estimates that less than ten of the 160 acres at the Shaw Creek homestead were suitable farm land. He and Jeanette really wanted to farm, he says, but the land they had chosen near Shaw Creek was not the place.

With his neighbor, a homesteader named Charlie Koppenhaver who was also from Pennsylvania, Robert searched the country a few miles east of the highway. He and Jeanette prayed to find four qualities in the wild land: a water supply, south-facing slopes, land that was easy to clear, and spruce trees large enough to build a cabin.

In rolling country five miles from the highway, the Walkers found a spring-fed creek with sweet water. Nearby was the site of an old forest fire with the remains of trees that resembled burned match sticks, which would be easier to remove than living trees. They found acres and acres of forest land that sloped to the south; some of these forests held spruce trees that Robert could barely wrap his arms around.

With the help of Charlie Koppenhaver, Robert rigged a basic surveying tool: he drove three nails to a wooden post and tied string between them to form a right triangle. Aiming the homemade measuring device at trees and other landmarks, he marked the corners of a new homestead. This time, it was not a 160-acre square. Instead, Robert chose what he saw as the best land. The resultant 160 acres is a patchwork of mated rectangles in various acreages. The Walkers' land has eight corners.

They filed again with the Department of the Interior,

which was in the process of voiding their Shaw Creek homestead because the Walkers had given up on clearing the land. Without any assurance they would receive title to the second homestead, the Walkers began the process of proving up.

"They did not have to give us a second chance," Robert says, shaking his head. "The personnel of the Bureau of Land Management office didn't make us any promises."

As Robert and Jeanette transformed burned forest into farm fields, the Homestead Act celebrated its 100th birthday. In 1862, Abraham Lincoln signed the legislation to encourage westward movement of people in a country divided by civil war. The act, now expired, enabled settlers to claim up to 160 acres of the wilderness that had recently become the U.S. as part of the Louisiana Purchase.

By 1962, homesteading rules had changed little: The Walkers had five years in which to clear a percentage of the land for cultivation and to build a "habitable" dwelling, habitable being defined not by law but by BLM inspectors.

Robert and Jeanette felled spruce trees to build their first log cabin. Their first daughter, Debbie, now had a baby sister, Rose. With two babies in tow, Jeanette still managed to do more than her share of clearing the fields. All through the sweaty tasks, Jeanette wore a dress and skull cap of the Brethren in Christ. Robert was a lean and strong 30-year-old, with a high forehead and large, strong hands.

The difficult realities of homesteading made the Walkers realize they could not fulfill all their dreams.

"We had hoped we could start a church up here, but we found out it was a much bigger job than what we ever anticipated," Robert says. "I thought we would move into a community in which there would be a whole bunch of other homesteaders near us and we'd all get together and we could find a church congregation, but the steady settlers here believed in a doctrine drastically different than what we believed in."

Meanwhile, the Walkers' congregation in Philadelphia was breaking with the Brethren in Christ. Robert and Jeanette decided to resign rather than belong to a church 5,000 miles away. They were suddenly religious orphans.

"It didn't bother me because I had become disenchanted with the idea of a manmade organization," Robert says. "I think it is a spiritual matter. Christianity is a thing of the heart. It's between an individual and God. If you belong to a denomination, fine, it's just that I won't belong to one because I don't see the value in it."

"A Christian is a Christian, no matter what," Jeanette says. "If a person loves Jesus and loves God, they don't have to do everything the same way that I do."

The break from the church also allowed Jeanette a break from the traditional clothing. She had found it impractical anyway; few women of the Brethren in Christ in Philadelphia walked five miles in a dress at 20 below zero. Jeanette now prefers cotton shirts, jeans, a set of Carhartts overalls when she's feeding the wood stove in wintertime.

Today, the temperature is 90 degrees warmer than the 20-below day when Jeanette hiked in a dress. Excusing myself for a second, I sit on the ground next to Jane and kick off my hiking boots. A breeze hits my socks; it feels like cool water. After waking to snow on the tent just two weeks ago in the Alaska Range, today's warmth feels like a luxury, and

Jane snoozes without shivering. With my feet free of heavy boots, I rest my head on Jane's pack and lie on the lawn. I ask Robert about what he and Jeanette needed to do to prove up on this land — a place now surrounded by state land, where one can wander for days to the north and east without seeing another human.

To meet the requirements of the Homestead Act, Robert and Jeanette cleared 10 acres by the end of their second year on the land, 10 more the next year. They purchased barley seed, having heard from others that barley did well during the short but intense summer of the Tanana Valley. They planted ten acres in barley, ten in "nip oats," another cold-hardy variety. The weather was kind; it rained when crops were thirsty, and the rain stopped when it was time to harvest.

Their first growing season was a success: barley and oats grew on stalks four feet high. As the crop flourished, two federal agents drove down from Fairbanks to see if the Walkers were proving up. The men saw some of the healthiest barley they had seen in the valley. As homesteaders were only obligated to plant crops — harvesting was not a requirement of the act — the government men left truly impressed.

After Alaska Senator Bob Bartlett shook their paperwork loose from the Anchorage office where it had stalled, the Walkers received the patent for their homestead in 1968, four years after they complied with the requirements. They were awarded the land and the rights to the minerals beneath it. There were a few catches, though. If the federal government had the need, the land could be crossed by a U.S. railroad, canal, drainage ditch, or telegraph line. None has appeared in 34 years.

Shortly after the Walkers moved to their second homestead, the family expanded. A son, Robert Jr., was the third child Jeanette gave birth to with no doctor present. Robert learned about delivering babies by reading nursing textbooks sent to the homestead by Jeanette's friends in Pennsylvania.

"While I knew there was a lot of risk involved, I would have never missed that for anything," Robert says, looking at crooked fingers that were the first to touch three of his four children. "Back in those years, men weren't allowed in hospitals. I felt childbirth was a natural thing. In that time, it was treated as an illness."

Jeanette says her faith carried her through. "We trusted in the Lord to help us," she says. "I wasn't afraid."

Robert admits to being terrified when Rose, their second child, emerged from the birth canal with the umbilical cord wrapped around her neck. But Rose remained stationary long enough for him to slip the cord away from her tiny head.

Now 37 and the mother of two daughters who chase ducks on the lawn, Rose walks up to the picnic table near which Jane and me are resting. Her flowing brown hair is clasped in a ponytail. She wears jeans and a T-shirt. She is lean, muscular, like her mother clearing the fields. Her forearms are freshly scarred. On adjoining property she purchased from the Koppenhavers, Rose is building a log cabin for herself and her daughters. To do so, she hoists logs that outweigh her by hundreds of pounds. "She's the hardest worker I know," her mother says.

As quickly as she arrives, Rose departs. Like her parents,

she has many projects in addition to cabin building. She and her parents team to create wood crafts to sell at Northern Treasures, a plywood booth at the Tanana River near where the pipeline crosses the river. To make tables and lamps, the Walkers use spruce and aspen trunks afflicted with burls — knots in the shape of pumpkins, caused by viruses. They slice sections from rotten poplar trees, knock out the punk, and decorate the donut centers with flowers they grow and dry themselves. Robert spins birch wood on the lathe, creating lightweight chalices and salt and pepper shakers. Northern Treasures is the Walkers' latest attempt to supplement their income by using what nature provides. Long ago, Robert and Jeanette learned that hard work wasn't always enough to overcome nature 160 miles from the Arctic Circle.

"We tried to subsist," Robert says. "That, of course in the truest sense of the word, is an impossibility up here. There's some things you have to purchase from someone else."

"Like fertilizer," Jeanette says.

Robert continues. "If the land had natural fertility, you could eat what you grow. But we've never found a way you can grow things without fertilizer."

The lawn padding Jane and me is underlain by soil typical of Alaska's interior. In springtime, the fine soil has the consistency of flour. Stomp on the dry loess and it reacts like a liquid, splattering away and leaving a crater. It's hungry soil, with little peat to provide nutrients and hold water. Robert remarks that sometimes the investment in fertilizer left little money for other essentials.

"The only regret I have is that we lived right on the edge of starvation for a number of years," he says, remembering weeks when the only meat for the family came from snow-shoe hares and grouse. "I did not enjoy it at the time, and it terrifies me now to think of it."

Jeanette thinks something good came out of those tough times. "During the whole time, we were dirt poor, but we were very happy," she says. "It taught me to think about what I do have, and appreciate it. I'm thankful for everything that I have."

After a second unsuccessful attempt to raise chickens, to feed the family the Walkers left the homestead in September 1967. They moved to Fairbanks.

Robert found work as a mechanic at Aurora Motors, a Pontiac dealership. Jeanette took the post office test and landed a job in town, eventually climbing the rungs to hiring supervisor. The Walkers stayed in the Fairbanks area for 12 years, all the time dreaming of how they could return to live at the homestead, which they visited on weekends. They wanted desperately to go back, but they didn't want to face the same poverty that drove them to Fairbanks. Nearing their 50s, the Walkers knew they had to return soon or be trapped in a suburban lifestyle.

Then, Jeanette says, the Lord took over. While she pondering her family's future, a Bible passage jumped out at her: *Return to the earth*. Trusting in the scripture, she handed her boss a resignation form and continued working until the summer, when the family would move back to the homestead.

Shortly thereafter, Jeanette called the Delta Junction post office to invite the workers there to a Fairbanks meeting. As the conversation wound down, Jeanette asked the clerk when there was going to be a job opening in Delta Junction. She didn't anticipate the answer.

"This fall," the clerk said. "I'm leaving. My job will be open then."

Though a clerk's pay was $300 a month less than what she was making, Jeanette pleaded with her boss to be transferred to Delta Junction. He agreed, tore up her resignation, and in July 1979 she began working in Delta Junction, just 20 miles south of the homestead.

Robert returned to the homestead and began farming and building the house. He wanted a job, but employment was scarce. A nearby Army base, Fort Greely, supported much of the Delta Junction community, but because Robert was a conscientious objector, he did not think it was right to work for the military.

"Christ says you should love your enemies," Robert says. "I don't really see how you can kill them if you love them."

Though Robert worked as hard as any man, he wasn't comfortable with his wife's role as breadwinner.

"It bothered me. It bothered me a lot," he says. "I knew I wasn't bringing a dime in and I was depending on her for money. It didn't matter how hard I would work . . . I wasn't even doing the cooking. I don't know how to cook. I'd starve to death if I was by myself."

Jeanette shakes her head and points to their home. "He built this whole house, he built the barn by himself, somehow putting those rafters up without help. In the meantime we were growing grain and hay."

With Jeanette providing the materials, Robert built the two-story house in which he and Jeanette still live. He planted brome hay, bought a few head of cattle, some hogs. No matter the route, the Walkers found it impossible to make money with the farm. Because the Internal Revenue Service considers farming a hobby unless the farmer shows a profit in at least two of five years, the Walkers in 1984 sold the cattle and the hogs, and their fields of brome hay went unfertilized.

"Finally we just quit to where we had nothing but a cat and a dog," Robert says. "I'm still stubborn, I still wish I could farm in Alaska, but I do know I can't farm and make a profit."

With no livestock to feed and the days of proving up long past, Robert now mows the fields for two reasons: to keep the trees back and to preserve the effort of the early years.

In 1977, when the Walkers were living in Fairbanks and commuting to their homestead on weekends, a road appeared near the homestead. The road, built by Alyeska Pipeline Service Company, passed just a mile from the Walker's house. Robert was astonished at the sight of truck after truck dumping gravel for the pad on which workers would soon assemble the pipeline.

"To me, it was amazing, because I didn't think they could build anything through a place like that," Robert says. "We'd been fighting permafrost for years and we knew how difficult it was to try to even maintain just a trail through an area where permafrost was. We wondered how they could ever manage it."

The mile between pipeline and homestead consisted of well-drained land through which Robert could build a road. He did, linking the homestead with the pipeline. Alyeska gave the Walkers a key to the gate across an access road near

Shaw Creek. As long as they lock up behind them when they come and go, Robert says, the family has no problem with Alyeska. He had to sign an agreement making him liable for any damage his family might do to Alyeska equipment or the pipeline. Alyeska is not liable for any damage it does to the Walkers or their property, but Robert says the lopsided pact is well worth the luxury of driving in from the Richardson highway.

"We figured beggars can't be choosers. So far, there hasn't been a lick of trouble."

Jeanette has invited me to sleep in the Walker home, but an irresistible campsite sprawls before me. I excuse myself from the picnic table and walk to the hay field. Jane follows me to a spot near the woods. I pitch the tent on bent blades of brome hay.

When I return, Robert is ready to gather water. The Walkers get their water from a creek about a quarter mile south of the house. A well driller once bored a hole 380 feet down; he hit water several times, but the soil surrounding the water was so sandy the water was impossible to extract. A pipeline from the creek to the house proved too tough on pumps, so the Walkers carry their water from creek to house. In the early days, Robert strapped five-gallon cans of water to his back. Now his truck carries 500 gallons in a plastic tank.

A road leads past the barn and down to the creek. Squinting because of the pain of arthritic hips, Walker limps toward the truck. He slowly pulls himself into a faded green pickup with chains on the tires. I get in the passenger side. Robert rides the brakes as the truck rolls down a path of sand. We follow the girls, who have raced down to the creek. Robert backs the truck to the bank of a creek, which is so small the girls would have no trouble stepping across, if dry feet were their goal.

In the back of the truck, next to the water tank, is a pump the size of a lawn mower engine. Robert links black plastic pipe to the pump. On the other end of the pipe is a screen cage the size of a coffee can that he lowers into the creek. Robert pull-starts the pump and sits on the tailgate to watch its progress. The girls splash each other downstream.

I take off my shoes and socks and step in the water; it feels as if I'm standing in a bathtub of ice water. Robert dipped a thermometer in the creek once. Thirty-four degrees.

My feet feel like aching teeth; I step out after a just a few seconds. The girls wade as if in the Bahamas. They shame me on dry land, too, running over spruce branches and hay stubble without wincing. My feet, too many years in shoes, are as tender as raw steak.

Through the years, the nameless stream that emerges from a hillside has always produced.

"It doesn't matter how cold it is," Robert yells over the noise of the pump. "The water's always flowing. I've pumped at 43 below, yet I prefer to pump water when it's not colder than about 10 below zero. It just works better. When it gets cold I fill the pump with hot water before I go down . . . It's really good water, no particular mineral taste to it at all. Doesn't require a lot of detergent for washing."

The girls have found a metal pot, which they dip into the creek. They take turns sipping. I drop to my belly and touch my lips to the stream, the first unfiltered water I have tasted on the trip. The creek is cold, earthy and odorless. I think of how rare this is — to be able to drink straight from a stream without wondering what people upstream have leaked into the water. Because this stream emerges from the ground not far from here, we are safe even from the threat of parasites that live in the guts of beaver and other animals. I gulp until the roof of my mouth aches, quenching my thirst with water that was once snowfall in the Tanana Hills. For this moment, things are how they should be. In drinking the water as it is, I become a part of this place.

I am invited to dinner. In a chair with a high back, I sit next to Rose. On the wall in front of me, behind Jeanette, is a print of a wolf in snowy woods. The Walkers have looked out to the fields to see a lone wolf, lit by moonlight, running with two of their dogs. They also have lost a few dogs to wolves less lonely than the one that romped in the field with the domestics.

Jeanette and Rose have filled the tabletop with plates of pork chops and mashed potatoes. The pork is from a pig they purchased and butchered themselves. The potatoes were grown in the homestead garden. I'm ready to eat, but I notice everyone is bowing his or her head. Robert, at the head of the table, says grace. He thanks the Lord for the visit of Jane and me; he asks for our continued safety on the journey to the Arctic Ocean. I join him in the Amen.

I realize I have a lot to be thankful for here. So much has gone right during 44 days and 280 miles — I've been healthy, Jane seems still to be enjoying herself, I've met nice people who invite me to dinner and show me what Alaska means to them. I was raised a Catholic but have since drifted into curiosity about God without commitment to any religion. I like the Walkers, whose faith is strong enough that it spills into their everyday lives. I pay attention to them because they might be tapped into something. I do believe in a greater power, and perhaps that power is watching over me and Jane. Maybe not. My Amen feels like a universal thanks, even if I'm not sure to whom.

After dinner, in the garage, for two hours I listen to Robert's tales of the homestead. He tells me the homesteading experience did not match the dreams he had when he flipped through *Alaska Life* as a young man.

"It wasn't anything like I anticipated it to be. It wasn't an experience that was satisfying enough to make me feel real good about it, but it made me feel good enough about this place that I'm living here now. I like living here. We're isolated to some extent, but we've got modern things. I can't think of anyplace else that I would enjoy as much."

I would like to have had Robert's timing. To have entered the country when surviving was more a physical than mental challenge. That time is gone, but I can still taste it — when I camp, when I hunt, when I walk with my dog.

I listen to Robert's stories until my eyes close, then say goodnight and walk with Jane out to the hay field. A half moon hangs above the Alaska Range. I crawl in my sleeping bag and notice my headache is gone.

Though I sleep in the tent past breakfast the next morning, Jeanette has saved me batter. She creates two waffles shaped like Mickey Mouse's head. After breakfast, I walk Jane down to the creek with no name. I dip my water bottle. When I drink this water, somewhere miles away, I will think of the Walkers.

Though the Walkers offer Jane and me a ride to the pipeline pad (they are going into Fairbanks today), I decline, wanting to linger on their homestead as long as possible. As they leave, I give Jeanette a big hug, steal a kiss on her cheek. When the Walkers drive away, I remember what Jeanette said about her decision to move back to the homestead 18 years ago:

"When I gave in and said 'Yes, I'll do this,' The Lord opened doors for me that I never expected. And he's taken care of us ever since."

I feel as if doors have been opened for me, too, just by doing the hike. People I would never have met are people I'll perhaps call my friends in the future. With luck, I'll return to the Walkers' homestead someday, to feel the beauty of a place that really appeals to me. To see a dream that was fulfilled, a dream that might have been mine had I been born a few decades earlier.

11 | Things that Go Bump

Day 45

I never imagined this hike would be a social exercise. While dreaming about the trip in the months before takeoff, I thought of solitary, contemplative days spent walking with my dog. Quiet time. Tonight, after walking 10 miles from the Walker homestead, I found the scene I imagined. On a narrow, wooded ridge, ten miles of wild Alaska buffer Jane and me from the nearest humans.

Here, the pipeline shoots northwest, toward Fairbanks; the Richardson Highway tacks west. The 12-mile gap between the two pathways gives me silence. I camp in an aspen grove with earthy ridges of green between the tent and the highway. The only noises are the whine of frustrated mosquitoes, Jane's breaths, the fluty call of a Swainson's thrush, and aspen leaves quaking above.

Jane and I are not the only large mammals sleeping in these woods. A grizzly bear left its pigeon-toed tracks in the mud of the pipeline pad, sharing our path for more than one mile. The prints were bigger than my boot, a size 11. The bear's palm pushed deeper into the mud than my foot. It makes me feel alone for the first time. Grizzlies rarely wander into towns, the way black bears do. The big brown bears need land away from roads, from houses, from barking dogs, from the smell of heating oil.

Here, I share these black spruce and aspen woods with my dog, the skeeters, the songbirds, and a large grizzly bear. This is what I imagined the trip would be like. This is me, camping without the security of another person next to me, a person with whom to rationalize sudden noises in the woods. Camping alone scares me. Even though a shotgun rests parallel to my sleeping bag, bears scare me. Not many animals remain that can scare a person, even in Alaska. But bears are stronger than us, bears have proven themselves as unpredictable as us, and a few rogues have tasted us. This is one of the few places left on Earth where I can feel fear of animals other than humans. It's here, even in the company of the silver behemoth filled with crude oil. Even though I missed homesteading time, I'm glad I live in this one, where we haven't yet eliminated all of the species that wither human arrogance with nothing more than heavy breaths.

What am I afraid of? When I worked for the Park Service, the 12-gauge shotgun was the weapon of choice to kill a charging bear. Not that anyone I worked with had ever needed to kill a bear. But the fear was so strong that we all fired 50 slugs at bear targets. From the shoulder, from the hip, with just five seconds from when the instructor said "go" to pull the trigger. If you didn't get 50 percent of your shots in the kill zones of the paper bear targets, you weren't allowed to carry a shotgun.

I'll probably never use this shotgun to kill a bear. My first shot is a dummy shell, a noisemaker. If a bear comes into camp, my plan goes, I'll send a boom its way. If the bear keeps coming, I'll jack out the dummy shell. The next shell is a slug, a heavy cylinder of lead, meant to kill the bear, or at least knock it down. If that slug doesn't do the job or I miss, I carry one more in the shotgun's magazine. But the shotgun is just a tool, only as good as the person using it. Out here, the gun is all that makes me stronger than a bear. Even with this machine that throws lead, I feel puny.

It's funny that I'm afraid out here by myself. If John or Smits were with me, I wouldn't be the slightest bit scared, even though I would be supposed to be the one protecting us. Alone, I wonder what I'm afraid of. I've never seen a bear attack anything larger than a ground squirrel. I'm afraid of the stories — the bear that attacked a dog team near Coldfoot and killed and ate most of the dogs while the musher escaped; the geologist on the Alaska Peninsula killed by a bear that should have been hibernating.

I'm afraid of getting close enough to a bear to smell its breath, of the moment when I realize my wounds are enough to kill me, when I give up. I'm afraid of not being able to understand why an animal would need to kill me when I don't want to kill it. I'm afraid of seeing Jane attacked, hearing her squeal.

Without asking, I've gotten all sorts of advice all along the trail. A man playing pool in Tsaina Lodge nodded at what he knew would happen. *Yeah, those grizzlies are the ones to watch out for. They'll attack you without warning. It's going to happen to you sometime on your trip.*

A young father who was living in the woods near Paxson Lodge coached me. *You're going to get only one chance when that bear charges. Blow it and you're dead.*

While I think those guys have read *Alaska Bear Tales* too many times, I'm still wary enough to carry a shotgun across Alaska. As my pack presses down on my shoulders, I always think of things I can get rid of to save even a few ounces. I recently gave away one of those emergency blankets made of foil; it couldn't have weighed more than a handkerchief. But here I carry seven pounds of steel and plastic in one of my hands, all day long. It's kind of dumb when I think about it, but fear won't let me put it down.

Fear is part of the deal out here, though. It adds an element I don't have at home, or while sitting in front of a computer at work. Sitting up in the tent at night while Jane barks at snapping twigs is an experience I can't duplicate anywhere else. Sometimes it's good to be scared, it makes you feel alive. Out here, alone and afraid, I'm alive.

We are visited in the night. I wake to the clamor of a large animal near the tent. Eyes wide open, I sit up like a jackknife blade, but the brush surrounding the tent is too tall for me to see what lurks nearby. Because no animal that was stalking would ever make this much noise, I decide that whatever it is out there has just stumbled upon us. I clear my throat and try animal avoidance technique number one, the declaration of our existence.

"Hey! I'm camping here, right in your path! Sorry 'bout that. Please walk around. I don't want to get up to shoot you!"

When I stop talking, the noise stops. The creature has heard me. It now contemplates its next action. It fulfills my hopes by snapping twigs with a noise that grows ever fainter. To my surprise, Jane has not opened her mouth during the encounter. She usually barks at strange noises. Jane has left this encounter, occurring in the twilight of four a.m., to me. She plops back down on her sleeping mat, emitting a groan.

Satisfied at the silence of the forest, I stare at the silhouettes of aspen trees. As new blood dilutes the adrenaline in my body, I realize that my words to the noise in the night are the only ones I've spoken all day.

12 | **North Pole**

Day 53

Close to home. Pavement and traffic and noise, all somehow comforting. Cars without mufflers, the bitter scent of burnt diesel, the artificial heat radiating from asphalt. I wince at them when I'm at home. But I grew up with them; I've spend a lot more time with them than I have sleeping in the woods with bears.

Smits is here, too. She joined me for a Solstice celebration with friends, out by Pump Station 8. She visited me once on the trail, dropping off supplies at the Gulkana River, but at Solstice I had time to linger with her, to remember what she smelled like, what it felt like to be with a woman.

She's giving Jane a rest, taking Jane to her house outside Fairbanks. I'm walking through the town of North Pole, not taking the pipeline because it goes through people's backyards and I didn't ask them if I could walk through like Alyeska wanted me to. But I don't need to ask to walk on the Richardson Highway. So I do, carrying just a day pack and water while Smits shuttles everything else to her house.

The highway at 2 miles an hour is a new place. I've driven it hundreds of times, but I never noticed the broken glass in the ditches or the way hot pavement smells like ammonia after a cumulonimbus dumps its load.

I'm near home, and I walked from Valdez to get here. Three-hundred-fifty miles. Half the summer of walking, and suddenly I'm where I live. I'm a different person — tan, lean, thousands of new views of Alaska in my brain, and this is a different place.

Things have changed here. Trees exploded with green leaves, replacing the rusty brown of the hillsides. Dragonflies, mosquitoes and spiders are hunted by songbirds that suddenly crowded the ravens and chickadees. Stars disappeared, the sun took its throne, and the moon hides.

For a few days, Jane doesn't walk with me. She takes a break at Smits' house, where all three of us sleep on the lawn in a tent (I want to keep my streak of nights in a tent intact. It's stupid when Smits has a nice bed just steps away, but staying in the tent means something to me. Smits thinks I'm odd, but still she sleeps outside with me.)

As I step through the flatness of a spillway the Army Corps of Engineers built to divert the Chena River from Fairbanks and North Pole, I miss my Jane's tail, beating the air as her nose picks up the trail of an animal I can't detect. I miss her antelope leap into the trees, in search of grouse and snowshoe hares. I miss the ring of her bell on her backpack, a constant reminder I'm not alone.

But this is not Jane country. I'll walk on or next to the Richardson Highway most of the day. Jane is much better off lounging at Smits's house, resting rather than roughing her pads on hot pavement.

I walk in shorts and a T-shirt. I carry a day pack with only the essentials — a quart of water, snacks, sunglasses. No shotgun, no camera, no Jane. Nothing to identify me as that guy hiking the pipeline. It's fun to be anonymous again, to see if people react any differently. Of course they do. A woman I pass doesn't even return my "Hi," though I suspect she might if Jane were here wearing her red backpack.

I part with the pipeline as it begins an underground path through back yards. I walk across the Richardson Highway and reach Saint Nicholas Drive in North Pole. Only 2,000 people live in North Pole; twice as many have homes in a 15-mile circle around the town. But I feel I'm in a city, at least an Alaska city. My welcome to the metropolis is an advertisement, shouted in black letters on four sheets of plywood: "Welcome to the Exciting First Baptist Church of North Pole."

Walking on sticky asphalt, I reach a North Pole landmark. A fiberglass Santa Claus, tall as a telephone pole and wide as a car, stares blankly at the grass median between Saint Nicholas Drive and the Richardson Highway. The giant Santa has blue eyes and a big butt. His concrete pedestal is protected by a chain-link fence topped with barbed wire. He's been standing here for years, impervious to 50 below, fading in the summer sun. He'll probably be standing years after I'm gone.

I avoid Santa's gaze, taking the entrance to Santaland RV park, an acre of gravel on which perch the rolling summer homes of visitors to Alaska. I hang a left on Rudolph Lane, past a sign, "Slow, reindeer at play!" The plates on the motor homes are from California, Missouri, Nebraska. Their owners have traded $21 for electricity, a drain for their sewage, "Santa's Vehicle Wash," and — unobstructed by trees or other vegetation — a view of their transient neighbors. The fee is part of $635 million tourists will spend in Alaska this year. Though oil and natural gas development provide most of the jobs in Alaska, with seafood harvesting following close behind, tourism is a significant number three. And North Pole courts the RVers without shame: Santa's Car Rental, Santa's Elves Bed & Breakfast, Santa's 5th Avenue Automotive, Santa's Flowers, Santa's Kids Daycare, Santa's Gallery, Santa's Kitchen, Santa's Senior Citizens, Santa's Stitches, Santa's Travel World.

North Pole, Alaska, is barely closer to the geographic North Pole than it is to Phoenix. Walking here, I am still about 1,800 miles shy of the top of the world. Santa didn't always do business here. Before World War II, the area was known as Moose Crossing because the largest members of the deer family frequently roamed this 10-mile gap between the Tanana and Chena rivers. In 1949, Bon V. Davis decided it was time to subdivide his 160-acre homestead here. Davis eventually sold most of his land to Everett Dahl and Kenneth Gaske, two land developers from Fairbanks who were anxious to reap a return on their investment. They decided to name the subdivision North Pole for reasons Davis documented in a 1970 article in *Alaska* magazine:

"A toy manufacturer might be eager to establish a plant right here so that his products might be advertised as being made at the North Pole. And someone might start a Santa Land that might become a northern version of Disneyland."

Disneyland is not threatened. The structure most resembling the enchanted castle is Santa Claus House, which stands white with red trim before me. Next to another tall Santa (unfortunately two-dimensional and made of plywood), a telephone pole painted like a candy cane holds a sign 30 feet in the air: "the North Pole." Tour buses are stacked three deep. Retirees file into Santa Claus House, which sells things Christmas every weekday except December 25, when Santa Claus House is closed.

13 | **Fairbanks**

Day 53

My partner is back. After a one-day rest, Jane joins me on a path that leads through Fort Wainwright, the Army base in Fairbanks, and to the end of the flatness of the Tanana Valley — Birch Hill.

The south face of Birch Hill is shaved to grass; soldiers stationed at Fort Wainwright use the 1,500-foot bump as a downhill ski area. Jane finds wild strawberries growing on the open slope. She stops to graze. A citrus smell wafts into the air.

Birch Hill allows a view of Fairbanks and the Tanana Valley. The Chena River, which Jane and I crossed using a one-lane bridge on Fort Wainwright, loops around the military runway before meandering through the heart of Fairbanks. On the west side of town, the Chena spills into the Tanana River, which then hooks southwest before bending north at the town of Nenana, eventually joining the Yukon River 275 river miles from Fairbanks. On the trip, I will cross all three rivers.

The Tanana is a striated ribbon on miles of plain between Fairbanks and the Alaska Range. The Chena, denied rain in the second driest spring on record, is a slow-moving slough amid piles of gravel, a river you wouldn't take your new outboard up at the moment.

The physical characteristics of both rivers led to the founding of Fairbanks 96 years ago. The Tanana does not flow deep in a single channel; the silty water chooses a network of parallel gravel paths depending on the season. The braids of the Tanana are often shallower than a moose is tall. This feature forced Charles Adams, the captain of the steamship *Lavelle Young,* to leave E. T. Barnette and his wife Isabelle on the forested bank of the Chena in 1901. Barnette, the owner of $20,000 worth of goods with which to start a trading post, had contracted Adams, against Adams' better judgment, to ferry his wares up the Tanana River from Saint Michael, a Bering Sea town at the mouth of the Yukon River.

Barnette planned on creating "the Chicago of Alaska." But he didn't plan to do it on the south bank of the Chena River. Barnette's original destination was Tanana Crossing, on maps today as Tanacross. Because the Tanana River was impassable beyond Fairbanks, Barnette never got within 100 miles of Tanacross, and Fairbanks now has three McDonald's.

Seeing the smoke from the *Lavelle Young's* stack, two prospectors rushed down from the hills to meet the boat on the Chena. The miners avoided a 200-mile hike north to Circle City on the Yukon by acquiring supplies from Barnette, who cleared a spot in the woods to wait out the winter and attempt to reach Tanana Crossing the next summer.

Events the next summer changed Barnette's plans. Felix Pedro, an Italian immigrant and one of the two miners who'd bought supplies from Barnette, found gold on a creek 12 miles north of Barnette's cache. Barnette, a man who knew when opportunity was upon him, sent his Japanese cook to Dawson City to spread the news of the rich ground of the Tanana hills near the Chena River. Though the ground was not all that rich (Barnette hoped instead to profit from the miners who came to stake the streams), a stampede was on.

As a favor to Judge James Wickersham, who was responsible for law and order matters for Alaska's third judicial district (300,000 square miles of land), Barnette named his trading post for Charles W. Fairbanks, a senator from Wickersham's home state of Indiana who would become vice president to Theodore Roosevelt in 1904.

Wickersham later returned Barnette's favor by establishing a courthouse in Fairbanks, a move that helped Barnette out-compete a trading post in the nearby settlement of Chena, which quickly became a ghost town.

Fairbanks sprawls below us. After Jane finishes snacking on the berries, we resume our climb up Birch Hill. The north side of Birch Hill is a cross-country ski area with trails cut through forests of birch and spruce, a 1,200-foot bump covered with snow from October until April. Birch Hill is where many people play during the winter, fending off Seasonal Affective Disorder with daily skis at noon, when the sun makes a shallow arc over the Alaska Range to the south.

The sun's not hiding now. Summer is here, and Jane and I have walked home from Valdez, 345 miles away. I aimed Jane's and my path for Birch Hill today because Birch Hill is one of the reasons I love Fairbanks. Today, people scramble over the hill in sunshine like ants in a hurry to make the most of good weather. A stage is set up in the Birch Hill stadium, an acre of lawn. Actors rehearse a Shakespeare play, *Cymbeline,* in the outdoor theater.

As the actors perform, runners in a 10-kilometer race pant behind them on the rolling trails of Birch Hill. With Jane next to me, I see the runners enter the Birch Hill stadium. We watch the entrants cross the finish line, then bend, putting their hands to their knees. I know a few of the runners. In a different summer, I'd be running with them. A local humor columnist finishes five seconds behind the winner. In a column, he wrote he would like to walk 800 feet with me to gain column fodder. I invite him. Finishing a few minutes later is my friend Andy, who also has an invite to join me on the pipeline hike. Andy accepted, and in a few weeks will cover about 50 miles north of Fairbanks with me. Another runner walks up to pet Jane after finishing. He shakes my hand, tells me what a great accomplishment it is to walk from Valdez to Fairbanks. It doesn't really feel like a great accomplishment; it feels like the way things should be. Waking on a bed of earth every day, walking 10 miles with my dog, feels like the most natural thing I've ever done. After walking 345 miles, it seems I could walk all my life. If she could talk, I think Jane might agree. For now, the world is ours, and time doesn't matter.

Day 58

In 34 years of life, I have never been this organized. At this moment, I know what I will eat every day for the next 17 weeks. Foil packs of freeze-dried dinners, gorp bags the size of basketballs, a dozen boxes of pilot bread, 17 jars of peanut butter, 11 spears of pepperoni and other future meals coat the ground floor of Smits's home, in the Goldstream Valley outside Fairbanks. Here, I've taken a three-day break from the trail to buy supplies and rest. One of my chores has been buying more than $1,000 in groceries to fuel Jane, me and our human partners the final 450 miles to the Arctic Ocean.

Now comes the hard part: measuring cups of raisins, oatmeal, Cream of Wheat, gorp, refried beans. Sorting candy bars, vitamin C tablets, rations of toilet paper. Counting discs of pilot bread, rolls of film, double-A batteries. Ciphering how many of these items I'll need for a six-day stretch, or an eight-day stretch, or a ten-day stretch with two people. Placing the items in 17 cardboard boxes that will remain in Smits's house until someone delivers them to me.

Smits to the rescue. Unlike me, she tends toward order. To her, sifting cups of brown sugar is not drudgery. We have another volunteer. John stays until 3 a.m. One of his chores is to roll a certain number of vitamin C tablets, depending on the amount of days the food drop will cover, into a foil worm.

Without John and Smits, I could not have started or maintained this walk. Measuring, bagging and sorting, they save me from insanity. They both work in their own interest, too, because they will both hike with me north of Fairbanks. John makes sure his food drop box is spiked with pepperoni. Smits's boxes are heavy with dried fruits and include lots of toilet paper. By the time we finish, two complete days have been devoted to future food drops.

Thinking of food, I step on Smits's digital scale. I weigh

154, four pounds heavier than when I started. I hoist Jane as a cowboy lifts a calf, stand on the scale, and subtract 154 pounds. At 63 pounds, Jane has lost the same number of pounds I have gained. She is a rock of functional muscle. Her sponsors at Eagle will be pleased. I owe my weight gain to the menu Smits prepared on computer for me in March.

Day 60

The walk away from Fairbanks begins in the rosy twilight of 10:50 p.m. I chose this hour for its coolness; this hour chose me because it took all day to finish the food drops.

Andy gives Smits, Jane and me a ride from Smits's house to a section of above-ground pipeline next to the Steese Highway. Here is one of the few places where people are allowed near the pipeline. Busloads of tourists take the ride over the hill north of Fairbanks to see the trans-Alaska pipeline, number nine of Alaska's top ten tourist attractions (the cruise ship route through the waters of the Inside Passage is number one, Mt. McKinley number five).

Near midnight, none of the 200,000 tourists who see the pipeline every year are present, but three locals pull in as we prepare to take off. Two women, fiftyish, one holding a bouquet, and two men. They have just been to the Turtle Club in Fox, a few miles north. They pose in front of a signpost: *Prudhoe Bay 450, Yukon River 97, Arctic Circle 156*. As I attach Jane's backpack, the woman with the flowers asks a question.

"Are you Jane and that guy?"

"Yup, that's us."

"We've been reading about you every week. I really look

forward to the Sunday paper now."

"Thanks."

"Can we have your autograph?"

I sign my name on four bank deposit tickets. Jane's four fans have stopped at the pipeline only because one of the men is visiting from Portland, Oregon. The women are from Fairbanks. One of the men lives in North Pole. I write my name and also JANE, with a tiny paw print. We talk about the trip for a few minutes, then they walk back to their car.

Smits, who will walk with me for three days, begins the walk north with Jane and me. It's the July 4th weekend, and she gets a break from her thesis for a few days. She's happy for the change, to get some sun on her slender arms. She wears leather work boots, nylon pants that mosquitoes can't poke through, a T-shirt. She's small and delicate-looking, but not frail. When we hike together, I'm the one who calls for the breaks. Smits is an Alaskan who has spent much more time outdoors here than I ever will. She's a good person to share some miles with, observant and not afraid to pause when she's interested in something. She'll leave me near Wickersham Dome, and meet up with me again in the Arctic, for the last miles. The last miles seem a long way off.

We head toward the sun, which peeks over the green hills in front of us. The air smells of spruce smoke.

After three days of food shopping, food sorting, column writing and getting used to driving again, walking is exquisite. Back to a simple world, one in which all that matters is to put one foot in front of the other. Back to a world where everything I need is fastened to my back, including a nylon home that will keep me dry in the heaviest rain storm. Back to the distraction of bird songs rather than TV or music interrupted by people trying to sell me things I don't want. Back to dark brown moose with thoroughbred lines who watch our approach with erect ears. Back to squadrons of dragonflies hunting the night air over gurgling creeks. Back to the delightful wobble of Jane's butt. Back to Alaska.

14 | **Heart**

Day 68

A few days after Smits catches a ride with John back to Fairbanks, another friend joins Jane and me. Andy Sterns is one of eight people who will share the hike. Andy drove north 70 miles from Fairbanks in my red Dodge truck. Because I've arrived at our meeting point a day early, I have waited for him an entire day, sitting in my mosquito jacket, made of nylon with a mesh hood. While I waited, I wrote a column, took a nap and thought of the many miles ahead. Just yesterday, I crossed the 400-mile-mark, only halfway to Prudhoe Bay. It's July 11th, and I wonder if I have enough summer left to make it the rest of the way.

Andy shows at 10 p.m. He parks my truck on the shoulder of the Dalton Highway. We stuff our packs with food, new insect repellent, a tent for two, white gas for the stove, and new underwear for me.

As we pack, Andy insists on carrying all the food. I don't argue. We walk one-half mile to a hilltop, a spot with a view of hazy blue hills that roll to the horizon like waves. Beyond those hills is the longest river in Alaska, the Yukon. Andy will walk with me almost all the way to the river, 50 miles north. About 10 miles short of the river, another friend will join me, and Andy will hitchhike back here to the truck.

I met Andy a few years ago, when he worked as a dog handler for Iditarod musher Susan Butcher. Andy was living with my friend Mari, whom I met in the Park Service. Andy and Mari shared a cabin in Fairbanks. Theirs was a musher's home — sled dogs staked in the yard, the interior a detonation of laundry, newspapers and outdoor gear.

Andy's truck has a similar feel, with an artificial floor of unopened mail, polypropylene running wear, and enough bagels, energy bars and stray slices of bread to sustain him for at least a week should he become trapped in the vehicle.

Andy does not own a comb. His hair sprouts like wild hay until harvest time, when he shuffles into a barber shop and grins at the barber, who smiles back nervously, wondering if the panic shows.

He and I are almost exactly the same size and weight — we're both about 150 pounds without much fat. We both get cold easily. He always wears a hat, has clear blue eyes and a ready smile.

As long as I have known Andy, he has held only an occasional part-time job. Most people know him as an Iditarod musher. He has run "the Last Great Race" two times, twice becoming Page 1 news despite not finishing one race and reaching Nome a week behind the winner in the other. Now, he is a college student, in the Teachers for Alaska program, though he's not sure he wants to teach. Finding a career does not matter much to Andy. Living matters to Andy.

Day 69

Andy carries a pack that's 15 pounds heavier than mine. Not only does he Sherpa all our food, he also carries the two-man tent and an Iditarod-quality sleeping bag, which is large enough to allow him to sleep in with bunny boots on should the occasion arise. (He couldn't find his lighter bag.) During the first night, Jane fell in love with Andy's bag, which is so thick he does not need a sleeping pad. Unable to resist its six-inch loft, she slowly encroached on the opening of his bedding, eventually nesting near Andy's head and forcing him partway onto the nylon floor of the tent.

As Andy lugs the bulk of our supplies, I notice again his choppy gait. When Andy steps north, his right foot arcs east. The shoe on that foot does not clear the ground. With each step, he pushes a tiny pile of gravel. His running style used to be even more exaggerated. The first time I saw him in a running race, he looked sort of like a baby running across a lawn with arms flailing. I didn't know much about him then.

As he hikes, his foot catches occasionally on raised bumps of gravel. He falls forward, hitting the ground with his knees and hands, sometimes his face. His heavy pack makes the impact worse. Without a word, he pushes himself up and bobs on. I wince when I see him fall; I want to help him up, but I don't. And I've learned not to ask him if he's OK. He's OK.

Andy leans forward with each step to compensate for his sluggish leg. When he walks through a grocery store, down the street, people notice. After quickly looking away, they silently invent reasons why he is different. Maybe they think he has a birth defect, or a degenerative muscle disease.

The first time Andy finished the Equinox Marathon in Fairbanks, he collapsed after crossing the finish line. As he lay on the ground smiling at the sky, blood trickled from his nose and his forehead. During the marathon's course of 26-plus miles, exposed tree roots repeatedly caught Andy's foot. Each time he fell, he got back up. After four and a half hours of tripping on roots and slamming to the earth, Andy finished. And he was in the middle of the pack. Despite his awkward running style, he's fast. He has finished the marathon three times.

One of Andy's favorite races is the 24-hour Mountain Bike Challenge, put on by the local cycle club around summer solstice. Because they know him, other riders hate competing against Andy in the race. Even though they may be stronger, they realize Andy will not let them rest. If they snooze, which most people want to do at least once in a 24-hour period, they lose. During one such race, in which the winner is the one who does the most laps in 24 hours, Andy completed ten laps — each with a hill climb of over 1,500 feet — while taking no more than a ten-minute break in the entire day. He outlasted everyone except the best rider in the state, who managed one more lap than Andy.

Along with all our food, Andy carries a gallon of water. I usually don't carry water, preferring instead to purify and drink it at the source, but water is suddenly hard to find.

"The map says there's a creek in about a mile," Andy says.

"The map's been failing me lately," I say, "I see the blue lines and then I get there and all I find is dry rocks. I knew water would be hard to find somewhere along the line."

Our first water source, Lost Creek, is a rusty slough. Even after filtering, it has the alarming taste of heavy metals. For the first time on the trip, I dump my water bottle after filling it, opting to tap the next blue line on the map, two miles away.

We find dry rocks.

"Damn! I haven't had a drink since tea at breakfast." I look at the map. "That's eight miles. I've never gone this far without stopping to drink. I'm getting a headache."

"Maybe there's something just around the corner," Andy says. He's right.

After another dry mile, we hear wet smacking. Jane laps a puddle. The creek on the map is not there, but Jane has found a pool of black water in the shadows. Andy and I take turns pumping quarts from the water hole. It tastes like dirt but surprisingly good. I drink a half gallon.

Hours later, during the quiet after dinner, we recline on soft moss in a protective cloud of Pic, a green coil that gives off mosquito-repelling smoke. Andy washes dishes after a Jane pre-rinse cycle. I hang the food from a nearby section of pipe to finish the day's chores. Jane snoozes at my feet. Andy pulls on a winter hat, made of soft pile. My hat is wool, thick enough for winter. The heat of the day drifts to the ionosphere. The temperature drops to 40 degrees.

With nothing to distract us, Andy and I talk. I ask him about the accident. I've never heard him talk about it, because he doesn't dwell on the past. His world is immediate — if today is good, he has a good life. This day is a good one, he's in his usual positive mood. He doesn't seem to mind when I ask him about the time he broke his neck.

The accident happened nine years ago, when Andy was a cross-country ski racer at Middlebury College. The Panthers had just competed in a skating race at the University of Vermont's winter carnival, in Stowe. Andy and a few other skiers were taking a cool-down lap. Andy raced a friend, hit a patch of ice, could not get a bite with the edges of skis just two inches wide.

Andy rammed into a tree, head-first. After it happened, he lay in the snow on his belly. He remembers being carried off the ski trails on a stretcher, his friends afraid even to speak to one another as he was carried past.

The medical explanation: A compression fracture, fifth cervical. In the hospital, he could not move his arms and legs. Four days after the accident, Andy was fitted with a brace that secured his head to his torso with the aid of four screws turned clockwise into the bone of his skull.

Two weeks after the accident, Andy stood. Impatient, he was scolded by a nurse when she caught him, arms rigid and legs dragging, using his walker when no one else was around.

He eventually controlled his muscles enough to work crutches, upon which he would race his friend Eric down the hall of the hospital. Eric, a skier, evened the odds by walking on his hands.

Forty-eight days after the accident, Andy was out of the hospital's rehabilitation center and into his own apartment near Middlebury. With the brace still screwed to his head, he developed his own regimen of workouts. His days took on a pattern: A morning session of exercise, followed by lunch and a nap, then another workout in the afternoon.

Three months after the accident, a doctor backed out the screws. The halo brace came off. Andy kept pushing himself, not listening to a trainer who said he would never ski again, not listening to a counselor who said things would be different now, with a disability. He avoided the counselor.

His apartment was in a converted woolen mill. The complex had a swimming pool, a long staircase. It was there he shed his crutches and learned to walk again. He enjoyed the stairs. Up and down. Up and down. He struggled to control a different body, legs that did not lift upon command. He adjusted, bending his torso, hoisting his legs with his arms when he got into a car or truck. His walking style drew stares.

"He never complained, never said 'Why me?'" says Andy's mother, Judi Sterns, who watched Andy's recovery closely, along with Andy's father. "It frightened me at times that he was so stoic."

Andy went back to Middlebury the next fall. He graduated a semester behind his classmates and followed a path west that eventually led him to Alaska. He was living in Jackson, Wyoming, skiing every day and working a landscaping job. In a Jackson newspaper, he saw an ad in the classifieds: Dog handler wanted in Alaska. *Live between Fairbanks and Anchorage, tending to dogs of Iditarod musher. Conditions primitive.*

Andy called, accepted the job, and moved to Alaska to become a dog man. Because he says there's always more to do in Alaska, he won't leave soon.

His walking and running become smoother all the time. Andy has competed in the Iditarod twice and participates in nearly every mountain bike, running, and ski race that happens in Fairbanks. Though not a sprinter, Andy has a quality absent in some other competitors. Some call it drive. Others, heart. Endurance is an understatement. The longer and tougher and steeper the race, the higher Andy places in the standings.

Here, he carries our food and shelter in an internal frame pack that hangs from his back like a baby orangutan. I don't slow my hiking pace to accommodate Andy. If anything, I'm walking a bit faster than usual, especially up hills.

"This is really nice," he says. "Good views from the pipeline. Quieter than I would have thought, too."

Andy has twice attempted the Iditarod. In his first race, Andy completed 1,096 of 1,100 miles. Near the finish, Andy drove his team from Safety to Cape Nome, where a moaning wind stung his flesh with snow crystals. His goggles fogged. When he took them off, his eyelashes stuck together. His dogs were doing fine, staying on the trail. Then their eyes frosted over. The lead dogs began wavering. When he separated his eyelashes, Andy could not see 15 yards ahead. Because he and his dogs were going blind, Andy stopped the team behind a few buildings that broke the wind somewhat.

When race marshal Bobby Lee drove out to look for the overdue musher, the wind chill was 90 below zero. He found Andy talking to his dogs, who were curled up into balls, covered with snow.

The wind subsided enough to allow Andy and the dogs

to see. When Andy went to rouse his dogs for the lope to finish, a few hesitated. When they stood, they wobbled. The worst were slightly shaking.

So damn close. Lee, the race marshal, contemplated extending the boundaries of Nome so Andy could be considered a finisher, but that would take time Andy and the dogs did not have. Lee told Andy his options — to mush the remaining few miles with the healthy portion of the team, or to pack all his dogs in Lee's truck and scratch. Andy looked at his dogs, then chose the latter. He became the musher who came furthest in the Iditarod without finishing.

"Andy Sterns, to me, was the unsung hero of (the 1995) Iditarod," Lee would later say, citing how most people would have limped into Nome to earn a finisher's belt buckle. For his near-miss, Andy earned his first headline: *Musher scratches 3½ miles outside Nome.*

The next year, he got his second headline. Andy and his team finished the Iditarod in last place, 49th, seven days after Jeff King won. He and his dogs finished the race in 15 days, the quickest red lantern time by more than twelve hours. On the front page of the Fairbanks Daily News-Miner: *Last place is sweet vindication for Fairbanksan shut out in '95.*

I once referred to Andy's dogs as slow; he quickly corrected me. "It's not my dogs that were slow, it's me hanging around checkpoints and being slow with my chores." It's true. Andy would not make a good tax accountant in April. But I'm really glad he's here with me now. These miles would be tough alone — the mosquitoes are worse than ever, and we walk through lonely country that seems like spruce bog after spruce bog. I find myself fantasizing about reaching Prudhoe

Bay, sinking into my couch, eating Ben & Jerry's.

"Sometimes I just wish this trip would be over," I tell Andy as we search for another water hole. "I can't wait till I get to the point where the worst is all behind me, till I've seen the worst bugs, survived the worst storms."

"Your trip is something like the Iditarod," he says. "You should take it from checkpoint to checkpoint, like from here to the Yukon. If you think too much about Prudhoe Bay, you'll miss the fun of what you're doing now."

I've noticed that my mood is directly related to how blue the sky appears. Lately, the sky has been clogged with clouds. It showers frequently. The raindrops moisten the grass on the pipeline pad. My boots absorb the wet. I sleep with clammy boot liners in my bag every night.

The clouds that coat the sky like greenhouse plastic have made it cool enough for the mosquitoes to thrive. Instead of just irritating late at night or early in the morning, the mosquitoes bother us all day. Jane's meanders through the brush are recruiting trips; she returns with squadrons of mosquitoes. The tiny devils follow puffs of carbon dioxide to human with plenty of skin exposed. When they find my tender spot, the small of my back, I can't do a thing but wait for them to fill up. My pack prevents me from touching that spot. I feel the pinpricks and think of blood leaving my body.

Celebrated in the stories of arctic explorers and on today's cheesy T-shirts, the mosquito has been an almost constant presence on the trip. They seem to be getting worse, which isn't a big surprise. Walk a straight line across Alaska, you're going to get nailed by mosquitoes somewhere along the way.

North of the Arctic Circle is worse; Russian scientists found that caribou on the tundra in Siberia each lose more than five pounds of blood a summer to mosquitoes. The researchers noticed that up to 10,000 mosquitoes could draw blood from a caribou at one time. Biologists think mosquitoes and other insects do their share of caribou herding, driving the animals to high, windy elevations and snow patches.

The problem is, of course, the female. Male mosquitoes drink nectar from plants to keep them alive, but the ladies also need blood's protein to develop their ovaries and make more mosquitoes (though the male does its part, latching on to the female in mid-air, mating without touching the ground, and sending the female in quest of blood). Some mosquitoes survive Alaska's winter by clinging to leaves and other stuff on the forest floor and counting on a good snowfall to insulate them until spring. They emerge, sluggish and clumsy, as the first wave of attackers. These "snow mosquitoes" are slow enough to pick off in mid-air, but the same can't be said for those that follow. The mosquitoes that hatch later, from eggs laid in water the previous summer, are quick and efficient. Artful dodgers.

In the British textbook, the Biology of Mosquitoes, the editors reported that mosquitoes hone in on victims' body odor and breath. Once a food source is detected, the female follows the trail upwind to its source. Then the bloodsuckers zero in on other cues, such as silhouettes, dark colors, and moisture in the air. English researchers found that mosquitoes responded to the cues of a young cow when it was 45 feet away. In his 1949 book, The Natural History of Mosquitoes, researcher Marston Bates described an experiment in which he released mosquitoes in a room with a mix of humans, pets and livestock. Bates factored in the size difference of each animal and jotted down the mosquitoes' preference, in order: Cows, goats, pigs, humans, dogs, cats, and barnyard fowl. That the mosquitoes prefer Andy and me to Jane is a hypothesis I have no trouble confirming. She emerges from the alders with a smile, trailing a cloud that happily stops when it reaches Andy and me, hitting with precision all the spots we missed with the Cutters.

Day 70

We wake to a gray world, to rain that can't be out-slept. After crawling out of the tent, we eat breakfast amid a humming swarm. Slimy black corpses flavor our oatmeal.

"Man, this sucks," I tell Andy, thinking if I get mad enough, maybe something will change.

He smiles, nods, and chews his oatmeal.

The only relief from the bugs is walking, but walking doesn't help. Not only do the mosquitoes join us for the hike, they stay with us when a gray wall of rainwater belts us and runs in balls down my back. As we descend into the valley made by Hess Creek, mosquitoes bounce off our eyeballs. They fly up our nostrils. They show no respect for repellent, and somehow they dodge raindrops that should smack them out of the air. Even Andy begins to crack.

"These are the worst bastards I've ever seen," he says. Because his pants hang low on his hips, mosquitoes attack the small of his back, too.

I am tempted to fire the shotgun, to send a clump of lead

through the living cloud. The concussion might knock out a few whines from my ear, a few tickles from my nose, a few pokes from my eyeballs.

Jane picks this maddening moment to flush a family of spruce grouse, except one. That one, a month-old chick the size of a pint of milk, comes to visit us in Jane's mouth. It is dead when Jane presents it to me. I grab it by the legs and carry it in my free hand, which can no longer swat mosquitoes. I have noble thoughts of cooking the bird, feeding the prize to Jane. After about 10 steps, I pitch the bird into the brush because I can't imagine stopping for even a few minutes.

Andy laughs.

"I was wondering when you were going to toss that thing."

I laugh too, but my laugh quickly dies. Tiny oppressors clog my breathing, turn my eyeballs to flypaper, crack my fragile psyche. Nothing works. We are bathed in DEET. DEET doesn't matter. They are an army of thousands, insane for our blood. The worst part is the unsteady whine — it's like a dentist pressing down with the drill, hitting a nerve.

At the bottom of the Hess Creek valley is a metal box the size of a house trailer, filled with Alyeska oil spill equipment to be deployed should the pipeline spring a leak near Hess Creek. We lean our packs against the box and dig for the bug protection. Mine is my mosquito jacket, which I never wear hiking because it makes me sweat as if I were wearing a garbage bag.

From his bulbous pack, Andy yanks a headnet that looks like the prototype, with strings that dangle next to his arms. I knot the loose ends beneath his armpits. Andy's eyeballs are barely visible through rose-colored mesh.

I call Jane and reach into her pack for doggy repellent. I squirt a stream onto the bridge of her nose. Because my hands are being attacked, I slop some on her jowls. She licks the nasty substance, then tries to spit out her tongue. The poisoning of my dog further grays my mood.

We walk to the bank of Hess Creek, a 20-foot-wide stream that empties into the Yukon after 50 miles of meandering from this point. I have three problems at Hess Creek: there is no footbridge, it is a significant wade across, and we have hiked only six miles today. I want more.

We have two options — to strip down, wade, and risk significant blood loss, or to walk to the Dalton Highway via an access road that would take us five miles out of our way. As I fret over the decision, another black cloud opens overhead. Raindrops assault the hood of my bug jacket and turn my world hazy by wetting the mesh in front of my eyes. Not knowing what to do, I stand there, frustrated.

Andy has an idea. "Why don't I pump us some water from the creek?"

I give him the water filter and he walks to the Hess Creek gravel bar, sits on wet rocks, and starts pumping. As Jane whines at my indecision, Andy makes a suggestion.

"Why don't we camp here for the night?"

I bristle, but don't answer. We've gone only six miles. *How the hell am I going to beat the snow to Prudhoe Bay if we don't keep going? Stopping is fine for Andy; he doesn't have the success of his trip at stake. He's always so slow anyway. No way we stop here, we're moving. We'll hike out to the Dalton*

Highway to get around this creek. Decision made.

Andy pumps water. I still haven't responded to his suggestion to stop. Jane whines at my feet. *OK, I'll let Andy get done with the water, then we'll start off again. I've made this decision, and I'll stick with it. If he would only finish pumping, we could get going. Why is he always so damn slow?*

Andy hands me a quart of purified Hess Creek. I drink while standing, so as not to relax too much or give Andy the impression we're stopping. *We have miles to make.* Andy draws the handle of the water filter up, pushes it back. A stream squirts from the beak of the filter into his plastic bottle. He pulls, he pushes, slowly, raising the level of his bottle by a fraction of an inch with each push. *I can do it so much faster.*

As he pumps, Andy speaks. Another Iditarod story.

This one is about the time he bypassed a village when he and his dogs were tired. The wind and cold made the village seem inhospitable, but where he stopped on the trail was worse. He spent a few hours shivering in his sled bag amid cold black spruce that waved in the wind like frozen fingers. Another competitor who stopped in the same place saw Andy sleeping. She poked him with a stick.

"Susan Whiton looked over and saw my face was blue. I woke up when she said, 'Oh my God, he's dead.'

"I think no matter what you do, you're going to make mistakes," he says, trickling water into his bottle. "I think what really matters is how you react to the mistakes."

His story makes me think. I look at the gravel bar he's sitting on. There's a nice flat spot for the tent.

"Sometimes the best decision to make is no decision at

all," he continues despite my silence. "Like when you really want to charge ahead but you sack out instead."

I'm whipped. Andy's words, his calm, and the beauty of Hess Creek melt my resolve to blast ahead. I pinch the plastic buckles of Jane's pack, freeing her. She agrees with the decision to stay here, bouncing after sticks I throw into the creek.

Shortly after I pitch the tent and Andy fills three more water jugs, the sun emerges. With it comes a light breeze that allows us to eat dinner on the gravel bar without headnets. I feel wonderful, light, as far as I can be from the despair of a few hours ago. Andy peppers our conversations with more comparisons between this trip and the 1,100-mile sled dog race from Anchorage to Nome.

"Iditarod is just like today was sometimes. It's either the best place in the world you can be or the crappiest. Maybe you need those crappy times, too. Makes you appreciate times like this."

Not to move turned out to be the best decision. In the morning, Hess Creek is sunstruck, sparkling in the warm breeze. It's 65 degrees. Mosquitoes are gone, and the sky is pure blue. Clouds must be in the same place the mosquitoes went.

The creek seems friendly now. After Jane and I make it to the north bank, I drop my pack and return for Andy's. It is hard for him to walk through moving water. Hess Creek wets him to mid-thigh as he slowly takes a step, waits, takes another. I watch him balance on an underwater log. He teeters in the current, almost falls. He looks at me and smiles. The water is gentle, he knows that. Jane and I could walk through it all day without falling. Andy won't fall either, but he has to concentrate on each step to prevent it. Once again, he forces me to be patient, to realize there really is no rush to this. Life goes fast enough anyway.

When Andy gets close to the bank, he grabs a stick I extend for him. I pull him to the bank. Under clear blue sky, we walk along the pipeline pad in silence. The quiet is broken by just two noises: the ringing of Jane's bell as she follows a scent through the brush, and the crunch of gravel, tiny rocks pushed north by a shoe that fails to clear the ground.

Day 73

Andy has left, hitching a ride with a trucker back to my truck. My next hiking friend is not here. I told him eight o'clock, last night, at this spot, Alyeska access road 76-APL-1A. Now, at 10 p.m., he's 26 hours late. Did he crash on the Dalton Highway? Did he never leave Fairbanks? Did he get the day wrong, or did I? I don't know.

I hate to wait, but here I have no choice. Though I have hurried for years, there is no way I can hurry here. This is a summer away from the agents of haste — telephones, fax machines, e-mail. A phone would help me here, but I'm glad there's a place without phones, and that I'm in this place. Here, life moves from zero to four miles per hour. I can't outrun mosquitoes, I can't outwalk rain clouds. If something moves toward me, I collide with it. Now, I have bumped into uncertainty, with no illusions that I have control over this situation. I do nothing but bide.

A short-tailed weasel pauses in front of me when I eat

lunch. In the weasel's jaws is a limp vole, almost as long as the weasel. I've seen weasels almost every day. Five fearless ounces of stretched hamster, the weasels don't run from Jane. I've had to call her away from them to keep her nose from getting bit. The short-tailed weasel is a type-A personality, eating 40 percent of its weight in voles and mice every day to stay alive. Biologists have found dens with a side chamber used as a pantry for slain voles. So tuned is the weasel for killing, it will continue to kill even when the hutch is filled, seemingly driven by compulsion rather than hunger. In that way, it reminds me of another species that fills its garages with stuff.

As I pump water from a wet spot in the tundra, a green Ford truck with a plywood sled dog box on the back pulls in access road 76-APL-1A. I'm surprised and pleased. Andy Sterns steps out of the truck.

My next hiking partner, Andy tells me, forgot where to meet me and drove up and down the Dalton Highway for a while before giving up. After leaving me yesterday, Andy drove back to Smits's house. There, he learned my friend didn't find me. Andy drove to my friend's house and grabbed the food box from the back of his truck. Then Andy turned around and drove 150 miles back to where I sit. He's slept a total of three hours in the two days since he left me.

"Hey, thanks Andy. You didn't have to drive back up here."

"No problem," he says, getting in his truck. "You needed that food. See you in October."

15 | You Have a Dog … Be Happy

Day 74

If you cross Alaska from south to north, you will eventually run into a wide, brown belt across Alaska's midsection.

With Jane walking next to me, I meet the Yukon River at midnight. We step onto a wooden-planked bridge, the only span across the Yukon in Alaska. It's a moody night, with dark clouds to the northwest spitting lightning into green hills. We walk downhill on the bridge, which is one-half mile long and sloped like a ramp. If we were in a building, we'd be 20 stories above the water.

The bridge holds the pipeline in a sleeve attached to the upriver side. Walking the bridge is usually a no-no, but Alyeska security knows who we are; as we walk, I hear the amplifier hum of loudspeakers and feel the movement of cameras on Jane and me. Security guards watch us from the TV monitors at Pump Station Six, where I accepted dinner and a shower a few hours earlier.

We reach the far end of the bridge, crossing the widest

river of the 834 on the route from Valdez to Prudhoe Bay. I walk to the rocky shore of the big river and drop my pack, then Jane's. I have a relationship with this river; it's time to get reacquainted.

While Jane sniffs around, I kick off my hiking boots, sit on a rock and lower my feet into the Yukon. My toes disappear under silt, the residue of Canadian mountains ground to powder by glacier and carried into the big river by streams cold enough to numb. The Yukon is born where the Rocky Mountains end in Canada, just 35 miles from the Pacific Ocean, but the path of least resistance takes it 2,000 miles west to the Bering Sea. In America, the Missouri (2,565 miles) and the Mississippi (2,350 miles) top the Yukon for length, but when superimposed on America the Yukon still connects Boston with Chicago.

The U.S. Geological Survey map shows 62 villages and towns on the river's path through Alaska. Some of those towns, among them Purgatory and Paradise, ghosted out long ago. The thousands of rivers and creeks that drain forests, muskeg and tundra flats into the Yukon add up to about 300,000 square miles. One-third of the flowing water in Alaska finds its way to the Yukon.

The channel that absorbs all that water is comfortable, warm when compared to the midnight air. I wiggle my toes, feel the grit, and think of my time on the river as a park ranger. In Eagle, where the river enters Alaska, I ran a boat between the town and Coal Creek, a derelict mining camp about 90 river miles from Eagle. There, amid the beauty and peace of this waterway, I discovered what the other rangers called "river time." River time happened when you were downriver, away from the office in Eagle. The Park Service required eight hours a day out if its employees, but the start and finish of the work day was a bit skewed on the river. To a person who never wears a watch, river time was quite sensible and liberating. Wake up when you wake up, eat breakfast, even if breakfast starts at 2 p.m. The summer sun allows a workday that begins at any time. We could haul barrels out of the brush at midnight, when it was cooler. We went to sleep at 6 a.m., just like the bears. We lost track of what day it was, because it really didn't matter. It still doesn't.

Every time I'm near the Yukon, the water makes me pause. It beckons me to sit and think of where all that water is coming from, of where all that water is going. In reaching this brown belt, I think of how far Jane and I have traveled, and where we're going. I catch yet another buzz from looking back and thinking of the miles that have passed under our feet.

The air dries my feet by one a.m. The heat of the day has fled. I can tell by the density of mosquitoes. As we climb the first hill north of the Yukon in the twilight of mid-summer, I think of just one thing: getting Jane and me away from the bugs and inside the tent.

The best tent site is underneath the pipeline. Right away, I see the flaw: an orange pile of bear manure, pulpy and filled with rose hip pods.

I know I shouldn't camp next to the bear manure, but it's already past midnight and the bear isn't here now. The bear dropped the manure today, perhaps less than an hour ago. Maybe I used up all my dumb luck two weeks ago, when

I camped next to an old bear bait station on Washington Creek. Maybe there's only six hours until morning, and what are the odds of a bear coming when I think it's coming? Ever since I was a kid, I've had a theory that if you want to prevent something bad from happening, like getting in a car accident, you just have to think about the scenario once and it won't happen.

OK. I visualize the bear that shat here. It won't be back.

Driven by the hum of mosquitoes, I pitch the tent in record time. The manure pile will be visible from the back window when I get in for the night. Immediately after the tent goes up, I zip open a gap the size of Jane. She squeezes through the hole, shedding mosquitoes as she slips in. I zip the tent shut behind her and walk back to my pack.

I pull dental floss and my tooth brush from my pack, which leans against a pipeline support. I stick my toothbrush in my mouth. Before I start brushing, I hear the noise I knew I wouldn't — an animal busting through the woods, headed our way. It may be several animals. I think bear.

Jane hears it too. Zipped in the tent, she barks her meanest bark, the throaty one with two syllables. The noise in the woods stops.

I hear another sound: A soft woof. Then the sound of claws on spruce bark, like the scramble of a frightened squirrel. In a forest of aspen surrounding us, there's one spruce tree. It's 60 feet high, and the sound comes from that direction.

Against a backdrop of rosy twilight, twin bear cubs scale the tree. They look like little monkeys. My first thought is that they're cute.

As I grip the plastic stock of my shotgun, I wonder where

their mother is. She woofed her cubs into this tree, but what did she do at the sound of Jane's bark?

I hear a noise that sounds like a hand saw cutting though a two-by-four. I look and see the mother bear. The hand-saw noise is her uneven breathing. She's in the same spruce tree, hanging in what looks like an uncomfortable position, with one forepaw sweeping the air and the rest of her claws attached to the tree. She's 20 feet off the ground; the cubs cling to the tree at 40 feet. They watch me free Jane from the tent, as does the mother bear, who continues sawing two-by-fours.

Jane barks. My fear changes to weariness when I think of my options: though I don't think the mother bear will mess with us, there's no way I can take the chance of camping under a spruce tree filled with black bear. We'll have to move.

I disassemble the tent in less than one minute. With Mama Bear still puffing away, I fit Jane with her pack, fit me with mine, and we start back toward the Yukon. I look behind me every 10 steps; no bears follow. The mosquitoes relish our decision to move during the coolest part of the day.

Jane trots in front of me, her mind already switched from the noise of bears to whatever scent she's following. Just by being herself, barking at a strange noise, she prevented what probably would have been an ugly encounter. The bears were coming straight for us, perhaps attracted by a scent but more likely just on the move, walking the same path as we were. A surprised mother bear with two cubs will defend those cubs until she either dies or kills something, and the sow was just steps from meeting me when Jane barked. If Jane hadn't, I probably would have needed to use the shotgun.

We walk with a purpose back toward the Yukon, the

mosquitoes covering Jane's ears like hair. I pitch the tent by the river and push Jane inside. After I hang the food and make sure the bears haven't followed us, I enter the tent and kiss Jane on the forehead.

Here at the Yukon River, after 74 days and 447 miles on the trail, I notice changes in Jane. She was a chunk, now she's a hunk. At the beginning of the trip, her body was a barrel. Now she is cut, like a weightlifter. Her coat, almost black when we started, is bleached blond by almost constant exposure to the sun.

Jane has reverted to puppyhood. Her chocolate nostrils are constantly flexing east and west. Her blurry tail threatens to lift her airborne. The smell of a snowshoe hare, the silhouette of a ptarmigan, are daily sensations. She revisits scents and images of wild Alaska and catalogues new ones as she spends every hour of the day outside.

She has bad days, just like me. Sometimes, when mosquitoes perch like drilling platforms on the bridge of her nose, I want to get her out of this, to get her back to the couch in my cabin. Other times, though, when she's bouncing like an antelope through the brush, I know this is the perfect place for her. It makes me feel good to have her along. She gives the trip a purity. She just sees, smells and reacts to what Alaska presents her, an innocence I lose while fretting because I didn't roll my tarp to the ideal tightness.

Sometimes I wish I could get inside her brain. When Jane sniffs at a pile of hairy manure, I wonder if she sees an image of the animal that made it. Sometimes at night, she'll perk her ears and growl at an unseen monster out there. It gives me the chills.

Jane's not a morning dog, perhaps because I'm not a morning person. She sleeps while I break camp; she sleeps while I eat breakfast. She wakes up when she hears me washing the cookware, licks the oatmeal from my cook pot, then goes back to sleep until it's time to hike.

At times, to ease her into the day, I carry her pack for a quarter mile or so. After I buckle the seven-pound load to her back, she walks slowly and stiffly in protest, trailing behind. She lags until she sights or scents a hare, duck, grouse or any other tasty animal. She then breaks into a trot in which her pads don't seem to touch the ground, and her tail becomes a rudder, slicing the air behind. The image picks me up every day. It makes me think of my favorite Charlie Brown cartoon, one in which Snoopy is lying on Charlie Brown's bed as he tries to sleep. Charlie Brown talks about how sometimes when he lies awake at night, trying to understand life, he hears a voice: "You have a dog … Be happy."

16 | Left to My Own Devices

Day 76

"No way, absolutely not," the blonde says, forcefully. "We don't want any money from Ned and Jane. Or you. What's your name?"

"John."

"John, nice to meet you. I'm Theresa. Don't put any money in there. Don't."

A striking woman of soft curves and green-gray eyes tries to prevent my hiking partner John, who joined me at the Yukon River and will continue to Coldfoot, from stuffing a $10 bill into a birch basket.

"You walk 800 miles, you aren't going to pay for a hamburger."

Theresa Mitchell is co-owner and cook at the Hot Spot, a cluster of small buildings on ground that was Alyeska's Five-Mile Camp 20 years ago. Today, the site is several acres of bare gravel surrounded by aspen and birch forest and connected to the dirt ribbon of Dalton Highway by two paths, now greasy with mud. On the western boundary between gravel and trees, an artesian well spits from a fire hose. The Hot Spot sits on the southern end of the camp. To reach it, we backtracked a half mile from the pipeline.

As Jane trotted ahead, I heard a woman's voice: *Is that Jane?!*

The stuffing begins. Jane, wet and fuzzy except for dry fur on her middle where her pack was attached, gets served first. She eats steak scraps from the dinners of two boys — Theresa's son Tyler, 7, and Sean, the 9-year-old son of Dean Morin, Theresa's partner in business and life. When Jane finishes the steak, Theresa steps out from the box that is the main building of Hot Spot to grill burgers for Jane, John and me. She drops lean meat on the outside grill. The aroma of singed beef fills the back of our nostrils. I try not to drool from the corners of my mouth. Jane has no such hang up.

Wearing faded blue jeans, a T-shirt with a polar bear on the front, and a gold nugget hanging from a chain around her neck, Theresa Mitchell is a surprise here, five miles north of the Yukon River. Her face and figure would cause men to look twice if she were strolling down Fifth Avenue in New York; here, gawks are common. John raises his eyebrows, I nod.

Jane is more interested in what's on the grill. Theresa sets a paper plate filled with steaming burger on the Hot Spot's wooden deck. Jane is on the meat immediately, not raising her head until only sodden paper remains. She bows again to eat most of the paper plate.

John and I receive similar burgers. On one side of a plate is the burger, topped with cheddar cheese. The opposite side is crowded with tomato slices, onions, and several leaves of lettuce. It's like eating a burger and salad at the same time. It's impossible to hold it with one hand.

"A lot of people say they're too big," says Theresa, spatula in hand, of her creations. "I believe in big. Everything's big at the Hot Spot. That's what people come to Alaska for."

We do not find the burgers too big, though I suffer a charley-horse in my jaw. The burgers fill a void in our bellies produced by five miles of hiking with packs loaded with enough supplies to get us to Coldfoot. The packs must weigh 80 pounds, creating a sensation like carrying an eighth-grader piggyback. A mist of rain, almost a fog, coats us as we relax on plastic chairs.

Theresa stands in the centerpiece of the Hot Spot, looking out at us from a red window that was once the door of a front-end loader. Her partner, Dean, had unbolted the door from junked loader, fitted it with Plexiglas, and painted the frame red. His talent for scavenging is evident everywhere: a building next to us was a former guard shack. In the years before non-truckers were allowed to drive north of the Yukon River bridge, pipeline security guards sitting in the shack would inform drivers they could go no farther north. A silver ashtray projecting from the wall of the Hot Spot is the style found anchored to concrete walls in hotel lobbies. A red plastic top from a cooler provides a rain hat for the ashtray. Dean found the cooler top on the side of the Dalton Highway, his workplace. He operates heavy equipment for the state of Alaska, working out of a highway-maintenance camp two miles up the road.

Groggy, Dean emerges from one of two tow-behind

trailers, part of the Hot Spot compound. He wears jeans, a black baseball cap with the emblem of a labor union, leather loafers with rawhide toggles.

As he pulls up a plastic chair to join us on the deck, the two boys are drawn to him. He is solid, with a linebacker's neck and — because he's missing two teeth — the smile of a boy. He talks with the cadence of a stand-up comedian.

"I tell people I work for T and T," Dean says, then pauses for effect. "I work for Tony (Knowles), the governor, and I work for Theresa."

"The real governor," Theresa adds.

"Yeah, Tony pays a little better, but Theresa's benefits are better."

In summer, Dean works 75 hours every other week for the state, uncounted hours for the Hot Spot. He says he sleeps three hours a night.

"You run on three hours' sleep?"

"I walk... There's chronically stuff to do. Picking up behind these guys, burning trash, hauling water, constantly making improvements to the place, painting, electrical, plumbing."

Dean Morin is rare in that he uses the stuff he gathers. The Hot Spot is a refuge for reincarnated junk. The building Theresa spends the most hours in each summer, the one with the grader window that frames her face, inspired the name of the business. Three years ago, Dean purchased the unit for $300 from a man named Wayne Anderson. In another time, it was a room where men on the North Slope gathered out of necessity: a water closet, with four toilets. The "Incinelite" johns used no water; waste disposal was performed by electric heating coils. The Hot Spot.

Dean pulled three of the toilets out and sold them for more than he paid for the building. At Theresa's insistence, he left one toilet in the building, "just for the ambiance."

"I picked the cutest one — the turquoise one," Theresa says.

Though Theresa chooses not to use the remaining privy, it satisfies a Department of Environmental Conservation requirement for an employee lavatory.

"We got a perfect score on the pre-opening inspection," Dean says. "I was elated with turning an outhouse into a restaurant and getting 100 percent on the inspection."

The couple did not browse hardware stores to outfit their business. From a friend, Dean purchased for $20 the grill on which Theresa creates burgers. He repaired the appliance in the cellar of the Fairbanks house he shares with Theresa.

"Take it from me, though, if you ever decide to do a propane barbecue, go buy a new one," he laughs.

The deck we are sitting on hung in another life on the outside of a Fairbanks hotel. As Theresa and Dean drove past one day, she spotted laborers stripping the building. "There's my deck," she said. Dean happened to know the contractor refurbishing the hotel, and Theresa's words proved prophetic, but not before she, Dean, and their three boys extracted hundreds of nails.

On top of the Hot Spot stands a metal tower, Eiffel in design. Dean thought of a use for the retired communications tower when he drove by 47-Mile Hill on the Dalton Highway and saw it standing there. He went to the company in Fairbanks that owned the tower. The same company also owned a shack next to the tower that was filled with old batteries. Dean told the radio company he would tidy their site in exchange for the 10-foot tower and the building, which, in his words, "was all tattered and beat to rat shit."

After a few repairs and a coat of paint, the shack became the Hot Spot's generator shed. The tower is now "Hot Spot Rig One," a miniature oil derrick on the roof that supports a 30-foot CB antenna. The tower allows Theresa to communicate with passing truckers, who buy most of the burgers she sells at the Hot Spot.

"Those truckers have been gold," Dean says. "One guy towed the Hot Spot building up here for us. Gave us a bill for zero dollars."

"And they've advertised endlessly for us," Theresa nods.

The truckers seem to appreciate an oasis on their 500-mile haul from Fairbanks to the oil fields at Prudhoe Bay. A place where an attractive woman serves them food and chides them about mud on their rigs. Shortly after the Hot Spot opened in 1996, appreciative drivers spread the word on their CB radios. It didn't take long before Five-Mile Camp was a regular stop on most truckers' trips to and from Prudhoe Bay.

"They are so tight," Dean says of the drivers. "You talk about a line of communication. You can tell a trucker right there at the Hot Spot window something you want to get to Prudhoe Bay, and it'll get there faster than by telephone.

"If they like you, they'll do anything in the world for you. If they don't like you, they'll do anything to you. They can be bad news."

"They like us though," Theresa says. "And we're lucky for that. We wouldn't stay open without them."

When Theresa started flipping burgers on July 4th, 1996, she had her doubts about whether she and Dean had jumped into a black hole on the Yukon.

"We had a lot of $30 days," Dean says. "We'd have a $100 day and that'd be a great big deal. But when you think about it, she was open from seven till midnight. You got a $100 day, you gotta figure $50 to $60 of that went for groceries. Forty bucks for a 17-hour day, that comes down to about $2 an hour ... And that's not considering any of my time."

"I didn't even want to look at that," Theresa shakes her head. "That first year, I was petrified. I was getting ready for rejection. I used to say 'This is ridiculous. Who in the world's gonna pull in here and want to eat here?' I was stressing over it.

"But then they just started coming. And they started coming, and coming, and coming . . . This summer, I'm out here in my pajamas in the morning because people started getting here so early. If they see a glimpse of me — 'There she is!' — I feel so guilty that I don't want to go back to bed. I get the coffee rolling and start making food. Before I know it, it's one o'clock and I'm in my pajamas still, and I can't get out of here."

On one particular day, the number of patrons exceeded the amount of thawed beef. Theresa had 30 burgers on the grill and cars and trucks stacked up past the artesian well. Dean solved the problem by slicing frozen burger with a Skil saw.

"Some nights I only sleep about four hours by the time

I wind down enough to go to sleep," Theresa says. "And all night I hear trucks and cars pulling in."

"A lot of the truckers haul ass to make it there at midnight," Dean says. "That keeps us up till one or two o'clock in the morning."

The Hot Spot sits on one of five "development nodes" on the Dalton Highway permitted by the U.S. Bureau of Land Management and the State of Alaska. Theresa and Dean operate the Hot Spot on land they lease from an Alaska Native who owns a small chunk of Five-Mile Camp, the gravel pad that was a pipeline construction camp 20 years ago. Even though the owner will only lease the property to them one year at a time, the couple consider themselves lucky to have found land for the Hot Spot.

"We started researching the possibility of any private land," Dean says. "With the exception of one parcel that's available for an exorbitant price up there on Kanuti Flats, there is none. Four-hundred and fifty miles of road and every inch of it is tied up by either state or federal government. There is nothing private available to buy."

Dean eventually got in touch with the land owner, who had taken the state and federal governments to the Alaska Supreme Court in order to acquire a patent to his allotted land. After eight months of telephone calls from Dean and Theresa, he finally agreed to lease the land.

The division of lands near the Hot Spot is confusing, even for someone who lives there. The Hot Spot deck is on private land. When one uses the outhouse, 100 steps away, he or she pauses on BLM land. People filling water jugs at the artesian well are standing on federal soil, but the well is owned by the state. A sign prohibiting the washing of vehicles at the well bears the logo of Alyeska Pipeline Service Co., which has a permit to allow its red tanker trucks to fetch the water supply for Pump Station 6.

Before they set up shop at Five Mile Camp, Theresa and Dean went to dozens of meetings. They learned that before they could sell hamburgers they had to satisfy many government agencies: EPA. DEC. DNR. BLM. DOT. They complied with all regulations, a process that almost burned them out before the first burger hit the grill. Now, some of their most consistent customers are individuals from those agencies they are constantly working to satisfy, individuals who don't miss a thing on the Dalton Highway. Dean looks to the sky, pulls out a memory.

"The first summer, a Suburban load of BLM officials went up the Haul Road on July 1. We came in on the third. On their return trip, they pulled in here. We were all set up. They assumed that we were on BLM property, that we just came in here and squatted. And the radios and the telephones went berserk."

"If anybody's aware we're here, BLM is," Theresa says. "They don't miss a beat."

Dean shakes his head. "They call this the Last Frontier, and you think you're remote. Absolutely, you're not remote. They come up in their helicopter, come over and eat all the time. They're flying over every square inch of that ground. BLM knows exactly what's going on."

This summer, Dean and Theresa will earn enough from the Hot Spot to purchase a small pickup truck, a new building for the Hot Spot complex, and a propane tank on skids.

"The things a girl will buy," Theresa says. Raised in Florida, she did not have a lifelong dream to work a spatula 55 miles south of the Arctic Circle. Drawn north by pipeline work, her father moved the family to Alaska in 1975, "at the height of the funkiness." Theresa was 12 years old, not particularly enamored with the north.

She married young, gave birth to Jason, who is now 11 and in Fairbanks playing football, and Tyler, a blond 7-year-old who arcs spit balls at me through a straw.

Sean, 9, shows his father a bird's nest he found in the woods. He is Dean's son from another relationship.

After wintering in Fairbanks for the school year, the boys spend most of the summer at the Hot Spot. Their playground is boreal forest that stretches unbroken for hundreds of miles to the east and west of the Dalton Highway.

"They've learned to be creative with sticks and stones and actually have more fun playing in the dirt and running around with a stick than asking Mom for six dollars to go to a movie." Theresa says. "They know where the berries grow, where the diamond willow are ... And they meet really nice people."

After Sean retrieved a few sticks of diamond willow for a Hot Spot customer, the man offered him a few dollars. Sean declined, but he later received two pairs of pants from the man. When she opened the package and saw the gift, Theresa flushed with embarrassment.

"These kids look like they've been through World War Four because they've been having Tonka wars in the dirt. They're just rugged looking. People see them and feel sorry for them, they think we live here all year."

Dean laughs. "The old-timers off the bus give them apples out of their lunches."

Dean Morin owes his Alaska presence to oil. He grew up in Eugene, Oregon, "if I grew up at all. I came up here for the gold rush — the pipeline construction. And never really left."

Dean was 19 when he manned a bulldozer to help cut the pipeline's path through Keystone Canyon, near Valdez. He remembers changing the character of one of Valdez's biggest tourist attractions.

"I pushed the first dozer load of mud across Bridal Veil Falls. Made chocolate falls out of them. We had tourists down there by the thousands taking pictures. Man, it was awful."

Dean has no fear of heavy iron. He runs road graders, bulldozers, backhoes, snowplows. Now a foreman for the highway department, he was transferred to the station seven miles north of the Yukon three years ago. Having worked on almost every stretch of highway in Alaska at some episode in his past, he often thought of opening a roadhouse while driving his snowplow. The Hot Spot fulfills the dream.

With this year's Hot Spot earnings, they will purchase items more romantic than a propane tank: Tickets to Cancun, Mexico, and two wedding rings. In November, long after the Hot Spot will have become covered with snow, Theresa will become Theresa Morin. Three years have passed since Tyler's fall down a flight of stairs led her to Dean, who lived in a basement apartment with a man Theresa knew.

"She brought 'Tiger' with her to visit her friend," Dean explains. "Tiger tumbled down the stairway into my basement apartment. Landed in a big heap. I scooped him up. She thought that was a pretty good deal."

"Yeah, he was pretty good with kids," Theresa says. "And that was it."

Theresa knew life with Dean was going to be different when she began cleaning Dalton Highway dust from the original Hot Spot building, which had been towed south to Fairbanks from Alaska's North Slope. At their Fairbanks home, Theresa snaked a garden hose from the kitchen sink to the outside. Because the temperature was below freezing, she used a space heater to keep the water in a liquid state as she cleaned the building. Before she could finish, her mother pulled up and saw her daughter coated with Dalton Highway mud.

"She had this terrible look on her face, like the house was on fire," Theresa says. "She said, 'You have bumped your head. What's going on here?' I thought about it and realized I was being broken in rather roughly. After that, I knew the Nordstrom's days of a girl like me were over."

At the Hot Spot, she has become a tourist attraction.

"I've had my picture taken more times than Portage Glacier," she says. "It was very strange at first, but after a while you wonder how many photo albums you're in across America."

"I'm going to put up a sign," Dean smiles, shows his gap. "'Photos: Two Bits.'"

John and I lean back into the plastic chairs, allowing our stomachs to process a pound of beef. Dean gets us up. "Hey, I got something to show you guys," he says. "Follow me back here."

We walk behind the salvaged guard shack, where Dean

displays his latest acquisition: a green state of Alaska, painted on two sheets of plywood that stand together like pages in a book. Painted across the top third of Alaska is a dashed line with the words ARCTIC CIRCLE. The sign is the old Department of Transportation marker for the circle, 55 miles north. The green Alaska is cleaved by two other lines, the pipeline and the Yukon River. The two arteries form an X, near the center of which we are standing.

Dean found the sign at the DOT camp, in a dark corner of a garage. As is his nature, he gave the sign a second chance.

"I just knew it was going to wind up in the burn pile if I didn't," he says.

"You'll have to put that up somewhere," I say.

Dean nods. "In fact, I'll do that this evening."

"Ambitious."

"Well, I've been snoozing since I got off work. I'd better do something to earn my hamburger for the day."

We pose for photos in front of the sign, Jane and me on the Yukon Territory side, Dean and Theresa in front of the Bering Sea. The sign is tall enough that none of our heads reach the Arctic Circle. Jane, never a poser, tongues a brown puddle as John snaps the picture.

Near midnight. Time to leave the Hot Spot, find a campsite along the pipe. Jane seems a bit confused at being saddled. As John and I walk away, Jane stands her ground on the Hot Spot's deck, like the captain of the Titanic. Dean notices.

"I do believe she's arrived," he says.

The Hot Spot sticks with me that night. Once Jane finally decides to follow John and me rather than expand to a 200-pounder on handouts of cooked beef, we find a buggy campsite a few miles up the pipe. While setting up the tent, John and I talk about Dean and Theresa's energy, about how Alaskan they are to recycle all that junk to make a gathering place on a lonely road, about how good the kids are. We talk of them later, as Jane makes a damp nest between our sleeping bags, her stomach churning as it works on all the meat.

"Those guys are tapped into something," John says. "You should see them in Fairbanks and check it out."

A few months later, I visited Dean and Theresa at their home in Fairbanks. I heard what to me was a most meaningful story behind the Hot Spot.

Not long after I got to their house, Dean mentioned that he and Theresa were addicts, and that the Hot Spot was part — but by no means the only part — of their recovery.

"The Hot Spot has been a tremendous asset in that respect," he said. "It's not the greatest advertising, but it's the truth."

Dean was addicted to "a whole array of chemicals," among them cocaine and heroin. Theresa struggled with alcohol. They were both in relationships with other addicts. Theresa also wrestled with depression that wouldn't let her rise from bed some days.

"I'm a good codependent and enabler, and most of us are control freaks," Theresa said. "To be out there (at the Hot Spot), and not be in control of too much of anything other than what kind of food people get, was really hard for me."

"For both of us, this approach was practical, but one hell of a challenge," Dean said. "We really struggled. It was no easy deal. The stress of the whole thing. Trying to learn how to be parents. Trying to learn how to be lovers. Trying to learn how to be business partners. A hell of a transition."

Dean and Theresa's story appealed to me, because I've seen addiction through the eyes of a boy, and later a man. I asked them if I could write about their problems and the struggle for a solution, and they accepted.

I sat on their couch, petting a small dog, wondering how they would react to the questions I wanted to ask: "When did you start using drugs?" "How low did you get before you sought help?" "Can you give me specific details of how you wrecked your life?"

I felt nervous and intrusive and would gladly have walked out the door if Dean or Theresa pointed that way. But they didn't. Dean, in particular, seemed like he wanted to talk.

What he said hit home in ways I couldn't have imagined. When he talked of his character while stoned, I felt like he was talking about me.

"It took me a while to come to this awareness, but my entire M.O. was avoidance of responsibility," he said. "Never commit 100 percent to anything. Always leave an escape route. It doesn't matter if it's a job, a relationship, kids — I bought seven abortions before Sean's mother said no way."

Just before going to interview Dean and Theresa, I read the comments of an editor and friend who looked at the draft of this chapter. They hit me with almost the same force as Dean's words. "What's your addiction, Ned?" my friend wrote. "You're approaching middle age and still live in a cabin and hold down a part-time job. Why?"

I had never looked at these issues before, though my family and a string of girlfriends no doubt have. Dean brings out jarring similarities between him and me; the strongest is that we both are trying to stay away from alcohol.

I quit drinking five years ago, on the morning after my friend Pete died. Pete was Chinese, from Hong Kong, a journalist going to school at the university in Fairbanks. We met after we both took jobs with the student newspaper. Though a few weeks passed before I could easily pluck words from his accent, his constant smile made me want to be around him.

Pete became editor of the Sun-Star, the college paper. Every Wednesday night, he and the staff worked straight through till Thursday afternoon to get the weekly paper finished and delivered to the printers. Bonded by the camaraderie of sleepless nights and the creative buzz of producing a newspaper, Pete and I became buddies.

As I walked home from the university one September night when the temperature dropped to nine degrees, I thought of Pete, that I should call him. The next morning, ten inches of snow covered the ground. An early winter.

I started a fire in the wood stove, then dialed Pete and got his answering machine. I called the Chinese restaurant where he occasionally worked. One of the little girls, the owner's daughter whom Pete often helped with homework, answered. When I asked for Pete, she started crying.

"My teacher is dead," she sobbed. "He died last night."

The man who found Pete was the last to see him the night before; he left Pete's apartment after Pete started guzzling vodka and acting "demented." On the soaked carpet was an empty quart bottle of vodka. The coroner's diagnosis was heart failure.

I remember seeing Pete's body at the funeral home, how his lips were wrinkled, how unusual it was not to see him smiling. I remember being so mad at him for leaving me, so mad at alcohol for helping him get away, I punched a wall and dumped four Mooseheads out onto the snow. I was a heavy drinker in the Air Force and shortly after, until Pete died. I haven't had a drink since that day.

My friend Pete also taught me something about time. Since he died, I've made an effort to do anything that tugged at me, not passing up opportunities just because it was easier not to. Pete had things he really wanted to do. He wanted to publish his own magazine in Alaska. He never realized his dream, and he never will.

Dean made me think of Pete again. I nodded my head at Dean's eloquence as he described the sickness that took my friend and, to a large degree, shaped me.

"It's a three-fold disease — it's mental, physical and spiritual," Dean said. "When you first start using mood or mind-altering chemicals — and I don't give a shit if you're sniffing glue, smoking pot or shooting heroin, or if you're a garden-variety wine sipper — when you first start using, anything spiritual goes right out the window. You quit developing emotionally and spiritually. I think that oftentimes that's why I react like a 13-year-old kid, because that's the age I started using chemicals.

"Then you start trying to shit everybody else about what's going on, and in the process you're really shitting yourself. So self-honesty goes to hell. So there goes the mental aspect.

"Finally, if you stick with it long enough and hard enough, your physical being starts going to shit. You start contracting hepatitis — which I've had three different times — you get sick. Now, all three aspects of the disease are running full-bore in you.

"I submit that recovery happens just about exactly the opposite. First, people set the chemicals aside, they start eating right, sleeping right, brushing their teeth. They start feeling better, taking care of themselves.

"Most people never make it past that point of recovery. They start feeling better physically, and all of a sudden they've got it whipped. And that was my experience.

"But if you start getting honest about yourself and what's really going on, and taking an honest look at what's taking place in your life as a result of self-abuse, you start putting things in perspective, your mental being starts getting back into focus.

"And finally, if you stick with it long enough, you become convinced of the good news and the bad news. The good news is, that there is a God. The bad news is, you're not it."

Theresa nodded from the kitchen. She was weary of my tape recorder, but she didn't tell Dean to stop. And I didn't want him to stop. Hearing him speak was like watching something appear before my eyes.

"It all boils down to self-honesty," Dean said. "Being honest with myself. I've suffered from this terminal unique-ness — thinking that somehow I'm a little different than all these people. That I can periodically use socially.

"Life has become kind of a search for the truth. For me, it's come down to My Way doesn't work. That's a tough admission to make after spending all of my adult life trying to convince my loved ones, my family, my employers, the law and everybody around me that I've got a handle on it. To turn right around and admit that I'm fouled up . . . is tough for somebody with a twisted ego. Arriving at that element of self-honesty. I can't do this alone. Left to my own devices, I'm fucked."

"When did you look for help?"

"I pursued recovery after I saw my father change. I watched him go through such a tremendous change in attitude about life that I got curious. Where in the heck are you going every night at eight o'clock? (Dean's father was going to meetings with other recovering addicts.)

"My dad said to me, 'Maybe you won't change this whole world to suit you, but maybe there's a remote possibility that you might change you to fit somewhere in this world.'"

I was a bit surprised that all the boys were in the room, listening calmly. They had heard this before. Their parents' past was not a secret. I also liked the rapport Dean and Theresa have with the boys, who are outgoing but not obnoxious. Tyler came up to me at one point and put his new pet — a baby chick — on my knee. I can talk with all three boys as if they were adults. We've had conversations — about Legos, about hooking the Hot Spot on wheels so Jane can tow it north. They laugh, they talk, they listen. They are good kids.

"As it turns out, all of the responsibilities I have elected to face have turned out to be the greatest blessings of my recovery," Dean said. "Every single one."

The R word slams into me again, only this time I feel

hopeful. Genuinely good. After agreeing to meet with them and other people in recovery that night, I got ready to leave. Dean had a few last words.

"Why do people have to go out there and die just because they don't know how to cope with life?" Dean said. "Pick some power greater than you. Believe in something. I think it's important that we all do."

Seeing Dean with the boys, with Theresa, and the energy he's put into the Hot Spot, I think these are the things he believes in, the people and passion that get him through the bad times, the days so bleak that maybe he feels like using heroin again.

He makes me think of the power greater than me that I've chosen. That power was most obvious on the hike — the mountains, the rivers, the plants that blossomed so quickly, then withered, dropped seeds, and returned to the soil. The miracle of our nearest star being 93 million miles away, just the right distance to keep this planet warm enough for people without boiling away the oceans. I felt that power every day while walking. I didn't always like the rain, and the bugs, and the days that were too hot, but I always knew they came from a power greater than me. And I believed in it.

17 | Arctic Circle

John, Jane and I follow the pipeline's path out of the Kanuti River valley to near the Arctic Circle, the dashed line on Dean Morin's new sign. Black clouds cruise overhead, but they drop no rain. Because the trees are more like shrubs here, we can see trucks pass on the Dalton highway, just 100 yards west. We smell that burned diesel. A tour van slows as it moves south. Faces press against windows. John waves.

The driver pulls over near the river, one-quarter mile behind us. The door folds open, tourists spill out. They wave to us, take pictures as if we are grizzlies stumbling along the pipe. I wonder if we should walk back to them, pose. No, the miles call. We keep walking north. A raven escorts us, leapfrogging pipeline support beams. As we reach the shoulder of the valley, the van disappears. We follow the raven.

Lustrous, black, and chock-full of personality, the raven is a bird I've followed before. Though they tend to be overshadowed by the glamorous migrants of summer, ravens are the kings of winter. At 50 below, when nothing else is moving and ice fog blankets Fairbanks, ravens give a dead world life. Rod King, a U.S. Fish and Wildlife biologist so enamored with the bird he calls it "Raven," once loaned me a receiver so I could follow the winter movement of a raven.

Like other ravens adapted to the cities and towns of Alaska, the one carrying a disposable transmitter on its back chose to roost with its chums 20 miles outside of town for some reason. Each morning, the raven commuted from a secret patch of spruce trees with the first dim light, heading to Wendy's, McDonald's, the landfill. If there wasn't a town where the Chena River meets the Tanana, ravens would probably follow herds of caribou, rooting for wolves to provide them with a carcass to pick. But a clump of 50,000 humans and the fast-food establishments that sustain us are now more reliable than wolves. The raven I followed fed from a woman's compost pile all day. It flew back to the roost at twilight, just past four p.m., rowing its jet-black wings through air that was 24 degrees below zero.

Ravens always remind me of how frail we really are, how a few animals have adapted to a life in the north without the need to burn the grease within the pipeline or the ability to trap its warmth between thick walls. Unlike animals that avoid winter by hibernating, ravens have chosen the risky strategy of facing winter in a land where the sun's warmth can't be felt for months. People who live in Alaska make the same choice. Rod King's public talks on Raven always fill the auditorium of the public library in December and January. I always go, just to see his grand finale: A raven he's caught earlier in the day. It's sad to see the noble raven in a dog kennel, but the bird is so striking — black eyes, black feathers, black beak — that it leaves me feeling I've just seen one of the most beautiful creatures on Earth. I know I'm not alone: a good proportion of Alaskans relate to ravens, seeing the birds as partners in the endurance test that is winter.

The raven gets bored with us and flies off. Ahead, the pipeline parts from the road at the crest of a steep hill named Beaver Slide. Ahead, the pipeline cleaves the backbone of three forested hills. Judging from the map, the Arctic Circle follows the crest of the middle hill.

We stop one mile shy of the dashed line, on Fish Creek, an arctic waterway in that its source and mouth are north of the circle; here it dips south of the line for about 10 miles.

John wanted to camp high, on the circle, but I was smitten by the water: Fish Creek is deep, transparent. Under a bridge manufactured in an British steel mill, grayling dimple the water's surface.

"Let's camp here," I say.

"No, let's climb this hill, get it over with," John says. "Maybe there's a breeze up there to keep the bugs off."

"This is a neat creek," I say. "I haven't passed many grayling holes like this one."

"You're not going to fish are you?"

"No, I don't think so," I say, looking at the water but knowing it's too late to fish.

"Then let's climb this hill," John says. "We won't have to hit it first thing tomorrow."

"Yeah, but if we go up there, we'll have to carry water up, which means we'll have to filter it here anyways. It'll take a while. Besides, we've already gone 10 miles today."

I take off my pack and lean it against the bridge. John hesitates, then does the same. "It's your trip," he says, making me feel a bit guilty. "All these decisions are yours."

He's told me that before when he disagreed, but he always stops short of arguing. John has memorized my patterns, embraced them, improved on them. When we stop for the day, he sets up the tent faster than I can. He volunteers for all the jobs I don't like: slicing greasy pepperoni, washing dishes, pumping an extra quart. He seems to read my mind. When mosquitoes discover the warm spot in the small of my back, he pulls out the Cutters. He's helped me with everything on this trip, from the planning to preparing food drops to people delivery. He wanted to walk the whole summer with me, but I didn't think I could take his honesty every day. He accepted less, with just a little griping. Now, he lets me call the shots.

On a gravel floor with the water at my feet, I boil a quart of Fish Creek to start dinner. Cooking is always my job because, like Theresa Mitchell, I need control. I have managed to let others work the water pump, pitch the tent, sometimes even hang the food, but the MSR Whisperlite is my exclusive domain.

John dutifully lights four sections of Pic and lodges them in the sand in a square around us. Standing almost in the creek, he looks at me suddenly with a pained expression. He begins a bow-legged trot toward the woods.

"What's up?"

"I just shit my pants."

If John didn't possess an extraordinary ability to ignore

discomfort, he would now be insane. He stands in damp grass while mosquitoes attack his naked lower half. Without urgency, he borrows my soap, washes downstream, puts on fresh underwear.

He carries his other pair of underwear with a stick.

"Do you mind if I bury this?" he asks.

"Sounds like a good idea."

John buries his underwear in the gravel of Fish Creek.

"What do you think happened?" I ask.

"I've never drank water that cold that fast," he says. "I'm not used to drinking this much."

"You feel OK?" I ask. "Got any blood left?"

"Yeah, I'm fine."

"Well, your underwear is now part of Fish Creek. An historic landmark, like a time capsule to be found in 50 years. Unless they get dug up next spring when the creek breaks up."

John sits beside me on a log and munches his freeze-dried dinner. We eat in silence for awhile, listening to the creek and mosquitoes.

"Sorry about that," he says.

Without ceremony, we cross the Arctic Circle the next morning. The magic moment occurs in one of the low points of John's and my time together: it's raining, mosquitoes are rampant, and the labor of climbing the hill from Fish Creek sours our shirts. As we pass the opening of a pipeline access road that marks the Arctic Circle, I hold my tape recorder to John.

"Any words to mark the crossing of the Arctic Circle,

Johnny?"

"You have to get the cover off my backpack to get the Cutters."

Jane and I have walked 506 miles to reach the Arctic Circle. Eleven weeks, four days. The invisible dotted line on which we stand is 66.5 degrees north of the equator, the precise point at which the sun did not set on June 21st. On the day we celebrated the summer solstice near Pump Station 8, our closest star circled the horizon here like an interested horse fly. In less than five months, on December 21st, biting insects will not be a problem. On that day, the sun will not rise north of here.

This day continues wet and breezy, with a cloud layer so thick we can't point to the sun. We walk on an arctic plateau broken again by tors, one of which resembles the Sphinx. The rocks and mist are primordial; it's easy to picture aboriginal hunters spotting caribou from the Sphinx's back.

Rain and wind combine to lower my core temperature. I start shivering even though I'm walking. I feel threatened enough to pull my raincoat over my pile jacket and put on my wool hat. John is unaffected; cold takes longer to reach him than it does me.

"Look at that," John says, stopping me with an extended arm.

He points out a dream image in the mist, near the Sphinx. Two cranes, turkeys on stilts, are walking the deck of tundra. We stop to watch them until they see a brown dog, then flap away. I wonder if we saw them at all. An arctic mirage.

Night 84

John and I eat dinner while sitting on top of a rock fortress, a molar of granite amid spindly birch and a floor of white lichen. Our view extends in all directions, undisturbed bumps, some furry with trees, some domes of rock. A hunter's view. The Dalton Highway is a ribbon with toy trucks that head to the oil field, or back home. Mosquitoes joust with the wind in their quest for warm me. Two have tired; they perch on my notebook.

The trucks, on a lonely stretch of Dalton one mile from our rock, don't distract us often at 10 p.m. John and I groove on thousands of square acres devoid of houses, radio towers, roads, televisions, restaurants, development nodes. As far as we know, we are the only creatures in our significant viewshed.

The moon, pregnant and pink, crawls slowly above the horizon. When Neil Armstrong and Buzz Aldrin became the first men to walk on the moon, the third member of Apollo 11 crew, Michael Collins, stayed in the Apollo command module, orbiting the moon in a loop that took two hours to complete. Collins spent 48 minutes out of each orbit on the far side of the moon, cut off from radio communication and from the sight of Earth. I've heard the astronauts criticized for not writing enough about their experiences, but Collins put a pencil to paper when he was on the dark side of the moon:

I am alone now, truly alone, and absolutely isolated from any known life. I am it. If a count were taken, the score would be three billion plus two over on the other side of the moon, and one plus God only knows what on this side.

John climbs down from our castle to go for an evening walk. Jane follows him to the next tor, about one quarter mile north. They become dark ants on a lunar landscape, the only movement to grab the eye. The sun transforms northwest clouds into the smoked flesh of Yukon salmon. The ridge between my rock and the sun is sharply outlined, as if drawn with black marker. I watch John and Jane scale granite teeth in silence, as if there is no air to carry sound waves. When I hold my breath, I hear the hiss of nothingness, a sound that can't be planned for. I'd hoped to find this lack of sound somewhere along the path of oil this summer. It found me.

Day 85

Tall spruce trees have returned to the landscape. They cling to the edge of Prospect Creek, another grayling stream that wets John and me to the knees when we wade across. A breeze gives us goose pimples as we dry on the far bank. It's a fine day, approaching 70 degrees. The spot where we relax has seen much worse days.

A National Weather Service thermometer that hung here once registered minus 80 degrees, the coldest temperature ever officially recorded in Alaska. There are colder places, but not by much. In 1947, a thermometer at a Yukon Territory outpost named Snag registered minus 81. The coldest temperature recorded on this side of the equator is minus 90, at Verkhoyansk, Russia. The world champ is 129 degrees below, measured in 1983 at a Russian scientific station in Antarctica.

Today's 70 degrees is well off Alaska's all-time high of 100 degrees at Fort Yukon, which is also Hawaii's all-time high.

Day 86

"Hey!"

A slimy gray body wriggles inches from my face. Willow fishing pole in hand, John dangles a grayling over me, waking me from a nap on the pipeline pad. He has just harvested dinner from Douglas Creek, which reflects blue sky as it leads the eye upstream to sharp, 3,000-foot peaks that hint at the Brooks Range.

Because the creeks are not as orderly as engineers, we have walked through the Jim River two times today. We forded Douglas Creek three times, stopping when I saw a large grayling hunting an underwater canyon directly beneath the pipeline.

Even though we don't need the food, the fisherman inside me makes it difficult to pass these grayling waters without wetting a line and using the dry flies a pump station guard gave me.

A willow stem as pole, I lost three of the flies to the smacks of grayling. I gave up after fly number three disappeared into the mouth of a grayling, choosing to roll my sleeping pad on gravel and fall asleep to thoughts of bad knots.

John took over, wading the creek with the nine-foot willow dangling four feet of fishing line. Patiently, he dropped the dry fly in front of grayling for two hours until he coaxed one to bite.

Rising from my sleeping mat, I unhook the grayling and wage a moral debate with myself. We don't need this fish. Our backpacks (especially John's) are stuffed with food. The grayling still squirms with life. Should I kill it, cook it for dinner? Or let it return to Douglas Creek to live out its life with a dull memory of being held in a warm hand?

Cooking the fish will spread its aroma, possibly calling a bear. The 10 ounces of flesh won't be a meal for us, just a supplement. I will have to make a campfire.

The fish is dying in my hand. It demands a decision, so I make one, pulling out my Swiss Army knife and pushing the shorter blade into the grayling's head. It will be the only fish we eat on the trail.

Unfolding a square of aluminum foil, I place the fish in the center after stuffing its middle with a chunk of butter. John continues fishing, staring at the water with the intensity of a man who needs calories to survive. He stands in water so cold it transforms his legs into stumps below the knee. Some primal instinct has awakened; he's locked in his task.

I gather a nest of branches and build a fire less than a yard from Douglas Creek. When willow branches turn to coals, I place the sheath of foil in the center of the heat. The butter hisses; the foil pack bulges.

John gives up. The grayling now avoid the man with the long stick who dangles the feathery morsel above them. John's lower legs are stained pink when warmed by 75-degree air.

Burning my fingers, I unwrap the foil. The grayling's skin sticks to the metal, exposing delicate rows of white flesh. John and I sit on rocks beneath the pipeline and pinch hot chunks between thumb and forefinger. The first taste, buttery and clean, makes me wish we'd caught a few more.

I swirl the flesh on my tongue while looking at the creek in which the fish was spawned, in which it rose for the last time to the silhouette of gnat. The creek, the blue sky, the mountains, all mean a bit more at this moment. This feeling of communion is why I like to fish, to hunt. We are a part of the country as we eat of it, as it fuels our bodies. We become the fish, the moose, the caribou. The killing is the least pleasant part; it has nothing to do with the excitement I feel when hunting or fishing. Killing is a necessary part of the process, the bad part. As grayling dissolves on the back of our tongues, we experience the good.

18 | The 3,000-Mile Commute

Day 87

Jane is the first to hear it. She rises from her mattress of sleeping bags, growls, then barks. John and I look at each other with big eyes. Soon, we hear it. A distant clunking that gets progressively louder. Something approaches, but I think I know what it is.

I pop my head out of the tent to see the source of the noise: Three men, on foot, with carpenter's levels. Cow bells dangle from their belts. The line walkers.

This is the second time that John, Jane and I have seen the line walkers, four men who walk and drive the 420 miles of above-ground pipeline. With three men walking, one leap-frogging with a truck, they check each pipeline crossbeam for level and eyeball the pipe's galvanized skin for bullet holes. The line walkers had walked south from Livengood to Pump Station 12 earlier in the summer. Here, they're working their way south from Prudhoe Bay to Livengood. At Livengood, they will have covered all the above-ground pipeline. Their summer's work is nearly done.

I met a few dozen pipeline workers during the journey, but there was something different about the line walkers, a lightness of mood, conversation punctuated by laughs. These guys have fun.

The blame goes to their leader, Dallas Wymore, 44, a man with Mark McGwire's forearms and a calm voice. I remember his relaxed tone from the two other times I saw him on the trip — first at Pump Station 12 north of Valdez, second at French Creek near Fairbanks — and from a phone call three months before I started the trip.

I called Wymore at a time when pipeline company executives were not excited about the prospect of a person walking next to the pipeline. *If he does it, everybody will want to do it. Think of the security headaches.*

Wymore, who has led the line walk for 11 years, was the first pipeline person who did not ask why I wanted to walk the pipeline. In a call that lasted 45 minutes, he told me his favorite section of the pipeline (Top of the World, a tundra plateau in the Alaska Range), what kind of mileage to expect (50 miles a day if I really pushed), and how his crew avoids bears (wearing cow bells, throwing M-80s, climbing onto the crossbars that support the pipe). At the end of the call, he wished me luck.

John, Jane and I crawl from the tent-turned-sauna. The sun has caught us sleeping late. It's one p.m. as we emerge to greet the line walkers.

The line walkers are in good spirits. It's a sunny day, with no mosquitoes, and they will spend most of it outdoors. As

John rises from the tent, Dallas and his crew take an extended break to talk with us.

"Are you guys hungry?" Dallas asks. "We're about ready to go to Pump Five for lunch. We'll bring you back something."

An hour later, John and I dragging to the point where we haven't yet taken down the tent, the crew returns with two Styrofoam platters. John and I eat cheeseburger patties sitting on slices of white bread, curried chicken in applesauce, French fries.

The line walkers — Dallas, Aaron Pletnikoff, Rick Bivins and Kevin Geller — sit in the shade of the pipeline with John and me as we dig plastic forks into the meal. I ask Dallas how long he's been a pipeline man.

"I started in '77 and have worked security for all but three years since then," he says, pinning a mosquito to his arm.

Dallas was a high school teacher in Nebraska when his aunt, recently returned from Alaska, told him and a friend that guys were making $10,000 a summer on this pipeline project.

"We thought, 'Why not work all year and make forty thousand?'" Dallas says. "We quit our teaching jobs and went for it. I didn't know anything about Alaska. Money was the attraction."

Fairbanks was where Dallas landed. Though the pipeline jobs were going to guys who had been there awhile, Dallas quickly filled an open slot at an office supply store in town. He trained to be a salesman until the man training him told him why he was leaving.

"He said he was going to work as a warehouse man on the (north) slope. When he told me how much he was making, I turned and said to him, 'Rather than me meeting any more clients, you should take me back to the office supply store. I'm going to quit. And I'm going to get one of those pipeline jobs.'"

Dallas grabbed a phone book and jotted down every listing that had to do with the oil industry: The pipeline company, contractors, Teamsters. He called every number and offered his services. No luck.

His life turned on a haircut. He told a barber he was seeking pipeline wages; his barber asked him if he had any experience with security. He did, having worked briefly at a prison in Nebraska. He applied with a company that bid on contracts to provide the security force for the pipeline. In less than one month after arriving in Alaska, he landed his pipeline job.

"I went from making $12,000 a year teaching to making $42,000," he says. "I couldn't sleep at night in the beginning because I didn't know what I was going to do with all that money."

Dallas Wymore is not a born security guard. He dislikes wearing a uniform (when on line walk duty he dresses in jeans, a T-shirt, and baseball cap, but for the remainder of the year he wears police blues and Wellingtons). He prefers a fanny pack to a gun belt. With his calm tone and gentle nature, it's hard to imagine him pointing a gun at anyone. In nearly 20 years of security work, he has never unholstered his weapon.

As we talk with Dallas and the crew, John and I notice

something. Dallas laughs with us, but his smile fades quickly. He looks tired, drawn, as if his mind is somewhere else. When we'd seen him at French Creek, 37 days and 214 miles ago, Dallas had told us about his schedule. Like most pipeline workers, he works two weeks on, two off. The major difference between Dallas and his crew is the length of his commute. In the 14 days he is not in Alaska, Dallas lives in San Diego.

For a decade, he has migrated 3,000 miles every two weeks. The reason for his peregrination is the most important in his life. His son Tyler, 11, lives in San Diego with Dallas's ex-wife, Pauline.

During his two weeks off in San Diego, Dallas gets custody of Tyler four straight days. They are the four days that mean the most to him, the four days that allow him to endure a ridiculous commute and less-than-inspiring work.

"When you look at him, and he's your blood, there's nothing like it," Dallas said. "It rocks you, goes directly to your marrow. It's got to add years to your life, and lots of light to whatever you have."

John and I finish our meals. Jane licks the Styrofoam. When the containers are clean, Aaron Pletnikoff, a line walker who looks like a high school basketball player, takes our trash and stuffs it in the back of the Alyeska truck.

I was to meet Dallas one more time, at another Pump Station. It happened a few months after I'd finished the hike. I returned with Jane to visit Dallas because he sent me a letter in Fairbanks and offered me the chance to see for myself what it was like to be a pipeline worker. After so many days of walking next to the pipe, I really didn't get a sense of what it was like to make a living from Alaska's oil, as so many do. So, carrying a projector and slides of the trip, I drove down with Jane to see Dallas.

I met him again in the first place I met him, the guard building of Pump Station 12, the last place where oil is pushed south. Valdez is 62 miles away. He wore his security blues, as he did the first time I saw him. A silver badge hung from the blue material stretched across his barrel chest.

The pump station sits in a valley surrounded by mismatched pyramids of the Chugach Range, mountains smooth with snow, powdery like a Geisha's face. The valley within those mountains is deceptively broad — a table of wetlands rising to the white mountains. Between the lowlands and the highlands is a belt of gray forest, a graveyard of spruce trees with no needles. The organism responsible for killing the trees is no larger than a grain of rice. The larvae of the spruce bark beetle kills white spruce trees by feeding on a tree's phloem, the water- and sugar-carrying tissue that coats the inside of the tree from roots to needles. Millions of these tiny insects thrived in these forests a decade ago, killing hundreds of thousands of acres of spruce trees that now wait for a windstorm to transform the land into a giant's game of pick-up sticks.

Sitting in the palm of this valley, the pump station stands out, industry where there is nothing else. The first thing you notice is the noise, the surf of jet engines that move the turbines that push the oil. Once past the security gate, you are in a compound of metal buildings surrounded by chain-link fence with barbed wire on top. No plants pop through the crushed rock—the greenery is all outside the fence. Inside the fence are red trucks, a few more buildings that look like spacecraft touched down on a lifeless surface. Not a scrap of litter.

Dallas was just finishing his shift. He took me to an immense green building shaped like an L, the Personal Living Quarters, better known as the PLQ. We clanged up metal grate steps to the door of the PLQ. The door was metal, 10 inches thick. Instead of a doorknob, it had a lever. It was the door of a walk-in freezer.

As the door clicked behind us, we were sealed in a room with cubby holes and hangers. We kicked off our shoes to enter the carpeted environment of the PLQ. Architects designed the PLQs for arctic conditions. Once inside and unshod, you don't have to leave until you go to work the next day. If you are a cook or a housekeeper, you don't have to leave at all.

A cafeteria-style restaurant. Rooms with one bed or two, a toilet and shower (leave your wet towel in the hall and the housekeeper picks it up). A weight room. Sauna. Ping-pong table. Washers and dryers. A stack of daily newspapers for the taking. A store offering shampoo, soap, aspirin, candy. No money required. Stuffed chairs surrounding a TV, constantly on. Cable.

Dallas led me to the dining area.

"Should be some good stuff tonight," he said. "The better cook is on duty."

Sitting with Dallas and two contractors at a round table near the TV, I ate honey-glazed chicken and beef tips with rice. When I finished, I returned for more. There was no limit. On a counter nearby were bags of chips, a bowl of fruit, pastries under plastic. In another pump station, my hiking partner John once saw a similar table: "This is a dangerous place for somebody who's been sleeping on friend's floors the past few months." I wonder why everybody didn't weigh 300 pounds.

Dallas and I finished our meals. He took my tray, opened a door through the wall to the kitchen, and slid it in. The room cleared out quickly after dinner. Twenty tables that were filled with pipeline people were soon empty. The workers, tired from 12-hour days, retreated to their rooms, their books, their HBO. Tomorrow was another 12-hour shift. Stay up late and you pay.

"It's absolutely Groundhog Day," Dallas said, referring to the movie with Bill Murray and Andie McDowell. "Every day is the same here. You get up at the same time, go to work in the same place, eat in the same place."

Two weeks of 12-hour days followed by two weeks off is a schedule not uncommon in Alaska. I worked it on the oil spill, but I never liked it. I felt like I was trading my life for money.

"You can graph peoples' attitude by where they are in the two-week cycle," Dallas said. "The first week is real tough, but when people have only three or four days left, it's like, 'You know this job isn't so bad now.'"

When the two weeks of work expire, Dallas said he feels high, the reward for two weeks of living away from loved ones, a familiar bed, pets. Another pipeline worker who was adjusting a valve one day told me: "They don't pay us for what we do here. They pay us for what we do without."

Dallas said most pipeline workers love the schedule that gives them half the year off. They say they could never go back to a nine-to-five job with two weeks off a year. A single man of 44, he's not one of them.

"It's hard to establish a relationship, even with a next-door neighbor, with a two on, two off. For me, nine-to-five would offer a stable relationship. I could do it tomorrow," he said, propping his massive forearms on the table. "I would have loved to have had that schedule with my son. I've heard often that it's not the quantity of the time, it's the quality. Or that because we're home for two weeks, we can devote our total selves to our children for two weeks. But your children don't need you 24 hours a day when you're there. If you were there every night, I can't believe there's a substitute for that. I have to believe that we as a group are rationalizing that we have a better thing being there for two weeks straight. I don't know if that's the way life was meant to be."

Tyler, Dallas's son, was then 11½. Tyler is the reason Dallas lives in San Diego but works on permafrost. He met Tyler's mother, Pauline, at Pump Station 6. She made him laugh, she made everyone laugh. Dallas, more reserved, fell for her. They married after seven years of dating. She was from San Diego. The long commutes began 10 years ago and didn't end five years ago just because he and Pauline divorced.

The migration became particularly difficult just after the divorce, in the volatile period when he thought the most important thing in his world was going to be taken away.

"It wasn't the divorce — I thought I was going to lose my son. I remember coming back to work, driving from Pump 10 to 9. I was ready to explode. After pulling over on the highway, I started yelling and screaming and crying. I thought I was losing him. I thought it was over. It's an agonizing thing, changing the life of this person that's so important to you. This person that you love so much, you always want to give them the best, and you just took away from that. You took from them part of what you had as a kid. You had your folks there, you knew you were loved … It was very very difficult in the beginning."

The evening sun scrolled down to near the tops of mountains, beaming through the dining area windows to the point where I squinted when I looked at Dallas. He noticed, and stood up to pull the shade down. He's a considerate man. I've heard it from others too. When I walked into Pump Station 9 in Delta Junction, a security guard there told me his time on the line walk was his favorite time of all because he got to work with Dallas, and because Dallas, his boss, treated him as an equal. Dallas is a good listener. At the pump station, I asked him to talk, and he was not completely comfortable. But he talked, about the purgatory of two decades of a job where every day is the same.

"It feels numb," he said, his brown eyes softening. "How many times can you say, 'Been there, done that?' It's like it never hits the nerve. Like life in the pump stations. There's no color here … Early in my career I remember going into a grocery story in Fairbanks on my time off and just being amazed at all the different color boxes."

He said he recently reached a point where he could quit. He has invested in a restaurant, in Wasilla, with a good partner. He has the money.

"I wonder myself, why am I still here? I think it's difficult to let go of without some absolute assurances out there."

From his words and actions, and the mountain of cookies on the counter nearby, I found myself comparing pipeline work to addictive behavior. The ecstasy of your last work day, the big paycheck, then the crash of coming back to work for two weeks, debating, "Is this is really the way to live?" I'm glad I'm not a part of that cycle. Some people can thrive here. Not me. Not Dallas, either.

"The pipeline was fun initially. It allowed me a totally different experience than the plains of Nebraska. But I think I never ever should have stayed for 20 years. I should have found a career. I should have found something that made me happy and that I was good at. And I don't know what that is.

"When I first came to work, I remember thinking to myself — probably when I was sitting on a pipeline gate and bored — 'What is it in money that's so important? Would you sell your soul to have it?' I guess in a way I've said yes."

Dallas looked away, toward the TV. I asked him what he wanted most.

"That my son would have a close relationship with God," he said. "To be in a good relationship is a close second. One in which every ounce of energy you put in comes back."

Dallas laughed with me earlier in the day after he just received a Dear John letter by e-mail. "The wonders of technology," he said. He admitted to being stung by the electronic rejection, from a woman in Wasilla, even though he knew the relationship was doomed. He calls himself a hopeless romantic, a person who, in the initial stages of dating, overlooks traits in his partner that will prove fatal later.

"I'm a fool," he said. "I don't think intelligently about whether the relationship should or shouldn't work. I'm way too quick to jump out here," he extended his arm.

"I wish I was like my son." A grin emerged. "Ty is just getting into girls. In the last 30 days, he has either dumped or been dumped four times. And he laughs about it."

Dallas is a handsome man, with brown eyes, a dimple in his chin, the body of a weightlifter. Working on the pipeline for 20 years has not ravaged him. He has a great sense of humor. He is an optimist. But when he meets a woman at home, just after working to a vital stage of courting, he goes back to Alaska. It's hard for love to blossom across 3,000 miles of air.

"A good relationship, I wonder if it's ever going to be there," he said. "I wonder what I have to do to find it. I wonder if I'm going to be smart enough to realize when I've found it, and be willing to work hard enough to continue to have it be that."

I knew there was a spark in Dallas, but I wasn't seeing it. He was tired, burned out. Without color. A gear in a machine that would be replaced when it wears out. We sat without talking for a few seconds. CNN filled the void. It was then 10:30 p.m., and the PLQ was deserted. Everyone was sleeping, getting closer to the five a.m. buzz of the alarm. Dallas, too, would hear the call, but he didn't seem anxious to leave the table. After we talked a while longer, he invited me to his room. He wanted to show me something.

We walked the carpet past posters in which cartoon characters urged us to wear safety glasses. The hallway had an antiseptic smell, no detectable trace of earth. We reached his room, a space he has to himself. When he is in San Diego, another worker with the same job occupies the room.

Inside, a small but comfortable nest with a TV, sink and mirror and one window with a shade pulled down like a closed eyelid. A picture of Tyler, wallet size, smiled from the wall above his bed. On Dallas's night stand was a paperback with the subject of adapting to the teenage years, when your child wants nothing to do with you.

Dallas sat on the bed, then bent and reached underneath. He pulled out a cane, three feet long and carved from blond wood. Willow, with erotic-looking raised diamonds of red and brown. Exquisitely finished, the result of many hours sanding, then varnishing. On the shaft were raised letters: "JACK."

"I used to carve one cane every tour," Dallas said. "Either that or I'd read one book every tour."

Dallas makes the canes for coworkers. This one, Dallas would give to Jack's wife so he can surprise Jack on his birthday. He has carved more than a dozen canes and has given them all away. One man cried when he received his.

"There's some parts to this job that have been very rewarding," Dallas said. "I like getting to know people out here, especially on the line walk. Like you and Jane, we get to know each other better than anyone else. Some of the funnest things that ever happened to me happened because of the camaraderie here."

Dallas explained the evolution of the "Boney Award," a prize the line walkers dreamed up to give to a crew member with a good work ethic and positive attitude. They gave the award to a man who was reluctant to let the other line walkers into his head. A man who was having problems at home but still smiled through his workday. He was embarrassed to receive the award in a corny ceremony at Coldfoot, but Dallas could tell the effort touched him.

"Frank said he threw the Boney Award away," Dallas said, "But I bet it's in his house, in a prominent place. And I bet he laughs every time he goes by it."

When I got ready to leave, I felt a sense of regret, as if I was leaving an old friend who I might not see again for years. Dallas is a gifted listener, someone who isn't just waiting to talk about himself while someone else talks. I thought of the pain he'd been through, the times in his Alyeska truck alone when he had no one to talk to about his son, his divorce, how terrible that must have been. But I know too that even on his worst days, he was good to the people around him, and he always listened.

I met Dallas one final time, after receiving an email from him months later. It was a cryptic message, requesting that I meet him at Fairbanks International Airport. Dallas had 20 minutes between the flight from Pump Station 6 to his plane that left for Anchorage 30 minutes after he arrived. He would spend a day in Anchorage, then fly back to the reason for his 3,000-mile commute to San Diego, his son Ty.

When I saw Dallas, dressed in jeans and speaking softly and politely to a ticket agent, he smiled at me. He gave me a narrow cardboard box as tall as my waist.

"This is an early Christmas present," he said.

I hesitated, a little embarrassed.

"Please, open it," he said.

I cut through packing tape with a house key, opened the box and saw what I was hoping might be there. A cane, carved from willow, with a handle made from caribou antler. Amid the raised diamonds on its shaft are two words: NED, JANE.

I think of Dallas in his room after work, spending nights stripping bark from a willow, sanding and carving block letters, varnishing. A task of patience, of love. I feel like hugging him, but I don't.

He listens with interest as I tell him about my life. Just before he leaves to catch his plane he talks about how his two-week on, two-week off job was eliminated at Pump Station 12, and how Alyeska wants him to get a place in Fairbanks so he can work a 40-hour week at Pump Station 12, just south of the Yukon River. With his son in San Diego, he won't do it. When I spoke with him at Pump Station 12, he told me he needed something to push him into a change, to start a new life doing something he really enjoyed while being with his son.

"I guess this is the kick I needed," he said. Then he turned and continued his migration to a 12-year old boy waiting in San Diego. I walked with my new cane back to my pickup.

19 | Someone to Share Things With

Day 87

If I didn't know this was the Arctic, if I were just trans-
ported here blindfolded and told to take a look, there is no
way I'd believe we were this far north. Ever since John, Jane
and I crossed the circle, each day has been more sunny and
dry than the one before.

The pipeline now curves through valleys between rocky
hills, the highest of which reaches almost 4,000 feet. Big
spruce have returned in the river valleys, following the bends
of rivers such as the Jim, a waterway too untainted to pass.

We slide our packs from our shoulders and set them on
a gravel bar in the middle of the Jim River. With clear water
rushing past, John and I recline on our packs and absorb sunlight. Jane curls for a snooze, comfortable on a bed of gravel.

The nice weather has relaxed me, fooling me into thinking that maybe the end of summer isn't right around the
corner. In his volunteering to set up the tent and take it down
every day, John has given me more time. Even though we

sleep in, we still get going quickly. Our conversations have been a great distraction. If I were by myself, I'd be thinking less of the mountains and other things John points out and more of the goal of finishing the hike. The miles have gone fast with John.

We spend a lot more time than we planned on the Jim River. There's something homey about the setting. I envision a cabin in the big spruce upstream, toward the mountains. A place I could visit when I needed to escape Fairbanks. A place to visit when I didn't need to escape anything. The wonder of this spot is that there's no cabin in sight, even on this transparent stream not one-half mile from the Dalton Highway. There are no cabins because the land belongs to the Bureau of Land Management. Sitting here, looking at the lack of no trespassing signs, the lack of any human sign, I don't mind the land being tied up by the feds. As it is now, under BLM rules we could camp in that spruce grove upstream and remain two weeks. The land is as good as mine. As a U.S. citizen, it is mine. I can't build a cabin on it, or order other people off, but nobody can order me off. As we sit by the gurgling river, I can't help but think that having this land locked up by the federal government is a good thing. It belongs to everyone. We'll die long before the spruce trees anyhow, so why the need to possess this wild country? Why not share?

Day 88

These warm arctic days have allowed us to bathe in the local rivers. Today, we skinny dip in the south fork of the Koyukuk, the major artery that drains this side of the Continental Divide. The clear water in which we wash will eventually make it to the Yukon, then the Bering Sea. In less than 100 miles, Jane and I will top Atigun Pass in the Brooks Range. When we do, we will follow waterways that flow north, to the Arctic Ocean. When we reach salt water, our trip will be done.

John senses that I've been thinking of the moment when I won't carry the pack around anymore. I can't deny it. The desire to relax, to have a consecutive few days without walking, is strong. I wonder what Jane thinks. She seems to be enjoying the outdoor life, but what kind of a strain is this putting on her 10-year-old body?

We climb a long hill, up from the South Fork, and crest a pass from which we have a view of Cathedral Mountain to the north. Coldfoot, we know, is on the far side of Cathedral Mountain. Coldfoot is where John will leave me to head back to the Yukon, then Fairbanks. Even though we have plenty of food and I'm still enjoying his company, I feel like it's time to make some miles solo, just me and Jane.

Day 89

John, Jane and I walk next to the pipeline as it crosses the Dalton Highway and meets the middle fork of the Koyukuk, a waterway the pipeline follows upstream for the next 50 miles. The river rolls in aquamarine humps of power. It carries water from the jagged peaks of the Brooks Range, the northernmost mountain range in Alaska that isolates the North Slope. The Brooks Range is beginning to rise here, as we embark on a narrow corridor through 4,000-footers. The sensation, oddly enough, is like walking in lower Manhattan with the concrete towers of Wall Street leaning overhead.

But there are no piles of grizzly shit in New York City. A pile of barely digested blueberries stops our progress. I toe the pile, which has the volume of a small pillow. Soft and fresh, not long from the bear's tract. More piles, damp and blue, decorate the pipeline pad near Rosie Creek, a tumble of clear water that drains the north side of Cathedral Mountain.

Effervescent water crashes down steps of rock to the Koyukuk. We stop to drink, thinking of the grizzly. Rosie Creek's noise increases our chances of surprising the bear, and I worry about Jane as she romps on the grassy shoreline of the Koyukuk. But her nose is better than the human ear will ever be.

It's John's final day of hiking. At Rosie Creek, he makes a decision to taste of Alaska, unprotected. It is his habit, when driving around the country, to stop at major waterways and drink them. He has sipped the Mississippi, the Missouri, the Yukon. Until now, he has used my hand pump to filter all his water. Now, he'll take a chance. He dips his plastic water bottle under a Rosie Creek waterfall. The water spills a quart in seconds, overflowing cold on his hands. He sits on a rock, looks out at the pulsing Koyukuk, and drinks 32 ounces of the country.

"I'll come back and sleep in the tent with you if I get Giardia," he says.

Sweating in dry heat, we climb a high ridge that parallels the river. Below, a yellow raft glides down the river, followed by another. We share peeks through the binoculars to glimpse the orange and yellow lifejackets of the rafters, who can see the pipeline but cannot make out three tiny creatures who walk its path.

As we near Coldfoot, John takes the final steps of his journey. My friend has walked more than 200 of the pipeline's 800 miles. From the start, John was my biggest cheerleader, even though he said he was a bit jealous. He was there at the beginning, in Valdez. He walked through the Chugach Range, three months ago, when the trees had no leaves. He ferried my brother Drew to the Alaska Range, loaning Drew his raincoat and other gear my brother needed to be comfortable. John was at the Solstice celebration at Pump Station 8. He and his partner Nadia had the flexibility to hike from Pump Station 8 into Fairbanks. His pink hat showed again as he picked up Smits near Wickersham Dome, bringing supplies on the same trip. He has shared this trail from the Yukon River, a distance of 110 miles. Some of those miles were not pleasant ones — miles of mosquitoes, soggy socks, soiled underwear. And now I prepare to dump him when he wants to go on. Why?

I wish I knew the answer. John has learned my habits, catered to my need for control, left all the decisions to me. Why does a person need to be alone sometimes? When hiking with another person, there's always someone to talk to, someone to bounce questions off, someone to receive your thoughts, to send back opinions. But when I have a hiking partner, I tend not to open up to people I meet along the way. I'm not dependent on strangers for conversation, for advice. Before I started, I wanted this trip to be about Alaska, 1997. Who lives here? What are they doing? Why do they choose to live in this cold, buggy, beautiful place? When I hike with someone, I think of myself as a two-headed creature, somewhat of an imposition on people I meet. I avoid getting to know strangers. I'm self-conscious about asking them questions.

I also crave a bit of solitude. My aunt, the nun, once told me: "There are two types of people in this world: those who recharge their spirits by being with other people, and those who do it by being alone."

Ahead, in the Koyukuk's trough between mountains, is the Coldfoot airstrip. We descend a difficult pitch to the valley made by Slate Creek. The pipeline is once again pushing us toward a clump of people.

John doesn't sulk or try to make me feel guilty about hiking without him, but he does give me his opinion.

"You're not going to learn anything about yourself by hiking alone," he says. "If it was me hiking, I'd take you along for the whole thing. I've spent a lot of my life doing things alone, and I've gotten to the point where I know what it's like. I prefer someone to share things with."

I like to share things, but I enjoy being alone too. I may indeed learn something about myself by hiking alone, when I am forced to decide when to stop, where to camp, what to cook for dinner. Alone on the trail I am forced to dwell where my mind takes me, even if it's to a past experience I might prefer to leave buried. In a very social world, I am looking forward to a few days without the distraction of conversation, or TV, or music. Where will I go? I don't know.

We part at Coldfoot, a truck stop and the last place to eat a cheeseburger before Deadhorse. After he recognizes Jane, a trucker gives John a ride south, toward where he parked my truck at the Yukon River bridge. As the truck disappears into its own cloud of dust, I feel sad to see John go and excited to face the trail alone with Jane.

20 | Coldfoot

Coldfoot debuted in 1899 as the town of Slate Creek, a haven for gold seekers. They were the spillover from the Klondike, bearded men who made it to Dawson City only to find the gold creeks full of wooden claim stakes. From the Yukon, some boated and sledded up the Koyukuk, following rumors of a few successful prospectors who had retrieved a few ounces of "sunburned" gold from the creeks that flowed into the big river.

Menacing peaks of rock and the early onset of winter above the Arctic Circle proved frightening enough to several stampeders that they reached here and turned back for points south. Those who remained commemorated the chicken-out by exchanging Slate Creek for Coldfoot, a name that lives on in its descriptive accuracy: many motorists choose to go no farther up the Dalton after gassing up here. The next fuel opportunity is Deadhorse, 250 potholed miles north.

In the days when lonely miners named the surrounding

creeks after their wives and girlfriends (Myrtle, Clara, Emma and Marion are nearby; Minnie, Jennie and Linda a bit farther north), Coldfoot boomed in 1902. At its peak, Coldfoot had two stores, seven bars, one gambling establishment, and ten prostitutes.

In his written account of Wiseman and the Koyukuk country, Arctic Village, Robert Marshall detailed the history of the area in 1930. Fond of statistical analysis, Marshall calculated a relationship between prospectors, gold production, and prostitutes:

Year	Prospectors	Gold produced, in Thousands	Prostitutes
1898	200	$0	0
1900	270	$10	72
1915	300	$290	14
1920	119	$90	0

Coldfoot today lacks the romance of Marshall's era — just 60 years ago — when he made Wiseman his base for Brooks Range hikes and became enamored with the people of the Koyukuk. The Coldfoot compound, now owned by a fuel company, is a place of function: a remote stop on a gravel road at which to purchase gas, eat a meal, have a puncture repaired. Tourists stay overnight, herded from buses to Arctic Acres Inn and across the dirt parking lot to the restaurant, where a man named Snowshoe Scott entertains them nightly with vocals and accordion. Also clinging to the Coldfoot development node is a tiny log cabin belonging to the Bureau of Land Management. Across the Dalton is a clump of trailers and massive garage that houses the truck drivers and grader operators of Coldfoot DOT camp.

Inside the restaurant, a 20-foot spruce log standing by the cash register props the main roof beam. Electricity powers a TV bolted high in the southwest corner. Three truck drivers sit at a long table with seats for nine. A sign on the table: "For truckers only."

Someone did us a good deed at Coldfoot, but I don't know who it is. After I eat a meal of greasy ribs, I ask the cashier if she might know who gave me a gallon of white gas about a week ago. Some Alyeska people at Pump Station 5 asked if John and I needed anything. I told them we were a bit short of gas for the stove. They returned with a gallon of Coleman fuel, telling me it was donated by someone in Coldfoot.

"Oh, that must be Dave, our head of maintenance," the woman behind the counter said. She promptly called him on her hand-held radio.

So appears a large man with a Fu Manchu mustache, dominant forehead and meaty handshake. I thank him for the donation.

"Hey, you're doing something I'd like to do," he says, with a smile, teeth standing like Chicklets. "I figure if a guy can walk 600 miles to get here, I'm going to help him out. If there's anything else you and Girl-dog need, let me know."

There is something I need. John and I clipped along at a good pace, arriving in Coldfoot a few days ahead of my scheduled food drop. Jane is down to two handfuls of food.

Brady jumps on a four-wheeler and rolls to a trailer he shares with his wife, Nancy and his pit bull, Mister. He returned with a Ziploc bulging with nuggets of Mister's food. He also included a can of meaty chunks. Jane's tail wags at the sight of her Coldfoot bonanza.

In addition to outfitting my dog, Brady insists I sleep in his boss's house, a frame structure next to his trailer. "He's not here now, and you can get a shower, wash some clothes."

With a streak of 89 nights in a tent, I opt for Brady's lawn, but I use his boss's running water, and I look forward to sitting at a table to write a few columns. I walk to Brady's lawn.

While Jane enjoys the carpet in the boss's house, I wash all my clothes and take my first shower since Pump Station 6. It has been 16 days and 115 miles since I've washed beneath a sprinkle of warm water. I really haven't missed the shower, but I do feel better when I towel off. As I feel the luxury of carpet fibers between my toes, Jane stretches on the padded surface, groans her approval of the accommodations. We rest.

Day 91

Mile is a word invented by the Romans. Milia passuum, one-thousand paces, was what it took a Roman soldier in full battle gear to cover a mile. A pace to the Romans was the distance a soldier covered between his right heel leaving the ground and striking it again. Two steps to a pace, 2,000 steps to a mile.

With nothing much else to do, I count my steps from pipeline mile 236 to 235. In the flat flood plain of the

Koyukuk, my boots touch the ground 2,451 times from one mile marker to the next.

21 | **Wiseman**

Day 92

I learned to hate gold miners when I worked for a few summers as a National Park Service ranger on the Yukon River, near Eagle. A large portion of my working hours were spent crawling into tangled brush to retrieve 55-gallon drums left behind by those who operated diesel-belching gold dredges in two remote watersheds.

The gold mining companies used two dredges the size of houses. The dredges now rot in place on stream beds that twist unnaturally, following the course of the machines. The piles of gravel left behind 50 years ago are as barren as the surface of the moon — all the mineral soil that would have supported new plants was captured in the belly of the dredge, because the soil might contain gold.

Our Park Service crew removed 900 drums from one of the watersheds. Drums we wrestled out of mosquito bogs and spruce forest often were filled with waste oil or some other funky substance that slowly but surely would make it from barrel to creek to Yukon River.

I've always thought of miners as alien creatures, wounding the earth in a ridiculous search for a yellow metal neither edible nor especially attractive. What gives these people the right to scar the earth like that? What kind of selfish, inhuman jerk could leave all this junk behind, transform a valley into a pile of boulders and then move on?

I was about to find out. I had never had dinner with a miner until I walked into Wiseman.

While hiking through Coldfoot, I asked three people whether going to Wiseman would be worth three miles of hiking from the pipeline pad.

"Definitely, go."

"You don't want to miss Wiseman."

"If you're looking to learn something about this area, go there and look up George Lounsbury. He's got a little museum there."

With Jane leading the way, we reach the heart of Wiseman, four log cabins that sink into an acre of lawn. We pass the Wiseman post office, inactive since 1956. The door frame is short enough to require genuflection upon entering. Jane sniffs the dirt floor and finds nothing edible. We exit, back to the light.

Heading east, toward the Koyukuk, we follow two tracks of dirt road past a log cabin with signs of life — three chairs of molded plastic stand outside; a hanging basket overflows with flowers.

"Oh, you must be Ned and Jane."

A woman wearing white clogs has emerged from the cabin with the flowers. Bobbi Lounsbury is the wife of George. "My husband is up at the mine at Union Gulch, but he wants you to stay here until he gets back. You have a tent, don't you? George said you can camp on the lawn if you like."

I opt instead for a private stand of willows near the river. Three steps from the tent door, the Koyukuk is a band of teal a quarter-mile wide. It runs between shoulders of mountains that seem to change every time I look at them. First green in sunlight, then a faint blue when a cloud's shadow passes. Though I'm technically in a town, the riverbank is one of the nicest campsites I've had on the trip. From my sandy platform, I hear a generator hum, the sound of a chain saw, but no cars. One hundred yards away, a green bridge crosses Wiseman Creek, so named for Peter Wiseman, one of the first to find gold in the area.

In *Arctic Village,* Robert Marshall wrote of Wiseman in 1933: I*n summertime a Wiseman street is represented by a brown streak through the surrounding reeds and willows ... At most places it is bounded by fences and cabins, except for the outside of Front Street which is the bank of the river.* His description is still accurate near the end of the century, except for a yellow bulldozer parked near my tent.

Marshall continued: *It is not, however, the minor dimensions of town which are most impressive in Wiseman. It is instead the huge expanse which separates this lonely settlement from the outposts of Twentieth Century civilization. It is 200 miles airline to the closest pavement, the closest auto, the closest railroad, or the closest electric light at Fairbanks.*

It is still 200 miles to the closest pavement, at the border of the Fairbanks North Star Borough on the Elliott Highway. Though people can now drive to Wiseman over the Dalton Highway, the Alaska Railroad has not extended north of Fairbanks. Electric lights are the option of the 12 adults who live in Wiseman year-round. The Lounsburys, summer residents of Wiseman who winter in Fairbanks, have a solar panel on top of their cabin. They do not need it much now, on August 4th, because twilight still lingers, even in the quiet hours when the birds roost.

A few hours before midnight, George Lounsbury returns from the hills in a dusty Dodge pickup. George is 53, with curly white hair and a boyish smile, a man of impressive girth and kind brown eyes.

He leads me immediately to a nearby set of mated log cabins, his "picture museum." A saloon in the days of Bob Marshall, the picture museum houses a collection of Wiseman artifacts gathered by George and his brother Jim, better known as "Clutch." As George displays a plastic-coated ledger page, upon which the saloon proprietor penciled in the bar tabs of local prostitutes, Clutch enters the museum.

A year younger than his brother but similarly proportioned, Clutch works when he can at the brothers' mine. His paychecks come from the state, where he works at Coldfoot DOT as a driver of large vehicles. With a full beard and baseball cap embroidered with CASE, the name of a company that manufactures heavy equipment, Clutch looks more like a miner than his older brother.

The Lounsburys have been close to gold all their lives. As young boys, they played in piles of rocks outside tunnels that reached deep into Ester Dome. Their father, born north of Fairbanks in 1910, mined the Dome until the early 1940s, when the price of gold tumbled to the point that blasting powder — suddenly rare because of the war — became a more valuable commodity.

Today, the brothers both have homes on the flanks of Ester Dome, about 15 miles from the core of Fairbanks, but Wiseman draws them north when the aspen buds burst in the spring.

Harry Leonard drifted north of the Arctic Circle in 1934 after stints as an assembly line worker in a Maine shoe factory, a cowboy in Texas, and a mechanic in Fairbanks. In Wiseman he stuck, remaining for the majority of his life. Originally from Maine, Leonard looked a bit like an Eskimo: shiny black hair and an oriental tilt to his eyes. He found a peaceful, solitary existence in Wiseman, earning his grub by scratching down to the bedrock of Archibald Gulch, a tributary to Nolan Creek. There, he once found a 20-ounce nugget that now rests behind glass at the University of Alaska museum.

George Lounsbury, then a physical education teacher at Lathrop High School in Fairbanks, met Leonard in 1971. George later purchased one of Leonard's cabins in Wiseman. When George flew his single-engine Bonanza to Wiseman, he always carried something for Harry Leonard — a few dozen eggs one time, a fuel filter for Leonard's bulldozer the next. Leonard appreciated the gestures of the young teacher.

Though his wife requested a divorce in Fairbanks before he moved to Wiseman, Leonard was never alone in his cabin or on the trails. He always had a friend by his side.

"His dogs were the most important thing to him in his life," George says. He offers a story about another miner's visit to Leonard's cabin:

"Another Wiseman character came over one night for dinner. He saw three plates on the table, but he knew there weren't three old timers in town that spoke to each other. He was having a hell of a time figuring who that plate was for. There was no road to Wiseman at the time. Anyway, they got ready to eat, and up sets the old dog and he eats right with them at the table."

Leonard believed the only thing bad about dogs was that they didn't live long enough. When his canine friends died, Leonard buried each under a cross painted white, complete with the dog's name and the dates of its birth and passing. I would have liked Harry Leonard.

And Harry Leonard liked the Lounsbury brothers. George, who quit teaching to work on the pipeline in 1975, flew up to visit Leonard as often as he could get away. Clutch had his friends who were pallet makers fashion a casket for one of Leonard's dogs.

When Leonard's age prevented him from cutting wood, the Lounsburys hauled loads of wood up from Fairbanks on the newly constructed haul road. In 1985, George reserved a spot for Leonard at the Pioneer's Home in Fairbanks. Leonard, who could no longer feed his wood stove or accomplish other tasks to keep himself alive, reluctantly came into Fairbanks. After a year of feeling out of place, Leonard returned to Wiseman. He wanted to die in the place where he had spent the best years of his life. But the strain of living a bush lifestyle was too much for a trail-weary 85-year-old.

He returned to the Pioneer's Home, where he died quietly in 1989.

Though the Wiseman cemetery had not been used in years, the Lounsburys arranged to have Leonard buried there, on a hillside above town. Leonard's marker is only a few spruce trees removed from the grave of one of his favorite dogs.

Leonard rewarded the Lounsbury brothers for their kindness and companionship by leaving them his claims on Union Gulch, six acres of Wiseman, and four buildings. The center of that six acres is what George refers to as the farthest north lawn in North America.

Standing where the lawn terminates near the Koyukuk, the museum has become a regular stop for tour bus drivers in the know. George keeps a schedule of buses due from Fairbanks and southbound from Prudhoe Bay. He tries to be near the museum when buses pull into Wiseman. When travelers exit the buses, George plays the part of Wiseman historian, a role that gives him pleasure.

"If people have come this far, either on a tour bus or in their own vehicle, they've got to be something special," George says. "It's exciting to be able to share the history of the place with people like that."

Clutch sweeps me out of the museum to give me a formal tour of the post office. Speaking with enthusiasm, he recites the history of the area at a speed faster than my brain can absorb. He ushers me from the post office to Harry Leonard's old cabin, its front porch sided with corrugated metal. From there we go to Clutch's house, the only structure made from milled lumber on the Lounsburys' property. There, Clutch shows me a newspaper article that has him riled. He holds up a 1915 copy of the *Dawson Daily News*. On the cover is a man's right hand, his palm hidden by a gold nugget.

"Here's something you might want to report on," he says, pointing a stubby finger at the photograph. "They call this Klondike gold, but this nugget came from Union Gulch, the same place we're mining now. I can prove it."

Clutch unearths a black and white photograph, one the Lounsburys acquired from the archives at the University of Alaska library. Though the image is reversed, it's obviously the same hand, the same 35-ounce nugget. Written below the nugget is confirmation: "This Nugget Found on Union Gulch, Koyukuk River, Sept. 3, 1901. Weight 35 Ozs 5 Pwts. Value $669.50."

"How can they call this Klondike gold?" he slaps the Dawson newspaper on a table. "I'm going to take that to Dawson when I go there for a hockey tournament this winter. I want to get a correction done in the newspaper."

Clutch has three burning passions — things automotive (the origin of his nickname), ice hockey (he plays forward in the 35-and-older league in Fairbanks) and dense yellow metal.

"Tomorrow night, you come up there with us, to the gulch," he says. "We'll teach you how to find gold."

As I relax in one of two barber chairs in Clutch's summer house at 10 p.m., George enters through the screen door. He receives Jane's greeting as if he were a shortstop bending to a baseball.

"Time to eat, guys."

Bobbi has prepared a feast, which she serves on a glass table under the umbrella awning. Red salmon from the Copper River at Chitina, German potato salad, buttered rolls, green salad. Chocolate cake for dessert. Bobbi passes a hunk of salmon. Like me, Bobbi is a migrant — originally from Madison, Wisconsin, she drove to Alaska with a poodle when she was 35. The frontier she sought was one of adventure and a chance to compete for a job.

"My dad had always thought about coming to Alaska, so I thought, 'Somebody's got to make it up there.' I felt it would be a whole new world for me. Thirty-five years old, never married, no real ties. I was inspired to come partially because I couldn't stand that my family all was in 100 miles of where they were born. Somebody's got to make a move. Let's face it, that's how so many of us got here. That's how the country got developed."

She met George three years after moving up; shortly thereafter, George purchased the cabin from Harry Leonard. "We hit it off immediately," Bobbi says. "Went out a few times and here we are."

At the dinner table, Bobbi, Clutch, George and I are joined by the Lounsburys' friend, "Tahiti Bob" Hoffsten. Tahiti Bob spends his winters with his family in the South Pacific. Summers are for ventures such as this, in which he parks his cowboy boots in Harry Leonard's cabin after spending his days searching for gold. Tahiti Bob is a decade older than the Lounsburys, but his hair is Ronald Reagan black. He speaks with a pleasing drawl he picked up in his hometown of Brownsville, Texas. Alaska first saw Bob Hoffsten when he was 25, when he traveled to Barrow to operate heavy machinery.

Tahiti Bob returns every year to scratch his itch for gold. He recently purchased a wet suit and a portable dredge. At 64, he will spend much of his summer submerged in icy creeks, sucking up gravel with a four-inch hose.

Tahiti Bob earned his retirement checks in large part by working on the pipeline. During 41 years in the operating engineers' union, he worked at every pump station except number 11. He spent many hours maneuvering a crane: lifting pipe into place, holding it securely until the 798ers beneath him fused the steel.

As we eat, Jane sits next to Tahiti Bob. He takes a shining to her, feeding her cake crumbs and then beginning a ritual that lasts more than 10 minutes: dipping his knife into the tub of margarine, smearing margarine on his index finger, presenting his finger to Jane, who then licks it clean. Jane follows Tahiti Bob's motions throughout the rest of the evening. When he relaxes with George in the chairs overlooking the lawn and the mountains, Jane stations herself at his right hand.

Day 93

Union Gulch — just south of Confederate Gulch — is where George and Jim Lounsbury look for gold somehow missed by Harry Leonard and a string of pick-and-shovel miners dating to 1901.

Tahiti Bob ferries me to Union Gulch in his pickup, a muddy Jane trying to balance on my knees and crotch for four undulating miles. We arrive at the mine: a steep hill-side to the south, disturbed earth to the north, a creek, small enough to step over, trickling between.

George and Clutch search here in hopes that their modern machines can do more than the hand tools and wooden sluice boxes of men who combined to strip Union Creek to bedrock in the past 96 years. These same men left their marks with wooden dams, into which Clutch some-times noses a bulldozer. The dams, built about every 100 feet along the creek, held water for the old timers' sluicing opera-tions. The Lounsburys have found these dams all the way up the mountain, to the headwaters of Union Creek.

Despite their primitive tools, the former miners of Union Gulch were ambitious and tough. George and Clutch don't expect to find another 35-ounce nugget.

"Those old guys didn't miss a hell of a lot," George says.

Enough gold eluded the old timers to keep the Lounsburys interested. Young Carl Burroughs, a bleached-blond Wiseman kid and nephew of Brian Burroughs, races to the rusty metal sluice box as soon as he is released from Clutch's black pickup. Squinting into the sluice box at the metal riffles — designed like ladder rungs to catch gold — Carl reaches his hand inside. He extracts a gold nugget the size of a child's tooth. With springy steps, he presents the prize to George.

"We've got to hire Carl full-time," George says.

"You're kidding me," Clutch says, shaking his head while extending his cupped hand to George.

"I'm not kidding," Carl says. "I know the color."

That a significant amount of gold is sitting in the open air of the Lounsburys' mining operation prompts George to recite a miner's commandment, mainly to keep Carl from exploring unattended sluice boxes.

"If anybody comes around here when you're not here, you just kill them," George says in a calm tone. "It's like somebody coming into your home and stealing from you."

"Uh-huh," Carl nods.

"That's how I feel about it," George continues. "It's not like it's easy work."

George tells Carl to put the nugget in a rusted gold pan. It is time to sift the hillsides of Union Gulch. The Lounsburys' operation is small enough to be operated by one or two people — a front-end loader operator (Tahiti Bob), someone to aim the hydraulic giant (Clutch), and someone to pull rocks out of the sluice box with a rake (three are eligible for this job — George, me, and George's nephew Jason, a tall 15-year-old with baggy jeans who is visiting from Wisconsin).

Years ago, Clutch helped Harry Leonard build the sluice box. From a raven's perspective, the box looks like a large funnel cut lengthwise and laid on the ground. The sluice box, as long as three pickups parked end to end, is wider at the top than Tahiti Bob's loader blade. Forming a trough in the shape of a V, the box tapers to a narrow channel where the gold will settle in metal rungs underlain by green Astroturf. Over the wide end of the sluice box, bars form a rib cage slanted like the roof of a lean-to. The ribs prevent large rocks from entering the sluice box when the loader man dumps a load of soil from above.

With the bucket of the loader, Tahiti Bob bites into the

black hillside of Union Gulch. He raises the load of soil above the cab of his machine, a Case 450 B, school-bus yellow. Like a waiter in a crowded restaurant, he weaves the load toward the sluice box. To his right, Clutch sprays a stream of water from his hydraulic giant — a device that looks like a firehose that swivels like an owl's head — into the mouth of the sluice box. At the tail of the box, George and Jason ready themselves with metal garden rakes attached to long handles crafted from spruce trees.

Tahiti Bob holds the load of moist earth over the ribs of the sluice box. George waves, and Bob tilts the bucket slightly, dropping yards of dirt. Rocks the size of Jane clang off the metal ribs as fine soil floods the sluice box. Clutch aims his stream at the gravel and rock; George and Jason pull rocks through a torrent of muck that spews from the far side of the sluice box. The liquid flows into the first of four holding ponds, terraced pools in varying shades of brown. The ponds keep the muddy water from entering Union Creek. After the water flows slowly from the first pond to the fourth, sediments stirred by the sluicing process fall to the bottom, and clear water can once again join Union Gulch, where Clutch taps it to power the hydraulic giant.

As Tahiti Bob returns to the hillside cut, Clutch calls me over to run the hydraulic giant. I grab the control bar, which projects like the handle of a slot machine. After Bob dumps another load, I direct the fuzzy flood of water at clumps of rapidly dissolving earth. Clutch grabs a rake and pulls the stubborn load into the neck of the sluice box.

Placer, "pleasure" in Spanish, is the type of deposit the

Lounsburys work at Union Gulch. Their father was a hard-rock miner who used dynamite charges to reach veins of gold clinging to quartz and other rock. In placer deposits, the action of the earth through the rising of mountains and hills has liberated gold, which lies where gravity leaves it, usually stream beds.

The gold works its way low, near a solid mass of bedrock. To get to that bedrock, miners need to strip whatever lies on top. Called "overburden," the layers of soil and moss and trees above bedrock vary from inches to hundreds of feet. For deep deposits, floating dredges the size of bus garages were often assembled on rich streams. After the dredges' moving guts sifted through overburden, boulders and rocks would be spit from the back by conveyor belt. Many of the creeks mined by this method decades ago are still lifeless boulder piles. Though the Lounsburys' operation is many magnitudes smaller, they still take earth from a living hillside, transforming it into a dark wound.

The act bothers me. I can't help thinking of the countless tiny creatures whose universe we are destroying in a search for dull yellow rock. Once, after shaking my head at yet another tailings pile near Fairbanks, I checked into the uses of gold for one of my newspaper columns. In the Minerals Yearbook, published by the U.S. Department of the Interior, geologist John Lucas wrote that about 80 percent of the gold mined in the world turns into necklaces and wedding rings. This despite the fact that powdered gold is one of the finest lubricants on the planet, gold isn't affected by magnetic fields, and it's one of the best conductors of electricity. Gold is in almost every computer and telephone, used as a coating for electrical contacts that never corrode. Manufacturers can afford to use gold because they can use such tiny amounts; it's more pliable than Silly Putty. One troy ounce can be pulled into a 50-mile long strand of wire or hammered into a sheet of gold leaf that covers 250 square feet. If all the gold ever extracted on the planet were gathered tomorrow and formed into a block, the cube would be about 60 feet high and 60 feet wide. It's rare enough to that people will move mountains in order to fill a Skippy jar by summer's end. Seems an awful waste to me. I ask the brothers what they feel.

"Having been born in Fairbanks and seeing many years of the mining done around here, it doesn't bother me at all," George says. "You drive out by Chatanika now and everybody's trying to find where these old miners did their work. Except for the tailings piles from the big dredges, a lot of this mining is not recognizable. It's pretty hard to destroy a hillside unless you're really working at it. It'll revegetate unless you're on a one-to-one slope. And you wouldn't be mining a one-to-one slope."

Clutch adds: "Stripping doesn't bother me because I'm going to reclaim it when I'm done. BLM makes you restore the slope before you move on. You have go get in there with a Cat and smooth out the ground to satisfy them. I throw on some grass seed for good measure."

I know if I'd been born on Ester Dome into a mining family, I would agree with George and Clutch. But I wasn't, so I think we're destroying this hillside basically for recreation. Even if we covered up the cut with soil tomorrow, it would take the rest of my life before the native trees and plants returned as they were before Tahiti Bob took bites from the hill. Though I like the brothers, I wonder again why anyone has the right to destroy nature for whatever we humans think is valuable at the time.

But George and Clutch's decision to strip away trees, plants and the countless tiny organisms in the soil is really no different than my decision to take the life of a moose, an act that some people consider horrible. Though I will never be a miner, I'm made of the same stuff as George and Clutch.

We have clogged and cleared the sluice box four times. The riffles are heavy with black, fine mineral.

Clutch ambles to his truck and returns with a spatula almost identical to the one Theresa Mitchell uses to turn burgers. Gently, he scoops the black dirt into a gold pan from the riffles closest to the wide end of the sluice box. With a mound of black in the silver pan, he walks to a washtub full of cold water and douses the pan.

"This is where the money is," Clutch says, dunking the gold pan in the tub.

"That's why we're so rich," George says, laughing.

"I'm not quitting my day job," Clutch says. "Matter of fact, I've got to get this done so I can go to my day job. My boss is going to wonder where in the hell I'm at."

Clutch sits on an overturned five-gallon bucket, reaches into the tub, and retrieves his gold pan. With a practiced motion, Clutch swirls, dumps, swirls and dumps. He repeats the motion for 15 minutes, pausing only to pad mosquitoes away from the pale gap between the back of his jeans and his shirt.

"I never put any mosquito dope on," Clutch says. "They

gotta eat too."

Dumping a brown solution over the edge of the washtub after every swirl, Clutch eventually works the pan until it contains a handful of black sand. That small pile hides the gold, the densest material in the bed of Union Gulch.

"That gold's heavier than anything else in these hills," Clutch says.

Using the water as separator, Clutch makes flecks of gold appear as if by magic. With each whirl, more of the sunny metal appears, like sprinkled parmesan cheese. Enough fine gold to cover Clutch's thumb print. I ask Tahiti Bob to guess how much. Including the nugget Carl found, Bob says about one-third of an ounce. About $100 of gold. In an hour's work.

The brothers don't need to mine. George's retirement from the state and the labor unions keeps him and Bobbi comfortable. Clutch will retire from DOT in a few years and enjoy a nice pension. Still, he dreams of mining full-time. The idea also appeals to George. Why?

"Everybody sort of strives to be their own boss," George says. "In mining, you can come close to it. Mining is some-what like being a farmer farming the land, only a miner is mining the land. It's a grass-roots type of thing where you really feel like you're a part of what you're doing. And you never know what you might find."

"My Dad mined, his dad mined, it's just in my blood," Clutch says. "I suppose if my Dad was a poet, I'd be into poetry."

The sun brightens the tips of sharp mountains as

Tahiti Bob and I drive back to Wiseman, Jane on my lap. We drive through a forest bright with intermittent spots of flame — willow and birch leaves that are the first to turn bright yellow, the first to concede to the coming cold.

The mountains, trees and lingering orange light affect me. "Wow."

"Huh?" Bob asks.

"It's gorgeous."

"It is," Bob nods. "I worked in this area a long time. Lots of times, sitting in that crane, I said 'I'm going to come back to this. I like this.' The beauty of it, all the mountains. Nobody around much. Once those tourists leave here, ain't many people here."

Wiseman is protected from immediate overcrowding by one of Alaska's paradoxes — of the state's 365 million square acres, only one million are privately owned. Surrounded by Bureau of Land Management land, Wiseman is a pocket of 25 private lots and a few Native allotments.

But time means change, even here. A century ago, Eskimos and Indians would follow caribou that migrated along the Koyukuk, only occasionally camping here. With the discovery of gold on Nolan Creek, prospectors stampeded to the area. The towns of Wiseman and Coldfoot were born, and prostitutes ran up bar tabs. In the middle 1970s, the pipeline road was built, followed by the pipeline. George says he is prepared for what the next century might bring to his favorite spot on Earth.

"Things change and you've just got to adapt to it," he says. "You never want to go out and buy a home and property with the thought that nobody's ever going to live across the other hill, because they are. Anybody who complains along those lines is probably better off not living in Alaska. They shouldn't come up here with the thought that this is the wilderness and that's the way it's going to be forever."

In this wilderness called Wiseman, there is one telephone. The phone, I have been told several times, is at someone's house, but anyone can use it. I need to.

George had given me directions to the phone, which is at the Reakoff's log cabin, near the Wiseman airstrip. Jane and I begin our pilgrimage through the night, now chilly as cold air rolls down from the mountains to crash silently into warm air over the Koyukuk.

We walk over Wiseman Creek to reach what the residents call South Wiseman, a cluster of cabins that each look as if the aging logs have a tale to tell. One does. The cabin once belonged to Victor Neck, a man with a secret.

Victor Neck was an athletic man, trim and muscular, with a whitewall haircut of the type required of U.S. Marines. If moviemakers were to make a film of Neck's life, they would cast Ed Harris in the leading role.

A native of Finland, the former Vihtori Niskanen was the only one of six children to leave his home country. When he was 18, Niskanen took a ship across the Atlantic. At Ellis Island, he changed his name and headed north. Victor Neck entered Alaska in 1907.

He first went to the Birch Creek mining district on the Yukon River near Circle City. Discovering no fortune in the heavily staked area, he drifted to the Koyukuk country. Around Wiseman, he found enough open country to set up claims on the Hammond River, Emma Creek and Myrtle Creek.

The country provided the lifestyle Neck was looking for — he built comfortable log cabins on all his claims and he bought one in Wiseman. Black-and-white photos of Neck inside his Myrtle Creek cabin show the lifelong bachelor lounging on his bunk while reading Physical Culture, a fitness magazine. He didn't smoke, and kept himself in excellent shape with pushups and sit-ups. On his walls were pages torn from the magazine depicting women in one-piece bathing suits. An avid photographer, Neck's Wiseman cabin featured the only dark room in the Koyukuk mining district.

The surviving miners of Neck's era remember a man who wanted to be alone; Neck would occasionally travel to Fairbanks, but he soon would return home to the Koyukuk, and he was happy to be away from anything resembling a crowd.

When Neck reached his 60th birthday, he developed an ailment he did not talk to other miners about; they guessed it was cancer. Neck went to Seattle for treatment, then came back to the Koyukuk country to live what he knew were his last days. He returned to his cabin on Myrtle Creek.

As the disease further crippled Neck, his closest neighbor pleaded with him to go to Fairbanks for treatment. Neck would not leave the cabin. A few days later, he stopped eating. Soon after, a visiting miner found Neck's lifeless body on his bunk.

When Neck's cabins were inventoried, searchers discovered, among other supplies, a Zenith radio, six rifles, $10 in cash, and 44 cans of razor clams. A few ounces of gold dust, worth $74 at the time, was found in the cabin in which he died. But the searchers, among them Harry Leonard, knew there was more.

Someone else knew of Neck's secret stashes. Not long after Neck's burial, a person hauled a chain saw to his Myrtle Creek cabin and cut a broad X across the floor. The treasure hunter pulled back on triangles of flooring and searched underneath. Nothing.

The legend of Victor Neck's gold lived on, but Jim Johnson considered it a myth. Johnson, now 74, purchased Victor Neck's South Wiseman cabin in 1958 for $450. The old-timers shook their heads when Johnson told them of his purchase from a younger Wiseman resident. That old cabin was worth $100, tops, they told him. He had been taken, the miners said.

Johnson, quick with a full-dentured smile, lives in Fairbanks these days. In the 1960s and 1970s, he spent as much time as he could at his Wiseman cabin. He enjoyed visiting the old miners, hearing their stories, complimenting their moose roasts and sourdough pancakes. In Wiseman and in small cabins off the Koyukuk, Johnson found riches without ever swinging a pick.

"I never mined. I can't even mind my own business." Johnson laughs. "I loved the lifestyle of the old miners. But I never had the gold fever. The old-timers used to tell me, 'Don't get involved, because more money goes into the ground than ever comes out of it.' For once in my life, I did something sensible."

Johnson kept his cabin tidy. Every Saturday afternoon, he dropped to his hands and knees and washed his wooden plank floor. Over the years, the floor began to sag so badly that all his washwater would run to the center. In 1970, he began replacing the joists, the ribs that support the floor planks.

On the day Johnson started the task, the Rev. Don Nelson paid a visit. Nelson, known as the Flying Minister, would fly his small plane from his home in North Pole to anywhere he thought souls were in need of guidance.

Johnson, glad for the company, greeted the pastor with a warmth customary of those who live alone in the Bush. Because all the furniture was pushed to the front of the room, Nelson pulled up a chair by the door. Johnson told Nelson of his plans to replace the cabin floor joists.

"Why don't you pull up that board over there?" Nelson asked. "It doesn't look like it's nailed in."

For the first time, Johnson noticed the oddity of the two-foot long plank. He caught the edge of the board with his fingernails. Johnson hinged the plank up; it was a motion Victor Neck had performed many times. The gap in the floor allowed Johnson to see a square wooden box. A flattened Blazo can served as a lid. When Johnson tilted the lid, he noticed the box was lined with asbestos paper. It was also empty, except for one corner. There sat a two-quart mason jar.

Johnson needed both hands to lift the mason jar from the box.

"I'll bet there's gold in there," the Reverend said. Though his heart pounded in his ears, Johnson still didn't let himself believe that gold was what made the mason jar so heavy. He thought it might be filled with water.

After he popped the lid, Johnson pulled out a canvas sack. Within the sack was another bag, made of tanned moose hide. Johnson peeked inside and saw what he dared not dream — gold nuggets of various shapes and sizes. Four pounds of gold nuggets.

Breathless, Johnson secured the thong of the moose-hide sack. Nelson congratulated Johnson for the discovery, and both drank their coffee in silence. When Nelson left, he patted Johnson on the back, congratulating him. Johnson closed his cabin door and pondered the significance of his sudden bonanza.

"At the time, I thought I should give Nelson 50 percent of this for sharing in the discovery," Johnson says. "Then I got a hold of myself and said 'No, I'll give him 10 percent because that's what they tithe the church.' Then I got a better hold of myself and didn't give him anything."

After wrestling with his decision to cut Nelson out of the find and wondering whether Victor Neck might have living relatives who would emerge when he cashed in the gold, Johnson decided the best action was to leave the gold in the moosehide pouch.

Though Johnson says he "didn't have 10 cents to my name," he resisted the temptation to trade his gold for dollars. Then began a remarkable period of abstinence — from the 1970 discovery until 1987.

His hesitation was rewarded. In that 17 years, the price of gold climbed from $35 to $450 per ounce. When at last he clunked the bag of gold on the desk of an assayer in Fairbanks, his find, 93 percent pure, weighed exactly 50 ounces. Johnson exchanged the gold for $18,500, a sum he desperately needed to supplement his summers of commercial fishing, firefighting, or whatever work he could find.

Johnson did not forget the flying minister. After he deposited his money in the bank, Johnson wrote Nelson a check for $1,850. Three months later, he received a thank-you letter from Nelson, who had forgotten the day in the Wiseman cabin when he pointed to a floor board with no nails. Johnson eventually ripped up the two other floors in his cabin to see if Victor Neck had designed any other such hiding places.

"I never found any more gold," Johnson says. "But I got two nice new floors out of it. That's worth more than the gold to me."

Walking past the House With the Golden Floor, Jane and I progress toward the phone. The Wiseman Trading Company is a rare two-story structure, a place at which I had hoped to buy some dog food. (Dave Brady, the compound manager at Coldfoot, told me the store was closed just before he gave me some of his pit bull's food.) A note covered in plastic on the door expresses the owners' regret that they were not able to visit with whomever reads the note: *We hope the rest of your vacation is pleasant and peaceful and that you will take time to acknowledge the hand of God in this land. God bless you!*

The tan earth road leads on, past houses made of logs with sheet metal roofs stained brown with the funk of stove pipes. Dogs, tethered in their owner's yards, bark at the sight of Jane, who is on a leash to protect her from wandering onto an aggressive dog's turf. A sign at the entrance to a cabin:

Private. A sign below: *Keep Out.* I'm a stranger whose dog causes other dogs to bark, which causes people to look out their windows. I would love to meet these people, to find out why they live here. But I think of them eating dinner, living their lives without having to pause for every wanderer who discovers Wiseman.

There have been many like me since the road opened. George showed me an Associated Press article, "Civilization Invades Alaska Wilds." Robert W. Weller wrote, in 1974:

The handful of people in Wiseman cherish their simple, wilderness life. But fate has played them a trick. Civilization has followed them to the middle of nowhere, to Wiseman's doorstep.

Now the rumble of giant earth-movers shatters the sleepy quiet. Construction workers, hundreds of them, are carving out a haul road to parallel the trans-Alaska pipeline — the largest private construction project ever undertaken by man, a $5-billion pipeline to carry crude oil from Prudhoe Bay north of here to the Gulf of Alaska.

"It's just like the main drag to Fairbanks," sighs June Reakoff.

From the windows of a log cabin with moose antlers weathering on the outside wall, June Reakoff sees me wandering on her lawn. She walks outside to help. Her house fits the description of the house with the phone.

Jane immediately rushes June, who rubs Jane's ears. Dressed in jeans and a loose turtleneck the color of the Koyukuk, June's hair is as white as the moose antlers hanging on the cabin. She is compact, neat.

She and her husband Rick came to Wiseman in 1967,

when the town was close to ghosting out. "I've seen this place change from when Wiseman was four old-timers and an old Eskimo lady," she says.

The Reakoffs have a son, Jack, who lives in Wiseman, and daughters Missy and Heidi, who also live in Wiseman but work in Coldfoot. June leads me to the phone. Attached to the Reakoff's log cabin is a plywood extension, painted yellow, that contains the Wiseman public phone. The phone sits on a table within an even smaller room that has a chair for comfort and a door for privacy. Notices of public meetings are posted on wood paneling: a typed phone list includes the numbers of all the Dalton Highway DOT stations and Alyeska's pump stations, from 7 to 1.

A tiny metal box on the wall glows with a green light. Next to the box, a sign instructs me that if the light is red, someone inside the Reakoff house is using the phone inside, and I'll have to wait. When the light turns green, the phone line is available. A toggle switch ensures privacy. The note writer requests that people always flip the switch to the up position when finished.

"In 1989, Alascom put the phone in here for people," June says. "We were the only ones in Wiseman with constant generator power at the time. It's really just a courtesy."

I use the phone to call Smits and my parents in New York. While talking, I look out at the Reakoff's freezer, a lawn chair, and stacks of old magazines. When I finish my calls, June returns from inside her house. She has something she wants to show me. She escorts Jane and me to the Kalhabuk Memorial Chapel, Eagle Wings Prayer and Praise Center, a sturdy log structure 20 yards from her home. She restored the cabin and named it for an old Eskimo lady she admired. She encourages all visitors to enter the log church, because she believes this land provides nourishment for the soul.

"Wiseman is a wonderful place," she says. "I feel it's a place where people can come and think about their lives. It's a place to find guidance and healing — even physical healing. A lot of people are in chaos right now. Here, they can go in the chapel and just … think."

"Can I take Jane inside?"

"Please do."

The air is cool inside the chapel, night air. I have 18 chairs to choose from; the obvious choice is a wooden rocking chair. Jane curls on a throw rug.

Moss fills the gaps between the sturdy log walls of the chapel. The sound waves outside — a humming generator, a crowing rooster — don't penetrate the walls. The only noise is from within: The soothing sound of Jane's deep breaths and the bends in my nylon pants as I move back and forth on the rocker.

I think back to the phone call with my father, who said he prays on his rosary every morning, asks God to help us avoid bears. I see the image of Robert Walker as he includes Jane and me in his grace before the meal of pork chops on the homestead. In the silence of the log chapel, I sift through images of people and places of the last 93 days and feel connected to them, as though Jane and I are in their thoughts as they're in mine now. I rock for awhile, fall asleep, then wake an hour later when Jane licks my hand.

22 | **Frozen Hell**

Night 93

On a horizontal pipeline support beam, printed with a crayon of the type used to mark logs, a name is written. I scribble it in my notebook:

Charles Woods, Bronson, Texas was here

Twenty-one years after Charles Woods left his name in Alaska, I found his phone number via the magic of the Internet. When I called his house, Charles answered on the third ring, surprised that his graffiti inspired a phone call two decades later.

"My name is still on that pipe?" he said in an accent that made me want to listen all day. "Well I'll be darned."

Charles was pleased to tell me that the pipeline bought him his first house. The house is in Bronson, a locale he describes as "extreme east Texas." Nested in forest country between Nacogdoches, Texas, and Natchitoches, Louisiana, Bronson peaked in the early 1930s, when the lumber mill burned and was never rebuilt. Today, Bronson, Texas, is a town of one blinking yellow traffic light, one convenience store, and one post office. In that post office, Charles Woods has kept the same box, number 307, his entire life.

From January through May 1976, his mail began to pile up. He couldn't empty his box because he was in Alaska, working as a welder's helper with Pipeliner's Local 798.

Now 46, Woods was a shaggy-haired-24-year old when he wrote his name on a pipeline support beam. Part of a "tie-in crew" that joined sections of pipe at road and river crossings, Woods began his five-month tour in Alaska at Franklin Bluffs camp, on the North Slope less than 100 miles from Prudhoe Bay.

"When I got off the plane there I thought it looked like frozen Hell," Woods said from his cattle ranch in Bronson. "Flat, couldn't see anything but ice. No mountains, no trees, nothing. Was like looking out across the ocean. I wasn't too impressed."

He was, however, stirred by the power of his union, which lobbied for catered meals and trailers to live in rather than canvas tents.

"We were the elite, the 798ers. Whatever we wanted, we got," he said. "We were the ones everybody was kind of jealous of."

Woods remembered the plentiful food, the isolation, and the opportunity for Dumpster divers.

"The waste was incredible," he said. "There were junk yards in every one of those camps. You could go out there and dig around in the snowbank and find anything you'd need — anything from a typewriter to a cutting torch. They had just been thrown out."

Though he and a friend toyed with the idea of coming back to Alaska to prospect the hills for gold, Woods knew it was only a pipe dream.

"It was just too damn cold, it really was," he said. "If you happened for just an instant to take your glove off, touch the pipe, when you pulled your hand back you'd leave some skin on the pipe."

Though his union card has long since lapsed, Woods didn't squander his pipeline wages. Returning home to Bronson, he purchased an old home, abandoned for a decade but still furnished with the previous owner's antique furniture. He lived there five years with his new wife Connie, until they sold the home "at a handsome profit" and moved back (with the furniture) to the farm land on which he grew up.

Woods gave up pipeline work when he found it difficult to bring his wife along on jobs. He went back to Steven F. Austin State University in Nacogdoches and earned his teaching credential. Today, he teaches fifth grade in Hemphill, 20 miles away, and tends to 70 head of beef cattle with help from his son, Brian. Each week day, he drives to Hemphill with Brian, a seventh grader, Charlotte, a high school sophomore, and his wife Connie, who works as a teacher's aide. The Woods talk about their days at school on the drive home. When they arrive at the ranch, Charles experiences what is often his favorite part of the day.

"I enjoy just being here on the farm when I get out of the classroom. It's peaceful and quiet here," he said. "The closest house is my mother's house, probably about 150 yards. Then the next closest house is a half mile up the road."

A few objects in the Woods's ranch house still remind Charles that he once spent five months above the Arctic Circle. He has a picture of himself next to the farthest north white spruce on the pipeline corridor. In his den is a flat piece of steel, about 20 pounds, in the shape of Alaska. With a cutting torch, Woods crafted the half-inch plaque from a section of pipeline. The steel Alaska was in his duffel bag when he boarded a plane in Coldfoot in late May 1976, on the day when he vowed never to return to Alaska, a place that was so different from Bronson, Texas, it could have been another planet.

"I remember leaving on that old rattletrap plane that day," he said. "That old plane was popping and jerking, really scary. It was not safe to fly on that plane. But I was ready to go home. Hell, I would have rode out of there on a buzzard's wing."

23 | **Out in the Sticks**

Night 94

"There's probably only one other family you might run into between here and Prudhoe Bay," George Lounsbury told me in Wiseman. "After the Halls, there's miles and miles of no one."

George encouraged me to stop in on John and Ethel Hall. "They're the farthest north miners in North America," he said. "Maybe the world."

As I walked to Wiseman, a mining claim inspector for BLM told me John and Ethel Hall were different: "They work much of the claim by hand — drift mining, where they tunnel into a hillside, following a pay streak... And it's the tidiest mining camp you've ever seen in your whole life."

The Hall's cabin nods above the horizon as Jane and I bounce through a plateau of tundra. We walk the tough route because I charged up the wrong road. Jane doesn't complain, but the effort to cross spongy tundra causes my legs to burn with lactic acid. Sweaty, tired and self-conscious about dropping in without an invitation, I reach the mining claim of John and Ethel Hall.

Flowing from a mountain pond that would not wet a moose above its knees, the blue line of Linda Creek makes a 90-degree bend here and runs straight for the Koyukuk. In the elbow of the creek is a well-drained bench of tall spruce trees, an airstrip cushioned with foxtails, and four attractive log buildings surrounding the airstrip. The rise on which we stand is surrounded by treeless pyramids of Brooks Range.

The buildings are quiet, but someone's here. Three beach towels hang from a clothes line in front of the main cabin. I lower my pack and lean it against a spruce tree, then release Jane from her pack. I hear voices inside the cabin. With Jane at my feet, I knock at the door.

"Oh, you must be the guy with the dog." A blond woman, about 30, sizes me up and wonders what to do with me. John Hall, tall and frail-looking, appears at the screen door with a smile. He has an allergy to dogs, he explains, or else he would invite Jane and me inside.

John's wife, Ethel, comes out the door to greet Jane and me. She shakes my hand with a powerful grip and offers me a trailer in which to camp for the night. I explain my 94-night-tenting streak; she points to the airstrip. There, I set the tent on silvery heads of foxtail grass.

Three of the Halls' granddaughters—Shelley, Melissa and Jacky Peterson, who met me at the door—are up for a vacation from their homes in or near Portland, Oregon. Also on the Hall claim are James McCarthy, Jacky's boyfriend, and a man known as Chumley, who stays in a guest cabin on the bank of Linda Creek and helps John and Ethel work the mine.

Chumley's parents named him Mike, but he was one of many Mikes in the Fairbanks neighborhood where he grew up. As the nickname began to stick, Chumley made friends with Tom Hall, son of John. That connection, and his ability to repair machinery, led Chumley to the solitude of Linda Creek.

Before I cook dinner, he shows me his cabin on the hill. Like the rest of the mining camp, his temporary home is orderly, inviting. Rainwater, stored in a 55-gallon drum outside, flows from a tap. I fill my water bottle.

Chumley leaves the rubber boots he uses for mining out on the porch. A few days ago, while sluicing, he noticed his right sock was absorbing cold water. He inspected his boot and found two holes at either side of the toe. A bear had visited during the night.

"Picked it up kind of dainty," he says. "Must have been a female." Now patched with shoe-goo, his boots once again repel water.

Chumley stands on the path to his porch and lights a cigarette. He surveys the mountains, lit by cloud-filtered rays of the sun at 11 p.m. The only noise is our voices, quickly absorbed by hillside.

Chumley is 44 years old, a finishing carpenter by trade. For 15 years, he rushed to work, rushed through lunch, worked past quitting time. He wondered if there was perhaps more to life than 14-hour days and the promise of the same tomorrow. He saw his chance for a change with the Halls. He told John and Ethel he was taking a vacation from work. If they wanted some help at Linda Creek, he would give it, in exchange for the pleasure of Ethel's meals and the opportunity to drop out of the rush for awhile.

"Not a lot of people get a chance to do this," he says, inhaling through a cigarette. "I feel very fortunate to be able to do it for a little while."

"What's the best thing about being up here?"

"Peace and quiet."

In the morning, Jane and I crawl from the tent to a hot, sunny day. Though we are two degrees inside the Arctic Circle, today, at 77, is one of the hottest days of the Alaska summer. From the airstrip, I can see the most distinctive Brooks Range peak on the pipeline's path. Sukapak Mountain, the ancient dividing line between the territory of Eskimos from the northern coast and the Interior Indians, protrudes like the tip of a sword from the tundra. When I walk toward it, the full mountain comes into view. It slants, like a 4,000-foot wave frozen in the act of crashing on a beach.

The Brooks Range is full of these mysterious, tilting white mountains. The white is from limestone, the remains of countless sea creatures that lived here when a shallow ocean covered the North Slope about 400 million years ago. When the sea dried up and all those shellfish died, they became part of a chalky mud that hardened into stone. Tectonic movement eventually forced the stone upward. Because limestone is rigid, peaks like Sukakpak teeter at improbable angles. If you blindfolded a geologist and helicoptered him or her to the Brooks Range, he or she would know where they were in seconds. If the limestone's not enough of a clue, the lack of trees and modest elevations (most mountains are 5,000-to-7,000 footers; Mt. Igikpak, 8,750 feet, is the largest) seal the deal.

I retrieve Jane's food from the passenger seat of the Hall's white Dodge pickup, where I put it to keep it away from the dainty bear. As nuggets tumble into her canvas bowl, stalactites of anticipatory saliva form at Jane's jowls. For the next 80 seconds, the snowshoe hares are safe.

Ethel Hall sees me through the window of the cabin. She leans out the screen door and offers me breakfast. I call back.

"I'd love some."

Though his grass is surely the greenest, George Lounsbury's claim of the farthest-north lawn is in doubt. The Halls have trimmed the wild grasses around their cabin to a stubble of green and brown stems. Such a yard would not satisfy the bylaws of an Orlando Homeowner's Association, but here is indeed a lawn. The Hall's cabin is a one-story log structure, rectangular and reddish. Two 55-gallon drums are poised on each side of the cabin, ready to catch runoff from the tin roof and save the Halls a few trips to Linda Creek. The cabin walls, made of spruce logs, are still covered with bark. The moss that was used as chinking — to insulate gaps between the logs — is hidden behind strips of steel flashing, installed to keep the red squirrels from stealing moss to pad their own nests. A bow saw rests on a nail under a ridgepole. Next to the door hangs a sheet of canvas with leather handles attached to both ends, a device to transport logs from wood pile to stove.

Ethel Hall, 65, turns eggs over easy on an immaculate gas stove. A Welbilt. The stove was purchased in the Yukon River village of Beaver by Mamie Boese. Mamie was an

Eskimo woman who was one of Ethel Hall's dearest friends until Mamie died little more than a year ago. Mamie and her husband, Earl, a white bush pilot and miner, built this cabin in the early 1960s. Mamie cut steel gas cans and fashioned them into the metal flashing that keeps the squirrels from the moss. John Hall was Earl Boese's silent partner — providing Boese with a "grubstake," some money to support the mine — until Boese died in 1977. The next year, John and Ethel Hall made Linda Creek their home.

It's a comfortable home. I lean back in a chair at the breakfast table, inhale the scent of bacon, and look around while Ethel cooks. An a.m. radio sits beneath a framework of copper wire, a device that improves the reception of Fairbanks talk radio, broadcast 280 miles away. A .22 rifle for killing squirrels hangs by the door. A refrigerator that keeps things cold by burning propane was carried from Oregon to Linda Creek in the back of the Hall's pickup. It weighs as much as a dairy cow.

"She's there till she dies," Ethel laughs.

Ethel Hall's shoulders, round as grapefruit, look as if they belong on a high school wrestler. Her forearms are ample, her hands powerful, ridged with veins. Her granddaughters like to walk up behind Ethel and clamp their hands on muscles honed by two decades of moving rocks and swirling water in a gold pan. Even Shelley, an athletic blonde, cannot do the things her grandmother does, such as moving a few five-gallon water jugs. Ethel's eyes, gray as slate, show conviction, the type of strength needed to search for gold using rakes and picks.

"It's pretty physical work up here," Ethel says, sliding

eggs from spatula to plate.

Ethel Hall traveled to Alaska with her first husband. They left Portland in 1951 to search for gold. Her husband worked for a gold mining operation just a few miles from where George and Clutch Lounsbury lived.

In 1975, she married her second husband, John Hall. A few years later, they began a life she "enjoys all the time" at Linda Creek.

"I love it here," she says. "I always have. I grew up rural in Oregon — no electric lights, no running water, no indoor plumbing. People say it's primitive up here. But it's not any different than when I was growing up. We don't think it's primitive. We've got propane refrigerators, freezer. Gas stove. We've got nice outhouses. We've got water that's easily available."

Visitors to the Hall claim quickly notice a pleasant contrast to life in cities and towns.

Ethel whispers: "It's quiet, there's no phone. When you know that no one's going to get in contact with you, you relax. The first thing people do is oversleep a few mornings in a row."

The Halls' life here is appealing. After being here less than a day, I feel I could chuck Fairbanks summers and be happy up here. The setting reminds me of what Robert Marshall wrote in Arctic Village:

The inhabitants of the Koyukuk would rather eat beans with liberty, burn candles with independence, and mush dogs with adventure than to have the luxury and the restrictions of the outside world. A person misses many things by living in the isolation of the Koyukuk, but he gains a life filled with an amount of freedom, tolerance, beauty, and contentment such as few human beings are ever fortunate enough to achieve.

The granddaughters are waking. Jacky, the woman who greeted me at the door last night, enters with James McCarthy, her boyfriend, following close behind. In my few minutes in their vicinity last night and this morning, they have been in constant contact with one another — his arm around her shoulder, her hands massaging his neck when he sits.

Two days ago, standing directly beneath the trans-Alaska pipeline, James asked Jacky to close her eyes. Satisfied she was not peeking, He pulled a ring from his camera case, then slid it on Jacky's finger. He asked if she would be his wife. Jacky accepted.

"I wish you could have seen the look on her face when they walked back up here," Ethel says. "She was glowing."

Jacky emits rays of happiness as she kneads James McCarthy's shoulders. She suspected McCarthy might choose this two-week period at Linda Creek to ask her that most important of questions, but her hopes dimmed when she couldn't find the ring.

"I thought there was no way he could pack a ring without me knowing it," she says.

Jacky's engagement ring traveled from Redland, Oregon, to the Arctic Circle in the toe of James McCarthy's right sneaker, hidden by a wad of sock. When McCarthy wanted to wear the sneaker, he transferred the ring box to his camera case until he found the spot.

The spot is a mile from here. Past the gravel strip of the

Dalton Highway is a canyon constructed by Linda Creek just before the stream enters the Koyukuk. After steeling himself to the decision, asking himself for the one-hundredth time if this was what he really wanted to do, McCarthy's heart pounded as if he had just spooked a grizzly.

He took Jacky's hand and led her on a walk to the gulch. When they arrived, he sprawled on the edge of the bank and adjusted his tripod. He set the self-timer on his camera and aimed the lens to the bed of Linda Creek, where Jacky waited for him in excited confusion. She'd anticipated this turn in their relationship since shortly after they met just more than a year ago. She was the coach of a T-ball baseball team. One of the players on that team was five-year old Camden McCarthy, James's son.

With the sun reflecting from Linda Creek, Jacky Peterson accepted the proposal. They hugged each other while hundreds of gallons of crude oil moved south over their heads.

Back at the breakfast table, Jacky's hands disengage from James's deltoids and they sit beside each other at the breakfast table. Here, they share scrambled eggs in bliss, feeling the excitement of a place that will hold special meaning for them for the rest of their lives. The cabin vibrates with their energy.

At ages when many of their peers move to more comfortable climes and more static activities, the Halls engage in drift mining. They began drifting — tunneling for gold rather than stripping the surface — when their pay streak disappeared into a hillside more than a decade ago. Rather than attempt to remove the 100 feet of frozen soil, trees, moss and other plants that covered bedrock, the Halls dug caves into the hillside. With two separate tunnels, the Halls follow the channels of a creek that stopped flowing more than 1,000 years ago.

After carbo-loading Jane with a few blueberry pancakes, Ethel Hall leads Jane and me down a pathway that leads to a plank over Linda Creek. We cross the creek just below its 90-degree bend for the Koyukuk, and arrive at the Halls' mining operation.

On a flat field of bare soil sits a small bulldozer, a metal sluice box, and two sheds built on wooden sled runners. The bulldozer is one of Ethel's favorite tools. She enjoys terracing the settling pond, pushing dirt with the D3 Cat. John, more comfortable with hand tools, is happy his partner enjoys the Cat work.

Shovels and rakes with tines like long fingers stand evenly spaced, like West Point cadets, against the shed. Hoses wound with identical loops are hung on long nails extending from the wall. Three gold pans are stacked face-down, so they won't collect rain. I tell Ethel that the BLM man told me the Halls' was the neatest mining camp he'd ever seen. She nods.

"The girls were laughing, 'Grandma, you put everything in the same place all the time,'" Ethel says. "Yes. I don't want to think about where something is. I know where it is. I don't have to look. I can reach for something and know it's there … John and I are perfectly agreeable. Neither one of us likes junk all over."

From a bin within one of the sheds, Ethel grabs a pair of metal hard hats fitted with lamps and battery packs. She also carries two flashlights.

"There's no light in the adits," she says, referring to the mine entrance.

Through doors of canvas tarp, we disappear into the hillside. Immediately, we reach a door, made of blue foam within a wood frame, that plugs the entrance to the tunnel and blocks the summer air. Ethel grabs the heavy door with both hands and horses it to the side. The cave exhales a blast of winter air as we, Jane included, walk inside. Ethel replaces the door behind us. The world goes black, pierced by skinny beams of light.

With living nostrils, Jane sniffs the musty scents of Pleistocene creatures frozen in the adit walls. As Ethel walks us deeper into the passageway, she shines her flashlight on a thermometer nailed to a wooden post. It's 28 degrees inside, the reason for the insulated door. The Halls are protected by permafrost; the tunnels don't collapse or need timbers for support because the hillside is frozen as fast as concrete. The active layer, the ground near the surface that thaws every summer, is just 18 inches deep.

"It's amazing to me that the trees grow up there," Ethel says. "No wonder they're all stunted and twisted."

The trees are now 90 feet of frozen rock and soil above our heads. As we progress deeper underground, we enter a room dug around a rock the size of a Volkswagen bug. The boulder fell from the ceiling one day, fortunately when the adit was vacant. The Halls named it Chumley's Rock.

The roof of the tunnel, just a foot above our heads, is the world upside down. The ceiling is multi-colored gravels, most the size of a fist or smaller. The image is familiar, but hard to place. After a few minutes, I recognize what I see:

We're walking underneath an ancient stream.

"The gold we get from here assays the same as Gold Creek gold," Ethel says. Gold Creek is the next drainage south, about a mile from Linda Creek. "The geologists say the creek shifted over time."

When the Halls started following a trail of placer gold into the hillside, they made a startling discovery: Deep within the hill they bumped into frames of spruce logs nailed together. The old-timers had been there, digging 100-foot shafts straight down from the top of the hill.

The first miners of the bench between Linda and Gold creeks were named Ace Wilcox and Tom O'Leary. In winter, they built fires to thaw the ground, then heaped piles of paydirt they would sift through in the spring and summer, when the creeks allowed them to flush gravel through their wooden sluice boxes.

"It's an odd thing," John Hall said of the early miners. "A lot of it they cleaned out, but some of the very richest spots we got into were cuts where they had just finished working."

Encouraged by the efforts of their predecessors, the Halls extended their tunnels with tools no more sophisticated than those used 70 years earlier. Using a network of steel pipes to which they attached a homemade sprinkler system, the Halls thawed the tunnel walls with the water of Linda Creek. John Hall, wearing a raincoat, picked at the sluggish ground with hand tools. He removed the paydirt with a wheelbarrow, rolling the earth out the mouth of the mining shaft to the sluice box, then dumping his load and returning for more.

As Ethel walks Jane and me back out to the daylight and warmth that coats us like a down blanket, I realize just how deep the shaft is. One day last year, while pushing a load toward the light, John Hall made a decision.

"I was figuring out the number of feet involved and I thought well, here I'm running over one-tenth of a mile every time I push this wheelbarrow out and back again," he says. "It was time to make a change."

John Hall is skeletal, lithe. He works with the fluidity of a man 50 years younger. He has clear blue eyes and a handshake that could crush rock.

John and Chumley are shoring up the roof of the other adit. Near the insulated door, warm air is reacting with the permafrost, occasionally loosening boulders and pebbles from the ceiling. The echoing thuds inside the cave voice the need for hard hats.

Cutting timbers on a radial saw and then carrying them into the adit for Chumley, John Hall moves with urgency, as if he knows by heart the fleeting nature of an of an arctic summer. Even though he is in excellent health, Hall feels autumn approaching.

"At my age, if I'm going to do something, I'd better do it," he says. "If I postpone it forever, it may be forever. I turned 73 in July, so, let's face it."

Hall's biggest decision of the past two years was to further mechanize the mine. He purchased a "jack-leg drill" to bore holes for dynamite (blasting took the place of thawing); an air compressor (needed to run the drill); and a skid steerer, used to haul dirt (replacing the wheelbarrow). Soon will come the need for a shop to work on the new machinery, and a larger generator to provide constant power rather than the portable unit the Halls now use on occasion.

"It's a big leap into the '90s here with a jack-leg drill and all this machinery," Chumley says, emerging from the adit for a cigarette break.

John adds: "Some of those summers with the wheelbarrow we didn't sluice more than 35 or 40 yards. Of course, we can get that out now in two days with the machinery."

That John Hall resisted the pull of machines for years was not due to lack of capital.

"I felt comfortable with a pick and shovel and a wheelbarrow," he says. "I'm really a 19th century person living in the 20th century, and about to move into the 21st. I'm kind of behind the times in my thinking very often."

Chumley exhales smoke. "But then again, it's pretty easy to fix a wheelbarrow," he says. "We broke a hydraulic line the other day. A trucker friend of mine who just happened to be going up to Prudhoe grabbed one for us in town."

"When you're 280 miles away from your source of supply, it makes it difficult sometimes, as you can well imagine," John says. "Same with Ethel and cooking. She's got to anticipate a whole month of groceries ahead."

John Hall decided to invest in new, complicated equipment because he and Ethel wanted to turn the claim over to someone who would enjoy the work as much as they did. They made an offer to Chumley, Tom Hall, and John's nephew, also named John Hall, three men who were ready for a change in their lives.

"Of course, I have repeatedly explained to them — probably to the point where they get nauseated when I bring it up — that there's a strong element of chance in gold mining," John says. "Pay streaks go along fine, and they give out. You look for them and maybe you find the extension, maybe you don't. There's a considerable element of chance. They know that, and they're all adults, so now they're making their choice."

Chumley, Tom Hall, and young John Hall are all in their mid-40s. All share a dissatisfaction with what they are now doing. John Hall works construction, Tom is a real estate broker. In what Chumley describes as simultaneous mid-life crises, the three men decided to try to support themselves by following the pay streak into the hillside. For Chumley, the decision was based on something that tugs at him.

"The money isn't the overpowering thing," he says. "Being born and raised in Fairbanks, I have this romantic view of mining. That's what built Fairbanks, and it's something I've always wanted to do. If I lived in California, I probably would never have thought about it. But because I've been influenced by the history — I saw the last dredge working around Fairbanks when I was a little kid — I want to mine."

He also wants to live in a place devoid of strip malls, giant chain stores and ringing telephones. "Fairbanks was a lot different place before the pipeline. Now I don't even like it there any more — too much traffic, too much bullshit."

The senior John Hall's word choice and steady cadence would not seem out of place in a university lecture hall. He tried college once, at a state university in Washington.

"I was going to be a forester, but I spent one summer working for the Forest Service and I could see right then that

I probably wasn't cut out for that kind of career. So I went into a liberal arts course. Took some history, some psychology, some philosophy — all very important things for a gold miner, of course."

In World War II, John Hall was a merchant seaman in the South Pacific. When he returned home to Fairbanks, he joined the Teamsters union and drove trucks, hauling furniture and other household goods to and from the two military bases near Fairbanks. As he was driving, he thought of being his own boss, a status mining could provide. When Earl Boese died in 1977, Hall had just retired after 20 years with the Teamsters. As the price of gold had also started to climb, the time was right for a move to Linda Creek. Here, he found what he sought in steady, physical labor and beautiful surroundings.

"Of course, it's not only the work but the lifestyle that goes along with it," John says. "Fairbanks has too much hustle and bustle for me. Though I was born there, and it's my hometown, it's grown too much. It's nice to get away for a half a year at least. Come out in the sticks."

But there is pay in these tunnels. The Halls find gold most frequently within a layer of soil the color of rust. They drift where the orange dirt takes them, hoping to find more nuggets like the one as big as the top third of John's thumb they pulled out a few years back.

"It was just under an ounce, 19 pennyweight," he says. "If we had a bucketful of those, we'd be quite comfortable with it.

"But you have to enjoy the work, too. I was comparing gold mining to putting up sheet rock the other day. Putting up sheet rock is monotonous, repetitious work. About 95 percent of mining is hard, repetitious work. But you could put up sheet rock all your life and there would be no nuggets hidden away anywhere. In a mining camp, looking at it realistically, you know you're not going to find any nuggets as big as your fist, but there's always the possibility it could happen. That's the difference ... Gold surprises you. You can't anticipate it. All of a sudden there it is. You can't explain why at that moment or why on that piece of ground."

Thumps from within the tunnel hasten John and Chumley back to work. They joust with the hot air of the day; the heat is winning. Carrying a timber as tall as himself, John disappears with Chumley into the tunnel.

At the hub of the mining operation, the sluice box, Ethel stands surrounded by a landscape altered by her family and a family before hers; piles of rocks and a brown settling pond interrupt the natural path of Linda Creek. Though the Hall's operation is less obtrusive than most other gold mines, it's still nature strewn about for yellow metal. I wonder if it bothers Ethel.

"There's a few miners out there who probably say 'To hell with everyone else' and just basically rape the land and move on," she says. "But we live in this world. What do they say? You don't want to soil your own nest? We won't leave a mess. We can't."

Ethel invites me back to the cabin for a cup of coffee. We cross the plank over Linda Creek and walk up to the cabin on the bench. The day is hot, dry. Jane pants. High summer in the Arctic.

The Halls will spend 10 months of 1997 here at Linda Creek. They arrived in February and will stay until December. When they leave, they go to a condominium they own in Fairbanks, on the Chena River. Over coffee, Ethel explains why they chose to go back to Fairbanks, John's hometown, for a few months each year.

"There's nothing to do up here when it's cold and dark. Too cold to mine." she says. "The sun goes down here November 24th and it doesn't come over the hill until January 24. After you've spent November, December and January with no direct sunlight, you know why our ancestors were all sun worshipers."

Ethel reaches to a countertop and hands me a plastic spice bottle that formerly held paprika. The container is deceptively heavy, like Victor Neck's mason jar. Tiny chunks of gold fill the bottle to its neck.

But I get a feeling money is not the point at Linda Creek. Rather than exchange for cash one of the best nuggets she ever found in her pan, Ethel wears it on a pendant around her neck. It's the looking for gold that's fulfilling, she explains. The looking, and the wrung-out feeling at night, the cool air amid the mountains, and the scent of moose roast wafting from the cabin at dinner time. In the two decades she and John have been at Linda Creek, the Brooks Range has become her home. Like so many other Alaskans for whom it is true either figuratively or literally, she can never return to where she started.

"All the places I grew up are bedroom communities of Portland now," she says. "It's all gone. All gone ... Alaska is home. It's where I'm comfortable. I'd rather live here than anywhere."

After a minute of quiet broken only by a chickadee's song through the screen door, Jane's bark sounds the arrival of John and Chumley, up from the mine to eat lunch. Ethel fires up the Welbilt to prepare the midday meal. She hums while she cooks. I believe her claim that she enjoys life all the time. I ask John if he does.

"In general I'm optimistic, but there's a tendency as you get a little bit older sometimes to get a little cynical about the way things go," he says, settling at the table. "I don't like the influence of the federal government in our life, which seems to be more and more oppressive to my way of thinking.

"Alaskans, for many years, were neglected by Washington D.C. At the time, people were protesting that. But now, looking back, I think it would be lovely if we were neglected again by Washington D.C."

The federal government affects the Halls every day. By federal decree, the water in Linda Creek downstream of the claim has to have arsenic levels well below those required of drinking water. Because they live on a federal mining claim, they do not own this land. A BLM sign on the road leading to the claim instructs people that they can use the claim to camp so long as they don't disrupt the miners' activities. A BLM inspector occasionally visits the Halls to determine that they are keeping the claim valid by actively mining, not just using the beautiful spot as a home. The Halls do their best to comply with a number of regulations, a strategy John Hall feels is more conducive to peaceful living than showing defiance of the federal government.

"We feel it's better to do the best job we can just to avoid conflict," he says. "There are enough problems in mining without looking for problems from elsewhere."

Like George Lounsbury, the Halls don't fear the inevitable alteration of their way of life. By upgrading their equipment, they have met the future.

"I'm kind of pretty well resigned to change," John says. "I was born in Fairbanks in 1924, and I saw what really changed the country was the coming of World War II. The war changed everything radically. Having seen that change, it would be unreasonable to think it won't happen again in some other way. Look what the pipeline did.

"As I've gotten older I've noticed that there are things going on I don't like but if I think they're an inevitability, I'm not going to get all in an uproar over it. I'm not resigned to everything of course. If there's something I can do — to change what might happen — I'll do it. After a while you realize there are things you can change and things you can't change.

"Nothing ever seems to work out precisely as you anticipate."

24 | The Shangri-La of the Trans-Alaska Pipeline

Day 100

A backbone runs the length of North America, poking through the land more in some places than others, a somewhat continuous ridge known as the Continental Divide. On relief maps of the western U.S., it's easy to see the edge, the theoretical point where a raindrop falls on one side to reach the Pacific while a drop landing a few feet away — barring evaporation, absorption or ingestion — winds up in the Atlantic. The divide follows the Rockies, forming the chin and lips of Montana before tracking north through the nostril on an obvious path along the crest of the Canadian Rockies. The line wanders through the Yukon like a drunk, drifting east to the border of Northwest Territories, stumbling back toward Dawson City, then making a run north for the Arctic Ocean. Before wetting itself in salt water, the divide submits to the final obstacle in its path, an east-west band of treeless mountains known in Alaska as the Brooks Range. After a dramatic turn westward, the Continental Divide follows the Brooks all the way across Alaska to the western coast.

Atigun Pass, at 4,739 feet the highest point in the pipeline's 800 miles, is where my friend James Hopkins, Jane and I crossed the divide yesterday. We camped in a valley known as the Chandalar Shelf the night before. The shelf is where the trees surrendered to the realities of frozen soil and a short growing season; we camped amid naked pyramids of mountain that looked deceptively close until white specks of Dall sheep, zigzagging like ants, gave the proper perspective.

James is from Washington D.C. He's a stockbroker, poet, and world traveler who still looks like the little blond boy he showed me in a picture of himself when he was 12. James is married to my older sister, who lives in Berlin. He will mark their 10th wedding anniversary here in Alaska. It will be their last anniversary, he says. They have lived thousands of miles apart for several years. Mary went to Europe to manage art museums and write while James stayed in the U.S. with frequent trips to Nepal, India, and other places that interest him. Their relationship was hard for their parents to understand, especially when they began dating other people, but they said they loved one another more than they loved any other person. James says Mary is still the first person he calls when anything good or bad happens, and she does the same with him. But the women James dates are not happy to find out he is still married. Mainly because of that, he will ask my sister for a divorce. As we load his pack near the Chandalar River from where he was dropped off, I ask James if the pending divorce makes him sad.

"A little bit," he says. "But I'm not going to lose her, and I'm certainly not going to lose you."

James and I get off to a questionable start. While wading through the upper Chandalar River, numb below the knees, James notices the safety on his pepper spray has fallen off. We backtrack a bit, but soon give up trying to find this tiny piece of orange plastic through a screen of willow leaves.

When we cross a channel of the Chandalar, the inevitable happens. As James bends down to tie his shoe, we hear the sound of a fire extinguisher. The crotch of his nylon pants turns orange, coated with oleoresin capsicum, a derivative of cayenne pepper designed to drop a charging bear by torching the mucous membranes of its eyes.

James quickly strips before the solution penetrates his pants. We wash them in the creek with biodegradable soap, but frigid water and weak suds don't hide the smell. James pulled the pants back on; my eyes water just walking behind him. When we string up the food on the pipeline after dinner, his pants go in the bag.

In the morning, clouds hunker over the mountains. Our path tracks north and disappears upward, into the white ceiling. As we break camp and begin a walk to Atigun Pass, a truck approaches on the pipeline pad. Out steps George Gray, a surveyor I met two days ago. George has just crossed the Continental Divide in his pickup. He has a weather report.

"It's raining like a bastard in the pass," he says. "You're going to have a shitty day."

George is right. James, Jane and I walk a long, shaley ramp up into a cloud. The rain, driven into our backs by the wind, is thorough in its soaking, wetting us through pants, through hair, to the skin.

Though the highest point on the pipeline, Atigun Pass

is far from the steepest ascent, but it's the most eerie. Lifeless rock and fog, fine shale underfoot with nothing green, all gray-black. The only spot of contrast is a patch of white on the mountain near the top of the pass, the remains of a Cessna that didn't make it through the fog.

The pipeline intersects the Dalton Highway on top of the pass. A van is stopped. James asks a man from Boston to take our picture. A white-bearded tourist whose every other word is *fuck* fumbles with the strange camera before finally snapping a photo of us squinting into the rain. As we cross the divide and descend to Alaska's North Slope, I worry about hypothermia.

Our loss of elevation doesn't bring warmth other than that of our burning thigh muscles. At the bottom, we meet the first waterway that drains into the Arctic Ocean, the Atigun River.

The river leads to an unexpected refuge, one that appears like a mirage. In a place where no people live, there's a house. It's green, the color of the shrubby hills that remind me of Ireland, except for the jagged black crags that rise from the hills. We walk to the house, which sits on a circle of gravel several acres in diameter. Stenciled above a door is the word "FIREHOUSE." We are at the only building that remains of what was a good-sized Alaska village 20 years ago — Atigun Camp. A sign once identified Atigun Camp as "Shangri-La of the Trans-Alaska Pipeline."

Atigun Camp was one of 29 towns-in-miniature built in the late 1970s to house the people who built the pipeline, the haul road, and the oil pumping stations. Atigun was one of the smaller camps, with about 300 people constantly in residence during the three years of pipeline construction. If we'd been doing this walk 20 years ago, James and I could have stopped in at the movie theater to watch *Jaws*. We could have dried our clothes and Jane's backpack in the power plant, taken a hot shower in the living quarters, found a room with a bed for Jane. We could have read *The Atigun Times,* "the Farthest North Daily Newspaper." We could have played foosball.

Here was once a community, a place where people ate, slept and worked while they earned the biggest paychecks of their lives. Pauline Rhodes, a woman my mother's age who now lives in Fairbanks, called Atigun Camp home in 1977. She worked here as a security guard during pipeline construction.

Now barren, this place once bustled. Pauline remembers it as one of the most exciting times of her life. "It was like living in a hotel, where you had room service and wonderful food," she said. "It was always clean. You'd be amazed at how nice and clean the camps were."

Pauline worked the night shift here, patrolling the camp in a pickup truck. She carried firecrackers in her pocket for one of her main duties: shooing grizzly bears away from camp.

Across the Dalton Highway used to be a diesel station for truckers, who would stop on their way to and from Prudhoe Bay for fuel and dinner. Twenty years ago, a German fuel pumper who was terrified of bears would call Pauline on the radio when it was time for him to cross the highway and walk a few hundred yards to the dining hall. On one particular evening, as Pauline and the gentleman carried full cups of coffee out to the truck, a large grizzly appeared in front of them.

"We were terrified," Pauline said, "but we knew we had to move very slowly and carefully. We turned around to get back in the barracks, and somebody had taken the door knob off the outside of the door."

The frantic German pried open the door with his fingernails. He and Pauline scrambled inside and slammed the door just as the bear charged.

"We just fell inside," Pauline said. "The bear hit my shoe with his paw just as I got in the door."

The Atigun bears recognized the food truck. They congregated outside the dining hall when they saw the driver backing in. The bears became so attuned to the scent of tuna fish and chocolate they learned to peel a truck like a banana. They'd pull weather stripping from truck windshields, wedge their claws between glass and frame, and lift the glass.

"It just looked so easy for them," Pauline said. "One night they pulled off seven windshields."

The bears became so persistent around food delivery time that Alyeska workers installed an electric fence around the zone where trucks backed up to the dining hall. Pauline said the first bear to get zapped laid right down like a bear skin rug. She tried to roust it by honking the horn of her truck, but the bear wouldn't move.

"We thought we had killed it, and we were scared to death, because that was a big offense to kill a bear," she said. "We got the camp manager up and took him out to see the bear. It disappeared. After that, we didn't have any trouble with the bears. It made me wonder if they could somehow communicate."

Trucks no longer deliver cuts of Nebraska beef to Atigun Camp. There are no ketchup packets, no jars of peanut butter; the garbage dump has long been bulldozed over. All the alluring, imported scents of Atigun have faded. The bears have returned to the hills, back to a monotonous diet of berries and ground squirrels. The young brown bears today have never developed the skill of popping a windshield, though it would not take them long to learn should another Atigun Camp appear, maybe for a gas pipeline or some other project that draws north workers, a few of whom will try to feed sandwiches to bears by hand.

This place will never be what it was before the pipeline — the belching trucks on the nearby Dalton Highway remind me that the road is here to stay — but the pipeline will in theory be pulled when it outlives its usefulness. Jane will not see that day. Because of technology allowing less promising oil fields to be tapped, James and I will likely not see that day.

We view these mountains, this former town, for just a few hours. We scan this field of gravel and the firehouse with eyes that will go dim in just a few decades. Jane's brown eyes already show the clouds of age. Even if she lives five more years, she will die soon. We, as transient as mosquitoes when compared to the mountains that hem us in here, will die a little later.

On the fringes of the gravel pad, in places where people once ate steaks and thought of home, willow shrubs poke their heads through sharp black shale. The plants are creeping from the edges. The natural invasion takes longer here than it would most places on Earth, because this is the Arctic. This place is cold, slow, and raw, but it is alive. The tiny seeds of willows, carried on their own cottony parachutes, land on the naked flatness that was Atigun Camp. Most of the seeds touch down in the wrong position, held above the gravel by the same fluff that allows them to move. They dry out and lose the magic within. Others find a crevice in the compacted soil. After they absorb the rain, a tentacle of root pops from their side. It extends like a drill bit, finding moisture and anchoring a new tree in the gravel pad. If the soil is poisoned with motor oil or another contaminant, it takes a while longer for bacteria to clean up the mess and prepare the site. But the site will be ready for plants eventually. The weeds will win in the end.

Wet and cold, we would surely settle for a room out of the weeds tonight, but there is no refuge in this ghost town. We turn the knobs of three doors on the firehouse, but they are locked. I try a key an Alyeska worker gave me, but it does not work. There is one room, a plywood enclosure, behind a door without a knob. We step inside to get out of the rain and find it cold, with a dirt floor that would muddy our sleeping bags. I go back outside and pitch the tent on the west side of the building so the firehouse blocks the spitting rain.

We return to eat dinner in the shed, leaving the door open in order to have enough light to see. The shed is uncomfortable and dirty, but it has a roof. We leave our packs, food, and wet clothes hanging inside, in a place where they would have been ravaged by brown bears 20 years ago. Those bears are long gone, though, and we sleep peacefully, Jane and I for night number 100, on the far side of the Continental Divide.

25 | To See the World

Day 101

Waking in the morning at Atigun Camp, we get a brief respite from the rain. I rush to break down the tent because it dried overnight and I don't want to carry it wet. James is game through all, smiling and letting me lead.

While we're eating breakfast, the rain starts again. Looking out the door, I see a motorcyclist pass by. He turns his head, waves, then slows down and pulls up to the firehouse.

The cyclist pulls off his helmet, freeing a mop of curly blond hair. His face is round as a dinner plate, and he has striking blue eyes.

"Can I cook my food here?"

Kai Sehoeve, 33, is from Germany. He has not been home in three years. Since 1994, he has split two continents lengthwise with his BMW motorcycle. He started his trip in Tierra Del Fuego, at the southern tip of South America. The northern tip of North America is his destination. He will reach it today.

With Jane wagging in anticipation next to him, Kai removes a plastic box from his motorcycle and brings it inside the shed. He opens the box and takes out a Coleman backpacking stove and a package of Top Ramen. His stove is black with soot. Soon his fingertips are black.

"I use unleaded gas in the stove," he says, trying to corral a wild yellow flame. "It's a bit dirty, but it works. I use the same in my motorcycle."

James asks Kai questions about his trip as Kai cuts up slices of pepperoni and hands them to us. I wonder if he's done the whole trip alone. He says he traveled two months with a friend, and his girlfriend joined him for awhile in South America, riding double on his bike.

I ask him a question everyone asks me.

"Why do you do this?"

"It's a way of life," he says slowly, with careful English. "There are people who have the feeling, when they are a week away from home, that they want to go back home. Other people get back home and they want to go back out, to see the world. This is me."

I bounce another question off him, this one about traveling alone. I have enjoyed being by myself on this trip, even craved it at times, but my warmest moments have been with John, Smits, my brother Drew, friends Harlow and Andy, now James. I used to read about hermits when I was a boy and wondered if I was one. As an adult, I wonder about the old miners, like Victor Neck, who apparently preferred their own company to that of others. After walking this far and discovering what seems to be an innate need to share experiences, I wonder if anyone really prefers to be alone. The man slurping Ramen noodles is qualified to answer.

"Sometimes it's good to be alone, a good experience," he says. "But not too long. I met a lot of travelers who have traveled totally alone for two or three years. It's not so good for the mind. They are a little bit crazy. They are used to being alone, so they are not good with other people."

I've met people like Kai before. As a park ranger on the Yukon River, two out of three floaters drifting by on spruce log rafts were Germans on extended holiday, feeding on adventure while someone else worked their jobs at home. Kai is an electrician. After three years of travel, his job will be there waiting for him if he wants it. He's not so sure if he does right now, just a few hours from meeting his goal of biking the length of the Americas. As he zips up his leather jacket and prepares to mount his bike for the final leg of his journey, he says he wants what a lot of us are sometimes afraid to reach for.

"It's good to change," he says. "To travel alone sometime, but not all the time. Just like when you are at home, it's good not to work every day. You have to change sometimes. It's good for your health."

26 | Sagwon

Day 113

Sagwon is a terrible place to walk a dog.

A clump of dead buildings that used to be a hotel, a mess hall, a generator building, workshops and offices, Sagwon is now musty and sharp, each step littered with broken window glass and upturned nails that threaten to puncture a pad.

Under a gray sky, Jane and I approach an abandoned oil exploration camp and airstrip that lived and died before the pipeline was built. Because the pipeline dips beneath the Sagavanirktok River, Jane and I took an airboat ride with two Alyeska guys to get here. Because the Dalton Highway is two miles away, cut off by the Sag, nobody comes to Sagwon anymore. I envisioned a ghost town, and was looking forward to meeting the ghosts.

As Jane and I walk across tundra reddening with the season, we dodge batteries with the word "CAT" printed in yellow. Fifty-five-gallon drums are scattered everywhere.

The buildings are all one-story, except for a cube of

control tower perched on another structure. All the windows are black, no reflection where glass used to be. My eyes dart from window to window, looking for silhouettes. I feel like someone is looking back.

The closer we get, the more junk we need to sidestep. More batteries, a dead flashlight, lumber pulled from buildings, food cans, beer bottles, wire, shards of window glass. The middle of the compound is a mess. Not only had Sagwon been abandoned, people had come in here and trashed the place. Because few teen-age boys fly Super Cubs, the vandals must have been adults.

I lean my pack against a building with a few rooms filled with scattered trash. A message is stenciled on a door:

QUIET

MEN ASLEEP

DON'T SLAM DOOR

Because my tent is wet, I set it up inside the building on a painted plywood floor. When I raise the tent off the floor by setting the poles on crushed cans, a breeze runs the length of a hallway and begins drying the tent floor. The north wind peels sheet metal from the roof, filling the compound with a rhythmic banging.

Looking down the hallway, with four doorways on each side opening to vacant rooms, I imagine sleeping in the tent here. I picture the ghosts of Sagwon emerging from those rooms as I sleep, walking down the hallway to the tent, my being awakened by Jane's growl ...

No way. I take down the tent, think about the time I'm wasting, and wonder what to do. This is my last night alone on the trip. Smits, in theory, will join me at Pump Station

2 tomorrow. For now, I have no one to share the tent in an abused ghost town that scares me as if I were eight years old. Only one structure — the control tower — is small enough that it doesn't terrify me with irrational thoughts of approaching spirits in the night.

Jane follows me over the garbage-covered floor of a sad building that used to be a terminal, where men and women would await flights home. Someone had cared for this place once. The interior is painted in pastels, green and blue. A wooden mail box: INCOMING, OUTGOING had been crafted with care. In the years since, someone armed with a can of black spray paint blasted a runny streak over the part that said US MAIL. The same person painted SAGWON on a wall, and perhaps contributed to the layer on the floor: torn sheetrock, cans, broken glass and scattered stationary for Interior Airways, Inc.

I walk up the only stairway in Sagwon, to the box of a control tower. It is painted pastel blue, over which a spray paint artist has dated his act to 1975. After Jane follows me up the stairs, I close a trap door and decide this is where we'll spend our night in Sagwon. The control tower is dirty, littered with, among other things, a lone sweat sock and fiberglass insulation, but the trap door makes me feel a bit further removed from the roaming ghosts. I set up the tent on the trap door. We're in for the evening.

I first saw the name Sagwon years ago, on a map of Alaska printed on a placemat at a Chinese restaurant in Fairbanks. The map contained several other non-towns, such as Gordon and Tofty, places that peaked briefly, usually until the easy gold in their hills and streams was mined or its price fell too low to keep people around. Sagwon, once a place but no longer a destination, owes its existence to a different type of gold: North Slope crude.

Before 1964, Sagwon's airstrip, a mile of smooth, crushed rock, was a dry channel of the Sagavanirktok, a braided river that reaches 180 miles into the Brooks Range and flows north to the Arctic Ocean. Pilot Jim Magoffin, flying out of Umiat, a tiny arctic compound to the west and a staging area for geophysical crews in search of oil, was looking for opportunity. His small company, Interior Airways, was struggling at the time. Because the federal government had just opened the North Slope to oil leasing, Magoffin knew the area was going to explode with exploration crews for the oil companies. He took off from Umiat in his Super Cub one day and searched for a place to build a new airport.

Flying over miles and miles of flat tundra, the sun mirrored in hundreds of lakes, Magoffin searched for a place east of Umiat, closer to the hotspots of exploration, a place far enough inland that it would not be often coated by the creeping fog from the coast.

Sixty-five miles due south of Prudhoe Bay, where the largest oil strike would occur four years later, Magoffin bounced to earth on a gravel bar, one of the Saganavirktok's ancient paths that was now above the high-water mark. He knew he had found the place for his airport. He stepped out of the Super Cub, grabbed a hatchet, and began clearing willows and moving rocks.

He flew into the site again and again, each time bringing more tools with which to clear a runway. With each trip, he could bring in more building materials because the improved runway permitted larger aircraft. Soon, he and a friend began framing the buildings that were to become Sagwon.

Magoffin was not overly concerned about to whom the land belonged. He knew it was federal land, a few hundred acres amid millions, and he would establish a base first, worry about the red tape later. This was pre-pipeline Alaska, a time when a person could do pretty much as he or she pleased on federal or state land without worry. They were days when men and women of action could do things without being regulated to death. Those days spawned many Sagwons, some of which later cost taxpayers millions.

Jim Magoffin is now a tanned, healthy-looking man of 81, with a full head of hair, black streaked with white. I met him once, at the float plane pond of Fairbanks International Airport. He was there tending to his Grumman Widgeon, a beautiful blue aircraft that lands like a duck, with its belly in water, but also has wheels for crawling on land. The plane, built during World War II, is entirely navy blue except for a gold Alaska flag painted on the tail.

"I still fly her all over Alaska," Magoffin said. He told me he had logged more than 29,000 hours of flying different aircraft around the world, 22,000 in Alaska. Among them was the initial flight to Sagwon, the flight that inspired him to pour big money into the arctic outpost, a gamble that paid off for Interior Airways.

"We invested more than one-hundred thousand, not including the labor," he said. "But it made millions of bucks for us."

Sagwon began as an airport with the name "Sag One," because the airstrip was the first to be built on the Sagavanirktok. When pilots on approach slurred the two words over the radio, the name evolved to "Sagwon."

Business was booming at Sagwon in the mid-1960s, so much that Magoffin scrambled to buy more and more aircraft, eventually purchasing five C-130 Hercules, planes with bellies large enough to carry a tractor-trailer truck.

As Sagwon peaked, Interior Airways had still not received a lease for the property. "We were just squatting," Magoffin said. "But nobody gave us any trouble. We applied to the federal government for a lease, but it never did come through. We very seldom saw anybody from the state or federal government. Practically everyone who came through worked for the oil companies."

I showed Magoffin some photos I took while at Sagwon, pictures of rusting barrels on tundra, of batteries scattered about, of trash within the buildings. He didn't flinch.

"Here's the sleeping quarters," he said. "Looks like they've kind of suffered a bit. It doesn't look too livable right now."

When the pipeline was being built in the mid-1970s, a biologist for the state Department of Fish and Game visited Sagwon. Congress had passed the Endangered Species Act in 1973, and Sagwon was of interest because of the bluffs that rise from the Sagavanirktok across from the runway, cliffs of the type preferred by peregrine falcons. The falcons, sleek raptors that migrate thousands of miles to nest, were on the endangered list. Pesticides they ingested in their travels caused large numbers of the birds to lay eggs with brittle shells that cracked under the weight of the mother bird. After chemicals such as DDT were banned in the U.S., the birds began to recover, but they were still hurting in the 1970s. The Fish and Game biologist at Sagwon reported in a memo on Feb. 5, 1975:

… (L)ow-flying aircraft (especially Hercules cargo planes) over the falcon aerie apparently resulted in the loss of young through cannibalism by the adults. Cannibalism of young is a common behavioral response of peregrine falcons to disturbance or stress.

In 1985, the Alaska Department of Environmental Conservation sent a few technicians to Sagwon. They counted more than 4,000 metal drums scattered around Sagwon in a shotgun pattern, 2,700 in one pile. They also discovered 20,000 pounds of explosives.

With nothing yet cleaned up 11 years later, passing Alyeska workers saw several muskoxen at the Sagwon compound. The massive, hairy creatures were lined up like pigs to a trough. When the workers walked in later to investigate, they found that the animals had kicked open bags of drilling mud, a compound used to lubricate oil-drilling bits. The muskoxen were using the drilling mud, some of which contained chromium, as a salt lick. Alyeska later dispatched a crew to gather the drilling mud and place it in wooden boxes.

After the discovery of oil near Prudhoe Bay in 1968, Sagwon faded. Seismic crews stayed in the new town of Deadhorse, just a few miles from the action. Though pilots still used Sagwon on occasion, most of the activity moved north. The peregrine falcons were enough to force Alyeska to route the haul road to the west of the bluffs and build Pump Station 2 four-and-one-half miles north rather than at Sagwon, the company's first choice. In the meantime, Magoffin knew Sagwon's time had come and gone.

"We just moved out," he says. "Our good period there was over. We moved out and concentrated on other things. Just like so many other little towns in Alaska, it became a ghost town."

Magoffin says he felt no responsibility to remove the airport from the land on which he squatted.

"It would have been a mistake to take it down because it was a good refuge for pilots in trouble," he says. "And there's been lots of them."

Magoffin retired in 1982. He had already sold the shares in his airline to Alaska International Airways, which became MarkAir. When it became time to clean Sagwon, BLM pointed the finger at MarkAir.

MarkAir, then Alaska International Air, received an airport lease for Sagwon in 1975. The lease required a $25 yearly fee and reports of business conducted on the site. In early 1985, BLM confronted the company by letter for the mess at Sagwon. On January 25, 1985, MarkAir sent a letter to BLM asking to get out of the lease. Six months later, MarkAir vice president for maintenance Chuck Gold denied the charge that MarkAir should pay for cleanup of Sagwon:

"The hazardous materials you note on the premises were not placed there by MarkAir," Gold wrote. "MarkAir had vacated and cleared the premises several years previous and has not returned since. The materials you mentioned as far as we can find out were placed after MarkAir's vacation and therefore not our responsibility."

BLM concluded that the majority of the junk was left at Sagwon from 1964 to 1975, at the time Magoffin's Interior Airways occupied Sagwon, not after MarkAir left. Though Interior Airways was the parent company of MarkAir, MarkAir went bankrupt in 1995. Susan Flora, an environmental scientist with BLM in Fairbanks and BLM's head of the effort to clean up Sagwon, says the agency stopped looking for someone to pay after MarkAir went out of business. She tried for several years to get federal funding to clean up Sagwon, but the site was not a government priority.

"There's no people there at Sagwon, no water wells, no day-care centers; it's really just a big garbage dump," she said. "The federal government was not tremendously concerned.

"When we find a site like Sagwon, we scramble and try to find who's responsible, then try to get them to clean it up," she said. "If we can't find someone, we see if we can find volunteers to clean it up."

Volunteers have stepped forward, Flora said. With a budget of $3 million, British Petroleum, Alyeska and ARCO have agreed to strip everything away from Sagwon by 2000: the drums, the batteries, the buildings, the General Electric record player in the crew quarters, everything.

"They find Sagwon to be a terrible embarrassment, even though they weren't directly involved in it," Flora said.

But they were involved. British Petroleum was one of the first companies sending the oil hunting crews up north. Alyeska is an amalgam of six oil companies, including BP and ARCO, that have all explored from Sagwon. The tainting of Sagwon seems to be attributed most often to the oil exploration crews, faceless, nameless scapegoats that scattered years ago.

At the airport float pond, I asked Magoffin if he felt at all responsible for the shape of Sagwon.

"Not really," he said. "When we were doing business there, we kept a fairly neat camp. That's the way we always did business, and our customers liked that."

His customers were crews of men who felt little responsibility toward the land they were exploring, he said.

"I can see how it happened," Magoffin said. "Because the crews worked out there in the middle of winter, with the wind blowing 30 to 40 knots, at 40 below. They weren't really interested in cleaning things up. They would just empty a barrel and throw it off the side."

Sagwon makes we wonder what gives someone the right to leave a place in such terrible condition. John and Ethel Hall, the miners at Linda Creek, can't leave their place like this. They can't even fog the water with sediment because the federal government will shut down their mom-and-pop operation. Sagwon and places like it are the reason it's so hard for miners and other developers today. Sagwon is an example of get what you can out of a remote piece of Alaska few people will see, then return to a comfortable home, leaving rotting drums to slowly leak their contents into the tundra and the river. Who's to blame? Is it the nice man who sat next to me at the airport float pond, the man who gave me an autographed copy of his book?

In the morning, the ghosts of Sagwon appear, perched on the open window panes of the control tower. Jane and

I look at each other from within the tent when we hear a deep glunk that sounds like a boulder thrown into a river. Through the walls of the tent, I can see the outlines of two ravens, standing side by side, who are perhaps curious to see signs of life in this dormant place.

I step out of the tent in my long underwear and the black birds squawk away, lighting on the remains of the hotel. Looking past the ravens, I'm surprised to see a moose cow and calf stripping willow shrubs in the distance. I didn't think moose ranged this far north. (Magoffin later told me he never saw a moose north of the Brooks Range until 1952, when he saw a cow standing knee-deep in the Arctic Ocean near Demarcation Point.)

My plan to stay dry in the control tower has failed. My nylon pants, the tent, and everything that wasn't inside the tent hold droplets of water deposited by a coastal fog that seeped in through the broken windows.

I take down the tent and walk down the steep staircase to pee and find water for breakfast. Walking outside, I dip my cook pot into a creek surrounded by 55-gallon drums and think about drinking diesel fuel. Back in the control tower, I hear Jane laboring up the steep staircase behind me. As she reaches the top, she tumbles. I listen in horror as her body bounces down the stairs and lands heavily, with the crunching of broken glass.

I fly down the staircase in three steps, pick her up like a fawn, and carry her up the steps in my arms. I lay her on the control tower floor, on her back, and check for cuts as she looks at me with frightened eyes. I run my hands along her legs, watching her face to see if she flinches, listening for a whine or whimper. Nothing is broken or cut.

I want to get out of this place. Nothing is changing the bad feeling I had when we got here. I have visited places that have made me feel good instantly — a friend's cabin in the woods, for example — but this place is bad medicine. Sagwon was created for profit and abandoned soon after. After being deserted, Sagwon was mistreated by men flying in and acting like angry children, smashing windows and breaking furniture just because they knew no one was watching them. The worst of human nature is on display here.

After breakfast, because there is the rare luxury of a chair in the control tower, I write my last newspaper column with the HP 200LX, which still works even though my fingers and toes are stinging with cold. As I type with one hand, I hear a familiar noise — the worrisome, repetitive screech of a peregrine falcon that has summered on Sagwon Bluffs with its mate, perhaps producing a few young. Sagwon Bluffs is once again a peaceful place, not a place where birds are driven to eat their young.

The falcon lifts my mood. Very soon, it will fly with its partner and young to somewhere quite far from here, maybe South America. Thankfully, I, too, am only a visitor in this poor, ghostly place. It's time for my own peregrination.

27 | **End of the Line**

Smits is here to wrap this thing up. She, Jane and I walk over a land with nothing on the horizon but sky, the coastal plain of the Arctic. After we ate breakfast across the river from 500-foot Franklin Bluffs this morning and walked north, the hills vanished. Looking north is standing on a ship in the middle of a green ocean. To the south, the Brooks Range is a set of teeth on an autumn-yellow jawbone of horizon. The map looks like Swiss cheese — a green surface pocked by hundreds of lakes, few of which we can see. The elevation countdown continues — 100 feet at last night's campsite, a gradual drop here, 10 miles farther on, where we are about 70 feet higher than the salt water of the Arctic Ocean.

We walk a gravel path through a tabletop of cotton grass and tussocks. To our left, the rock bed of the Dalton Highway silhouettes trucks against the sky. They look like toys. With just 10 miles to go, we part from the Sagavanirktok River as the pipeline crosses west over the Dalton Highway. I'll miss the Sag. The river provided excellent campsites, easy water, and the unexpected pleasure of a herd of muskoxen that appeared like moving haystacks on Franklin Bluffs as we drank tea this morning.

Away from the river, where we walked on gravel bars for variety, there is no other path than the pipeline pad. Two steps off the gravel and cold water covers the ankles. For the final 10 miles Smits and I will stick close to the pipeline. The rule doesn't apply to Jane, who's in Labrador heaven: lots of puddles, filled with geese and ducks that are sometimes hesitant to fly, even when a brown dog with a backpack swims toward them like a snorting battleship. Jane's flights across the tundra have been a pleasure to watch. She has sent hundreds of barking ptarmigan into the air since we crossed Atigun Pass 20 days ago, probably the first domestic canine to worry these birds. Not many dogs walk up here.

"I have to stop for a minute," Smits says. Unlike me and the other boys I've hiked with, she has to take off her pack to pee.

"Let's stop at that next valve," I say. "It's Lou Gehrig, the iron man of baseball."

The next valve in the buried pipeline is number four, Lou Gehrig's uniform number when he played for the New York Yankees. In counting down the miles, I've also counted down the valves that regulate the flow of oil in the pipeline, starting from valve 125 near Valdez. As the valve numbers got below 50 just north of Coldfoot, I've thought of Yankee players who wore the same number as the valve. My hiking partners have endured descriptions of number 44 Reggie Jackson's three home runs in the World Series, number 17 Mickey Rivers stealing two bases when I went to my first game, number five Joe DiMaggio's 56-game hitting streak. Smits pauses on the tundra as I tell her about the fatal disease that ended Lou Gehrig's consecutive game streak.

"Who's next then?" she asks, walking back to her pack. "Who's number three?"

"Babe Ruth."

When I was just out of the Brooks Range, near Toolik Lake, a pipeline worker named Mike Anderson told me about North Slope weather: "When you get out of these mountains it'll get a bit warmer, but then the wind picks up as you near the coast," he said. "And it never stops. Ten to fifteen miles per hour all day, all night."

Mike Anderson was right. As we near pipeline mile 10, the wind slams into us from the east. We lean into the wind so hard that if it were to stop suddenly, we would fall to the ground. Breathing takes effort; it's like sucking air from a vacuum. As I look for a spot to pitch the tent for the last night, there is nothing to shelter us from the wind — no trees, no shrubs, no mounds of earth. Just tufts of long grass and lakes with whitecaps, flatness and horizon.

As we walk on, the horizon suddenly disappears as fog races in from the ocean. The sun, with us for much of the day, dims to a 15-watt bulb, then disappears. As we walk on, I worry about pitching the tent; I've never put it up in a wind this big, probably about 20 miles per hour. Smits and I have walked 12 miles today, Jane a little more, mostly because there wasn't much worth stopping for.

Finally, I see what I was looking for in the fog — the

orange-and-black marker for pipeline mile 10. Beneath it is an anchor point, where four support posts stand together and the pipeline is bolted down rather than allowed to slide. The posts aren't much of a wind break, but they are all we have.

As I pull the tent from my backpack, Smits points out dark figures in the fog. Three caribou are nosing the ground less than 200 feet away. Because the wind is whipping our scents due west and the caribou are north of us, the animals remain calm, with heads bowed. We stand and watch them for a few minutes. Jane finally spots them and erupts with a few barks. The caribou raise their graceful heads and look at us, then start moving closer, heads up and mouths like the letter O. Even as Jane barks, the animals move closer. Finally they intersect our quickly moving smells, then splash off into the flats with smooth strides, looking regal as they run through sodden humps of vegetation that would make any human cry out in frustration.

"You know caribou means peaceful in Inupiat," Smits says, her tone as soft as a little girl's. "It's kind of fitting that three were here to greet us — one for you, me, and Jane."

And it's fitting to have Smits here, wrapped in a raincoat that serves to block the wind, wearing a winter hat on the last day of August. She was there in the middle, walking with me outside Fairbanks. She was there at the start, 119 days and 790 miles ago. She was there before the trip, helping me plan meals, sort food, pack it into boxes. When the start of the trip neared and I was feeling overwhelmed, she was the one who told me I had plenty of time.

I'm grateful Smits has put up with me. She's one of several partners I've had in Alaska. The relationships lasted from a few weeks to five years. Smits and I have been together two years, while living in different houses. She's endured my moods and my need to be alone sometimes. I've endured hers. When I wrote in a newspaper column that Jane has been with me through "three pickup trucks and seven girlfriends," Smits signed her next trail note "number 7."

Smits and I will always have the memory of these days in the high Arctic, no matter what — walking together, feeling her soft, warm form on my shoulders as I piggyback her across creeks, sharing an encounter with a surprised red fox near its den, her words of wisdom: "When you sit by the river, listen to it flow, and watch the little swirls of foam, you really need nothing else."

Maybe this is as good as it gets for us. I want more, even though I'm afraid to reach for it. I want someone to spend my life with. At least that's the ideal, one I could have had several times if not for an invisible wall in my brain that doesn't allow me to get past a certain stage in a relationship. It's a barrier I'd like to tear down, but it's made of powerful stuff. Maybe, as my father wrote me after I told him about another unhappy ending, "there's nothing wrong with a single, fruitful life."

I remember back to the beginning of the trip. Keystone Canyon, where I walked away from Smits with tears in my eyes, wanting someone permanent in my life, craving for something that was mine. A constant in the unpredictable miles ahead.

Now, I've spent so much time by myself on this trip that I'm less afraid of the Big Alone. I've walked through that gateway of loneliness that pushes basic trainees to propose to their high school sweethearts over the phone. I think I've realized that we're all alone anyway. No matter how close you are to another person, most of the trail is walked solo.

I step on the tent corners while Smits inserts the poles. As soon as the tent becomes a dome, Jane trots inside. Smits follows. Their weight is the only thing keeping the tent stakes in the gravel. The wind is so extreme that sitting outside is not a pleasure. It's 35 degrees; even with all my layers on, I shiver from the chilly knives that cut through my raingear.

I was a good boy on the entire trip, staying true to a regimen of cooking and eating a good distance from the tent. Tonight, with the wind pressing down on the ribs of the tent, I set up the stove just outside the tent's entryway. There, I cook dinner. Jane eats inside the tent, another no-no. When the water boils, Smits and I eat our freeze-dried dinners, the last trail meal, inside nylon walls that have protected me across Alaska. I'm asking for trouble, introducing food smells to the tent, but tonight I would rather face a polar bear than the wind.

After dinner, I go out to hang the food over the pipeline for the last time. As I release my parachute cord and the wind hurls it over the pipeline, three white-fronted geese take off from a nearby lake. They try to fly away, but hang in the wind, frantically beating their wings. They are living kites, and I feel bad for making them spend the energy to escape me. After tomorrow, I won't bug them.

In a week, we'll all be farther south. This place won't allow humans to walk around on the tundra for much longer. With the clothes we're wearing now, if we walked the same path in six months, the cold and wind would kill us.

I wake the next morning holding Smits's hand. She sleeps next to me, only her arm and her head exposed. Last night's wind has become today's gale. The tent pulses with each gust — poles bend and recover, bend and recover. The rainfly, holding up admirably, has come loose in a corner. The nylon claps with each gust, a noise that woke me many times during the night but was not enough to make me leave the cocoon.

I dress in all my gear and leave the warm tent. The wind sucks heat from my body. I quickly recover the food bag, my hands turning to stone despite wool gloves, and dive back inside the tent. It is colder today, on the day we will run out of pipeline. My little thermometer says 33. It is the first of September, the fifth different month I will scribble in my journal while on the trail.

Inside the tent, Smits stirs. Jane rises when she hears the bell on her pack. As I pour Jane's food into her bowl, I hear what sound like rice grains smacking into the tent. The noise is chunky rain that aspires to be snow, driven at 20 miles per hour. It's a good day to stay in the tent, but tomorrow might be worse. Winter is here on top of the world, and I'm impatient to get off this ride. Despite the caribou and the geese, the landscape holds little joy for me. It's the wind's fault. The wind doesn't care how frail we are, it doesn't care that we're just a few miles from accomplishing a summer's goal. It's just out there, waiting to numb us when we collapse our flimsy shelter. Waiting to kick our butts.

It wasn't supposed to be this way. This trip was supposed to get easier every day. Waking up to snow on the tent in the

Chugach Mountains was to toughen me up for the Alaska Range; the Interior mosquitoes were to give me a tolerance for swarming insects down the trail; river crossings were to be easier than the Dietrich, which swept Jane one hundred yards before she found the bank. This was all supposed to be a building process. I thought by this point I would have seen it all — the worst insects, scariest animals, swiftest rivers, wettest feet, worst weather. Nope. The worst weather waits outside the tent.

It's funny how much this trip parallels life when I'm not hiking across Alaska. At the start of a new job or relationship, I crave the time when things settle down. I want to master a routine, get control. I want things to be comfortable and easy. Then I get there, get bored, and start all over again. Hearing the crystals smack into the tent, I remember again that I'll never really get control of anything, that every day has new challenges regardless of what I did yesterday.

Unlike every other day of the trip, everything is done inside the tent this morning: breakfast, Jane's washing of the dishes, the stuffing of sleeping bags. Smits loads her pack inside; I pack mine, and it waits only for the tent. Despite her 120th objection, I strap Jane's pack on. Smits I look at one another.

"You ready?" I ask.

She nods, then smiles, showing the gap between her front teeth. "Let's go."

We exit our warm cave and face the spitting snow. It smacks our faces so hard that we simultaneously turn away. We quickly get to our predetermined tasks: Smits releases the tent poles from front grommets, me from the back.

Packing the wet tent numbs my hands. As I snug the heavy tent inside the top of my pack, I can't wait to get walking. I'm shivering despite wearing all my layers. The wind pelts us with wet snow. With the tent down, there's nowhere to hide. No comfort here. It's time to walk.

The last miles are the hardest ones. The wind is square-on from the north, the direction in which we walk. Watching the scenery is out. Every time I raise my head to look forward, wet snow hits my eyeballs with enough force that I wonder if it's scratching my corneas. Scolded, I continue to look down at gravel that is wet on one side, dry on the other. The rocks are the size of ball bearings, causing our ankles to roll in boots still heavy with yesterday's water.

The ground is turning white, giving the feeling of winter, of the end. The only places that are not white are the troughs of water that cut frequently across the pipeline pad. Some are knee-deep. A few days ago, when there was sun, I stopped at the stream crossings. I took off my boots, put on my Surf-Mocs, and carried my pack and shotgun across. I returned, carried Smits over on my back, then returned once again for her pack. The exercise kept our boots dry, and I liked the feeling of carrying Smits. Today, I don't dare strip down. I know that once I get cold, there's no warming up. Today, we depend on our internal stoves to keep us warm. My stove is telling me not to push it.

We decide to cross the streams in our boots, making wrinkled white feet even wetter. We cross quickly, trying to take the shallowest route, but I can feel the ice water reaching my toes by the second step. For all the discomfort, crossing creeks this way is strangely liberating; during the course of the trip, there were so many moments of agonizing over stream crossings, trying to find a route that wouldn't get my feet wet. I have an irrational phobia of wet feet, avoiding the sensation whenever possible. Here, plowing through water gives a feeling of freedom, a so-what to the internal warning against getting my feet wet. I accept what I can't change. This feeling has been a long time coming.

And this day is different from all the others. Because we can't hear each other over the wind, Smits and I don't talk. Jane, coated with snow and looking like a polar bear cub, marches behind us because that's her only option. She is not having fun today.

The miles tick off slowly. We see the marker for eight, then six. At mile six, a surprise. An Alyeska truck shows up. I walk to the cab and see a man with safety glasses, beyond him a familiar hat, nuclear pink. John smiles from the warmth of the cab.

Rob Merdes, the Alyeska manager of Pump Station 1, is driving. A freelance photographer is sitting next to John. Merdes, unable to hide his alarm, looks at Smits and me. I can see by his eyes that he thinks we're in trouble. If we had to camp here with a wet tent, we probably would be in trouble, but as long as we keep moving I feel OK.

"Want some coffee?" Merdes asks. Smits and I hold Styrofoam cups with wet mittens. John gets out of the truck to join us, squinting as snow pelts his eyes. It's good to see my friend, the man who shared a quarter of these 800 miles. He yells over the wind.

"Alyeska had a big welcoming committee scheduled to fly up and meet you at Pump Station 1 yesterday," he says.

"They canceled because you're so slow."

I'm happy for that. Having Smits and Jane and John here is perfect. John caught a flight up with the photographer. He told Alyeska he was a journalist, going to do a story for the *Fairbanks Daily News-Miner* about the pipeline hiker reaching Prudhoe Bay. John is acting, but says he would really like to write a story.

After we drain our coffee, John and the photographer escape back into the truck. Merdes drives back toward Pump Station 1. An Alyeska worker a few days ago told me a big party was planned, but when he told me who was coming — the higher-ups at Alyeska and other people I don't know — I hoped it wouldn't happen. Some of the same people who were scheduled to be at Prudhoe Bay were the people who did not return my phone calls when I was trying to get permission early in the year. Though the trip has been good press for the pipeline company, that's not why I decided to walk 800 miles.

I'm glad the plane load of Alyeska brass never started toward Prudhoe Bay, but I remember pipeline workers made me happy almost every day of the trip. Guys like Fritz Savoy, a man who looked and sounded like Joe Walsh of the Eagles. Fritz gave me coffee on a cold day near the Sagavanirktok and told me if I needed anything to hike to the highway and tell a passing motorist to get in touch with him; or Garry Chandler, who let me use his office at Pump Station 2 to fax columns back to Fairbanks and allowed Smits and me to dry the tent in an Alyeska building. There were dozens of pleasant encounters with the worker bees of the pipeline. They always had a smile, and always parted with the same question: *Is there anything you need?*

One numb foot after the other. Walking into the spitting snow has become nothing else. Though distracted with thoughts of the end, our hiking gets no easier. The wind will not give up. I find myself looking for the next milepost marker like I do in a marathon for which I haven't trained: I think of distance, miles and feet, making each mile incredibly long.

"This feels like a really tough Equinox," I yell to Smits. The Equinox is a marathon in Fairbanks considered one of the toughest in North America for its 4,000 feet of elevation gain.

"To me it's like yoga," she shouts back, "where the instructor tells us to stretch one muscle as if it's the only thing we'll do all day."

At mile 2, more mental relief. Another pipeline man, Joe Dwyer, a fatherly type with kind brown eyes, is driving. Joe gives the promise of sanctuary.

"We've got a hot shower waiting for you, a place to wash your clothes, and a room for the night, Jane included," he says.

I thank him, feeling new energy, and I pick up the pace. Smits matches me. I look over occasionally and catch the image of her teeth, smiling at me with that endearing gap. Jane trails behind obediently. We have walked without stopping today, another first. Usually, I stop every two miles or so, to pump water, have a snack, give my shoulders and hips a break. Not today. Stopping is no fun. Jane doesn't want to, either. When we pause to pee behind the poor wind-block of a pipeline valve (number one, Billy Martin), Jane whines at the lack of movement. Today is a day to get this over with.

One mile left. Fifty-two-hundred feet to go, four million feet behind. I think back to hiking solo next to the Dietrich River south of Atigun Pass, deciding the clear river and the spears of spruce trees and the naked mountains were the most beautiful images of the trip. But that image won't endure like the three caribou with Smits, Ethel Hall's smile as she pushed a cup of coffee my way, Andy Sterns's shuffle through the mosquitoes, or the taste of unfiltered water from the creek at the Walker homestead.

Pump Station 1 emerges from the fog and wind. From the top of a narrow tower, a flame battles the north wind. Looking ahead, I see the pipeline dip underground at a chain-link fence. A red truck idles at the fence. I see a pink hat inside.

With 10 yards until we reach the big black 0, one more obstacle blocks our path. Creek number 834, about mid-calf and just warmer than ice. Smits splashes through in leather workboots; Jane, seeing the truck and sensing the end, makes short work of it; I walk through slowly, then slap Smits's hand to mark another successful crossing, the last.

We stop walking at mile zero. I pull Smits to me for a kiss, then give Jane a smooch on her forehead, smelling warm, wet dog. John and Joe Dwyer step out of the truck. John gives a hug; Joe shakes my hand and puts the shotgun in the back of the truck. I lift my pack, then Smits's, into the wet bed of the truck. We climb in the pickup, feeling warmth other than body heat for the first time in days.

The end of the line does not bring a sense of

accomplishment. As heat from the truck's fan bakes us, all I feel is relief. To sleep in the saturated tent tonight would have been uncomfortable at best. I'm glad the walk is over, at least for the day, and that I don't have to sleep on the coastal plain tonight.

Alyeska treats us like the pope. John gets his own room, as do Smits and I. Jane is perhaps the first dog ever to overnight with permission inside Pump Station 1.

After we shower and dry some clothes, we attend a gathering inside the dining hall of the personal living quarters. Rob Merdes presents us with a cake. In blue icing: "Congratulations for Making it to the End of the Line Ned and Jane." The director of the Geophysical Institute where I work in Fairbanks, Syun-Ichi Akasofu, somehow made it to Prudhoe Bay through weather that grounded the Alyeska higher ups. He gives me a state of Alaska plaque, cut from the half-inch steel of the pipeline. A few Pump Station 1 workers are at the party. One is Peter Robinson, the father of my friend Harlow, who walked a few days with me.

But the trip isn't over yet. I want to walk from ocean to ocean, and the nearest salt water is eight miles away. I ask Merdes if he thinks it's possible. He calls the big man at British Petroleum, a Scotsman named Frank Musgrave, who grants permission for me to hike the gravel roads of the oil fields to the Arctic Ocean, so long as I have an escort.

The next morning is not snowing but still flat gray and windy. Merdes drives me to milepost zero on the pipeline. There, I kiss Smits, give Jane a pat, and shake John's hand. As planned, they will return to Fairbanks in my truck, which was ferried to Deadhorse by the people at Pump Station 2. I will walk on to the Arctic Ocean alone and make it home by myself when I can, hopefully with a ride from a trucker. As my red truck takes off, I wave goodbye to my hiking companions and begin the final push to the coast.

Though the snow stopped, the cold wind and fog persist as I start the last day. Merdes, my escort through the oil fields, waits for me in his red truck one-half mile away from Pump Station 1. As part of the agreement, Merdes will keep an eye on me; though I know the oil people don't trust me not to run amuck through the oil fields, the official reason for my escort is to protect me from bears. There is a polar bear watch today, and Merdes told me brown bears often hang around a dump site I'll be passing.

Except for my clothes, the last day is a stripped-down version of the walk: No shotgun, half my backpack empty, no tent, no Jane. This is not a dog's place — narrow piles of gravel elevating trucks above wet tundra, metal pipelines everywhere, drill rigs rising like radio towers. Everything is ugly, cold and functional. If people ever live in a space station on Mars, it might be a lot like this.

I have been briefed to stay on the gravel roads, not to take any short cuts across the tundra. With Merdes just out of sight ahead of me as I leave Pump Station 1, I take my first short cut across the tundra, a few dozen wet steps to a small pipeline that leads me to Oxbow Road, where Merdes waits.

As I walk past his truck, he rolls down his window.

"Is everything OK?"

I tell him the first mile was free of bears. I'm now in a highly regulated world, a world of trucks and oil and opulent

Operations Centers serving clams and mussels for dinner. No one besides me is here for recreation, and I wonder even what I'm doing here. If I worked up here, I would be inside today, sealed in one of these buildings away from this wind and bleakness. This is a place totally foreign, uncomfortable, especially to a person on foot. Like everyone else here, I just want to do my business and get out.

Merdes drives ahead to the landfill. I see him stop to idle perhaps a mile ahead, no hills or bumps to hide his truck. As I walk the road, trucks pass. Each driver cranes his neck at the unusual sight of a person walking through the oil field. I remember the sign at the Valdez marine terminal, the one that said walking was prohibited.

With the looks I'm getting here, I might as well be a dairy cow. I wave to each driver; they all wave back. A van stops. A black man with rose-colored safety glasses asks me if I want a ride to the Deadhorse airport. I thank him and say I'm just walking. His brows form a V.

"Walking? Up here? What for?"

I tell him. He smiles.

"Allright then. You finish that walk, man."

Minutes later, another truck stops, an ARCO security truck. A man in a shiny blue uniform and safety glasses so dark I can't see his eyes waves me over. I laugh.

"What am I doing here?" I ask the question for him. As I walk over to explain, the guard's radio squawks:

I've got a report of a man with a backpack on foot, between the borough dumpsite and drill site 15. He's off the roadway on the tundra. Could you go out and check out what he's doing?

I tell Jerry, the guard, what I'm doing and point out

Merdes truck ahead at the landfill. Jerry, chuckling, makes a few radio calls, confirms I am not a terrorist with a bomb in my backpack. He explains the fuss.

"You've got so many different facets up here — BP, ARCO, Alyeska — sometimes the word just doesn't get across. What they're worried about is liability. These trucks up here throw rocks at you, you might get hurt on the oil fields and ARCO's responsible … And we've got a lot of bears up here right now, especially around the dump."

Jerry usually works on the "West Side," from the Kuparuk River Field, but today he decided to patrol the East Side.

"Have you done this before — stopped somebody who was walking or anybody else that seemed threatening?"

"Well, we've had 'em. One guy stole a vehicle out of Deadhorse and took off down the haul road."

After I snap his picture, Jerry diesels off to finish his patrol. I walk until I meet Merdes at the landfill, which has no bears at the moment. Right now, this place seems thoroughly lifeless; I haven't even seen a bird through the grayness.

After hiking seven miles of raised gravel bed, I start down the final path, an access road for a pair of pipelines that sit on a series of T platforms. At the end of the road is the tail of Prudhoe Bay, the Arctic Ocean.

Merdes hangs back, letting me walk the last quarter mile alone. In the final steps, I descend to the sea, finishing a gradual drop from the trip's high point, 4,700 feet at Atigun Pass. Nearing the ocean, I strip off my pack and lean it against a trailer filled with oil spill equipment. I pull on pile pants in the wind shadow of the trailer, preparing to meet the ocean.

Leaving my pack behind, I walk to the southern tip of

Prudhoe Bay, named in 1826 by a British explorer for one of his buddies, Algernon Percy, a naval officer who held the titles of Fourth Duke of Northumberland and First Baron Prudhoe.

My final steps take me ankle-deep into the Arctic Ocean. Froth hisses around my boots. Gentle waves push salt water over my boot laces. I look out to a sea of liquid lead, met by a ceiling of gray. A gull cries, the first wildlife I've seen today. It hangs above me for a few seconds, then flies north toward the open ocean, toward the damp smell of seaweed.

I reach down to the clear water, dunking my gloved hand just above the gravel of the ocean floor. Bringing my wool glove to my mouth, I suck out the water, swish it in my mouth, then swallow. The water is bland, earthy, not like the bitter salt of Port Valdez, which I tasted 120 days ago. The wind blasts mist into my face. I look down at my leather boots, now absorbing saltwater so efficiently that the arches of my feet feel its chill. I look north, at a horizon that leads to sea ice, to the North Pole, then northern Scandinavia. I have gone as far as I can go. There are no more steps to take.

28 | **Going Home**

Deadhorse

I'm wet and cold and more alone than ever before, standing on the side of the Dalton Highway, the strip of gravel that leads home. Home is 450 miles away. My goal is to get a ride to Fairbanks with a trucker, sit at the trucker's table at Coldfoot, see what it's like to drive over half of Alaska in 19 straight hours.

The truckers aren't stopping. Maybe it's my black raingear, worn to cut the wind over my pile pants and jacket. Maybe it's because Jane is no longer with me, having traveled back to Fairbanks with Smits and John. All I know is that the truckers are passing me by. Nineteen of them since I optimistically staked a spot in the gravel at 6:30 a.m. I feel stupid for not returning with Smits, John, and Jane.

There's now no other choice for a ride back to Fairbanks. On September 3, the tourists are long gone, and the rest of the vehicles, pipeline red pickups and state dump trucks and graders, aren't going to Fairbanks.

I stand and wait. I learned to be good at waiting on the hike. Twice, I waited two days for friends along the Dalton Highway. Both times, I forgot the day I'd told them to meet me. So I sat, and read, and wrote columns on the little computer. And wondered where they were, if they had had an accident. With no phone, all I could do was wait, invent reasons why they weren't there. Our 8 p.m. meeting time would come and go, and I would wait. When I got into my sleeping bag, I decided they would come tomorrow. They did.

This wait is less certain. These truckers don't have to give me a ride. Yesterday, I walked to the headquarters of two trucking companies in Deadhorse, told them they might have read about my trip in the newspaper. Both men nodded, then gave me the same answer: *We can't give you a ride because you're not covered by our liability insurance. If a driver wants to pick you up on the highway, that's his business.*

None of the drivers is making me his business. I'm getting pissed when they pass without waving, but it's ridiculous to be mad. I'm asking for a big favor, and I'm asking these men to take a risk. I smile and try to look non-threatening. I drop the smile after the trucks roll by.

Deadhorse is depressing. A clump of metal structures on a manmade island of gravel, surrounded by soggy tundra that would wet you to the knees if you chose to leave the rocks. Everything here — the airstrip, the store, the Prudhoe Bay Hotel — is built strictly for function, to keep men and equipment running on top of the world. Like Dallas Wymore said about the pipeline camps, there's no color here. Even the sky is industrial gray. The only beauty here announces itself with honks — the migrating geese and tundra swans, moving arrows pointing south. I wish I had wings.

Because there are no trees, shrubs or other living obstructions, I can see trucks approaching from a mile away. A truck comes once or twice an hour, speeding my heart rate and prompting me to lean my pack against my legs. When a trucker turns left onto the Dalton Highway, he is 100 yards away. I hike my right arm and smile until I'm passed, when I inhale diesel and listen to the driver work the gears away from the top of Alaska.

I keep track of the trucks with the toe of my boot, pushing rocks into numbers. As I begin to form a "20," something happens that I'm not prepared for. A trucker downshifts, then rolls to a stop.

I run to the truck, grab a chrome handle, yank myself to the door, and open it. A driver I recognize nods at me. He is on the radio, talking with someone from Prudhoe Bay who wants him to come back for a load.

When he finishes his radio call, he tells me the bad news.

"I wasn't stopping for you. I was just stopping because they want me to backhaul some stuff."

I'd met the driver before, when Jane and I walked through Happy Valley, about 80 miles south of Prudhoe Bay. I remember him because he has a lisp, fleshy jowls, and a white moustache that makes him look like a walrus. He asked me at Happy Valley: "What kind of brain damage do you have to have to want to walk up here?" He also said it would be difficult to get a ride from Deadhorse with a trucker. I remember him saying he would give me a ride if he saw me. Does he remember?

"I gotta go back and get a load for the ride south," he says, arcing tiny drops of saliva to his seat. "If you're still here after they load me up, I guess I'll give you a ride."

I dismount and watch him turn his flatbed rig around. It disappears on the horizon toward the oil fields.

Two trucks pass me in the three hours since the walrus departed. The rain has started, making my raingear shiny. I'm getting wet and cold, but I know a ride is coming. I finally hear the whine of a far-off engine.

There it is. I recognize the rig from its exhaust pipes, fluted away from the cab like a swan's head. After he makes the left, the driver slows to a stop. I pump my fist. Yes!

I grab my backpack and step on the running board. As soon as I look at the driver, I know something is wrong. His face is wrinkled like a raisin.

"Is your pack wet?" he asks, spittle flying.

"Yeah, a little bit. Where should I put it?"

Now the raisin has swallowed a lemon. He looks as if he's in extreme pain.

"I'm gonna take a nap on this trip."

"What?"

"I'm gonna take a nap about 100 miles down the road, and I don't like anyone in here when I take a nap. You can't be here on the seats when I'm takin' a nap. And you sure as hell ain't sleepin' in the back with me!"

I stare at his ample belly, his contorted face, shiver at the thought of sharing a bunk.

"You want me to stay outside when you sleep then?"

"I think you better get a ride with someone else." He

334 • Walking my dog, Jane

squints. "I don't like takin' passengers. And those other guys don't want to take you, either. I told you when I saw you before," he gestures with a chubby finger, "you come up here, you take your chances."

I back out of the cab, burning inside. Before I step to the ground, I tell him I understand when I don't. I ask him to spread the word about me needing a ride on his CB when I know he won't. As his rig disappears from view with an empty passenger seat, I wish him engine trouble and severe intestinal cramps.

Now what? Nine p.m., starting to get dark. No trucks will leave during the night; the drivers will nap here. I could spend a night at the Prudhoe Bay Hotel if I had $70. I don't. I sent the tent back with Smits and John. Time to search for a hovel.

Just as I shoulder my pack, a pickup approaches. Out steps a man with a baseball cap and a beard to his Adam's apple.

Joe Reynolds is manager of GBR welding shop, the metal structure nearest to where I've been making numbers out of rocks.

"I've seen you here all day," he says. "Kinda late to be traveling up here."

I tell him my saga. He offers me a spot in the GBR man-camp for the night.

"You're not going to catch any more rides tonight."

I dine on chicken and niblet corn with welders and tire men. Another Joe, from Tennessee, has a pony tail and a skill for repairing large tires. Steve is a welder from Idaho who tells me episodes of his life while chain-smoking Gunsmoke cigarettes, which he purchases on an Indian reservation for six dollars a carton. Steve shows me a room I can use in the man-camp, a series of connected trailers. My mattress is next to the weight room.

Over dinner, I tell the men my tale and they listen with interest. Joe the tire man vows to somehow get me a ride in the morning. His offer is a comfort. Today was not a great day of hitchhiking: 15 hours of standing, making numbers of rocks, throwing rocks at a post, occasionally crossing the road to pee on a ramp of gravel. Twenty-four trucks passed.

But the day was salvaged. Because of the generosity of men I didn't know two hours earlier, I sleep on a bed instead of inside some metal shed.

Joe the tire man comes through the next morning. He walks up to me at my spot with good news.

"I just fixed this guy's trailer axle and patched one of his tires. Put in the good word for you. He said he'll give you a ride. I'll bring him over."

Charles Hartman is the last tourist of the season. I missed him the day before because he was hidden within one of the Deadhorse metal buildings, in the waiting room of Prudhoe Bay Fleet Repair. The patient was his fifth-wheel trailer, a 25-footer he tows with a Ford diesel pickup. The trailer has four wheels and two axles. After Charles hit a large pothole, a bolt broke. The front axle shifted so the two front wheels of the trailer met the road at an angle less than perpendicular. He began dragging the trailer rather than rolling it, which wasn't good for the tread of his trailer tires or his gas mileage.

Now, his trailer is fixed, and Charles is ready to head south.

"Good to meet you," Charles says. He is a tall, slender man, with a full Cherokee nose and a new beard. "If you want to, you can come put your pack in the trailer."

I hesitate for a second. What if the next truck is the one that will bring me to Fairbanks? Nah. I've been at my perch for two hours, my rocks are arranged in a "2," and a cold wind is blowing. I give up on the trucker's table.

I follow Charles to the Ford and trailer, and ask him what brought him to Deadhorse. He started in Los Angeles, driving with his girlfriend Diane. They entered Alaska on the Top of the World Highway, coming from Dawson City. The pair went to Chicken, Tok, Denali National Park, Anchorage and Seward. Then back to Anchorage, where Diane flew back to El Centro, California, and Charles continued alone.

He is 58, recently divorced after 20 years of marriage and 7 years of separation. A mortician, Charles just spent the last year in Japan, working for a funeral service and trying in vain to find greenery. Though nomadic at the moment, he calls Indiana home.

Charles's truck is neat and clean, with a passenger seat scooted back far enough for me to stretch my legs. His trailer is coated with gray mud after a 48-hour drive up a highway that took me 52 days to walk. Many people Charles has talked to in Deadhorse think he's a bit daft for pulling such a large trailer this far north, on a gravel road famous for destroying tires and vibrating wheels out of alignment. I find myself wondering, too; is he adventurous, or a bit loopy? Probably a little of both.

Before starting south, we eat breakfast at the only place in town, the Prudhoe Bay Hotel, a place where the rooms smell like burned tobacco and workers leave their rubber knee boots outside the door. We eat a buffet breakfast that costs $15 each. Charles won't let me pay for his meal. "You can catch me down the road," he says.

We leave Deadhorse without ceremony. As we pass the spot where I stood hitchhiking, I see my rocks, still arranged in a "2." Thinking of the cold wind that penetrated every piece of clothes I had, I tell Charles how much I appreciate his truck.

"Well, I appreciate the company," he says. "It's been a while since I've had a traveling companion."

He tells me that when he dropped off his girlfriend Diane at the Anchorage airport a few weeks ago, she asked if he would miss her. "No" left his lips before he could catch it. She pursed her lips and frowned, making him feel guilty.

"I know exactly how you feel," I tell Charles. "I've had that experience a few times, though I usually say nothing instead of no, and the silence is probably worse."

"Saying no is pretty bad, too," Charles says. "But after thinking about it I'm proud of myself for being honest."

After he told Diane he didn't miss her, Charles spent the next two weeks traveling through Alaska without saying a word to anyone but people to whom he handed money at restaurants and gas stations.

"It's all about my needing to be alone, in the out of doors and away from people," he says. "The year in Japan I was around people 24 hours a day. I could never find a place alone in nature."

On our trips, Charles and I both found places alone in nature. He found his on the drive to Prudhoe Bay, but he picked me up because he'd had his fill of alone time. He wanted somebody to talk to. So did I.

Within 20 miles of Deadhorse, the ride turns into a wildlife safari. I see two living brown balls on the tundra — bears — and point them out to Charles. He pulls over. The barren ground grizzlies trench for ground squirrels without being bothered by an idling diesel truck just 40 yards away. It's fun to see them now, these creatures I avoided on the walk. Though I was a bit disappointed not to see a grizzly on the hike, I imagine Jane next to one of these creatures and shiver.

The miles tick away, a bizarre sensation after moving so slowly the past four months. The countryside is totally different when seen from the seat of a truck — fleeting, odorless, like a movie.

Charles says he's glad to have me along because he misses the animals while dodging potholes. And the animals are here: a pair of muskoxen with horns resembling slicked hair parted in the middle; a bull moose near Pump Station 2, just 60 miles out of Prudhoe Bay; caribou floating across tussocks; the white dots of Dall sheep as we enter the Brooks Range.

Near Toolik Lake, Charles looks at his rear-view mirrors. He checks them again before pulling over.

"I think we've got a little problem," he says, shifting to park.

It's the trailer axles again. Another bolt has given way. This time, the rear axle is cocked so that the right rear tire is six inches back from where it should be. Once again, the Ford is dragging the trailer rather than pulling it.

Charles squints as he estimates we are equidistant from both Deadhorse, to the north, and Coldfoot, to the south. Since he is overfamiliar with Deadhorse, he decides to try to drag the trailer to Coldfoot, even though we'll need to crest Atigun Pass with the increased resistance.

Things get worse. One of the cockeyed trailer tires is expanding at the bottom, a slow leak. I help Charles change the tire. When we're done, he has no more spares for the trailer.

If Charles freaked out now, I wouldn't blame him. Males are genetically programmed to fret about things mechanical on a road trip, especially on a road like this, with the nearest help 150 miles away. But Charles doesn't swear, he doesn't shake his head. He laughs, says, "You get what you get." He drives, pushing in a tape of Art Bell's "Dreamland" given to him by his cousin in Fairbanks.

The crooked axle changes the nature of this drive. Charles creeps along with one eye on the rear-view mirror out his window. On the flattest straightaways, our top speed is 17 miles per hour. We will not make it back to Fairbanks today.

Good. I'm not ready for Fairbanks. I'm not ready to give up this trip, to release this summer. Four months of walking every day. Four million steps across Alaska. Sunny days, rainy days, buggy days, snowy days. Nights of sharing with friends, the bitter smell of sweet-and-sour chicken, tea and chocolate for dessert. Meeting good people from Valdez to Prudhoe Bay, now beyond. Entering their lives for a few moments, taking what they give, maybe giving something back, a diversion if nothing else.

I watch the pipeline's mile markers slowly pass from my seat in Charles' truck. Mile 155, where my brother-in-law James built a rock cairn for the spirits who live in these mountains, where he told me he will always love my sister even though they will divorce. Mile 172, where I saw the headlights of my red Dodge cut through the fog as Smits and John came through late with supplies. Mile 210, where Thelma and Bob Bowser gave me a Diet Coke and Jane a package of orange crackers filled with peanut butter. Mile 270, where John and I ate a grayling while listening to the creek in which it had lived.

Fifteen miles per hour is a good clip for me. Charles allows me to indulge in my memories, smiling when I point out a campsite or talk about a hiking partner.

As we roll slowly back into fall, back into trees with yellow leaves, back to the familiar musk of highbush cranberries, I realize the trip is over — no more walking, sleeping in a different place every night, anticipating the view around the next corner. Like a blast of warm air, a sadness hits me. I stop talking. Charles doesn't force conversation.

As we roll to Sukakpak Mountain, jutting white like a shark fin above the Koyukuk River, Charles pulls over for the night. He shares a meal with me, cooking up chicken patties on the trailer stove. We are just 30 miles from Coldfoot, where the trailer can be fixed. Charles is thankful we've made it this far yanking a trailer that doesn't want to roll.

At dinner, Charles tells me he came to Alaska because he was not ready to go home to Indiana. "My year working in Japan changed me," he says. "I feel like I can't go home until I understand the new person."

Seven years ago, he and his wife separated. He had to leave his home, sleep by himself for the first time in two decades. He avoided people he knew when he'd see them in the grocery store, because he knew they would ask him how his wife was. Then, he'd have to explain again. "It was the dark night of the soul," he says.

The dark night flushed from him anything comfortable — his bed, his home, his habit of working long hours at the funeral home. He searched with manic energy for something to relieve the pain. He tried counseling, support groups, weekend workshops on past-life regression.

"At first, it was one big blob of pain," he says. "Then, I began to sift through my life and identify situations and events that caused me to form my beliefs. These beliefs were formed by a child's brain, one with little understanding."

Now, Charles says, he's a different man.

"A man who accepts, appreciates, forgives, enjoys and loves himself, his body, his sexuality, his height, his weight, his mind, his attitudes and his family, even his ex-wife."

After dinner, I use water from the Koyukuk and my handkerchief to wash the mud from the trailer windows. I'll sleep on the trailer floor, and, after a summer outside, the muddy windows make me claustrophobic. When I finish, I look at the beauty surrounding us — Sukakpak rising to the east, the forest vibrant with orange and yellow leaves, a chill in the air that excites me. I'm returning to my favorite time of year, autumn. For the first time, I look forward to getting back to Fairbanks.

In Coldfoot, we don't get to sit at the trucker's table, but the trailer's axle is once again true, and all the spares hold air. With bellies full of a breakfast for which Charles let me pay, we continue south. The Brooks Range is behind us now, but we still have a long drive to the Yukon River. Long is fine with me. It's a crisp fall day, perfect for reflecting and anticipating the best part of the year in Fairbanks — the season of searching for moose, seeing your breath in the cool air, running the Equinox Marathon.

On the Ford's dashboard are seven dials. One points out the temperature of the transmission. As the Ford creeps up Beaver Slide, a mile-long ramp of gravel, the needle leans far to the right. Charles pulls over to let the transmission cool. I get out and walk away from the truck so I don't have to smell diesel fumes. I pick up baseball-size rocks and pitch them into a patch of willows.

As we wait for the transmission to cool, a big rig approaches from the top of Beaver Slide. The driver is barely moving; he stops right next to Charles' truck.

"Havin' a problem or just sittin' there?" the driver asks. He has a lisp.

"No, just waiting for the transmission to get down to normal temperature," Charles says. "Thanks for stopping."

Charles and the driver chat. I recognize the compassionate trucker as the walrus. He has already driven to Fairbanks and back. I wait for him to recognize me. If he does, he doesn't say anything. Nor do I say anything to him.

As the walrus drives north for what is perhaps the thousandth time, I mention to Charles that the truck driver was the villain who left me hanging in Deadhorse.

"Seemed like a nice guy to me," Charles says.

The transmission at an acceptable temperature, we crawl over a hill. The pipeline comes back into view. It's unavoidable on this road, a road built so the absurdity of a pipe across Alaska could become reality. Seeing the pipeline makes me think of what, if anything, I learned while walking a path that wouldn't appeal to a lot of people.

Travelling light is a good thing. When you carry your home on your back, you realize pretty quick that you can live without things. Of my original list of things to carry, I chucked half of them by the finish. Only a fist-size first aid kit rode for free — everything else I used every day, or it went back to Fairbanks with a hiking partner. Though at times I longed for a new tent, I found out I could be happy watching my dog's tail wag, listening to a friend, eating a nice hot meal at night. I didn't miss music, I didn't miss TV, I didn't miss sex (much), I didn't miss the rush of buying a new canoe. Everything I needed was out there, whether I was with someone or alone with Jane.

And what of the pipe? I began to bond with it. On the edge of wilderness and technology, most nights I enjoyed both. I'd look for a section of above-ground pipe to hang my and Jane's food; I felt satisfied that I didn't have to climb two trees to accomplish the same goal. Though I camped away from the pipe when I could, in many places the gravel pad beneath it was the driest, most level tent site. At times, the pipe provided a sort of security. Unlike nature, the pipeline is logical, understandable, predictable. I love the moose and bears and weasels and beetles, but I'll never understand them.

I felt an attraction to the pipeline, even though I didn't want to. The pipeline often had workers crawling over it, people I was happy to see, if just to say hi and watch them pet my dog. As much as I think Alaska would be better off without the pipeline, I couldn't separate myself from it. Not when my tent is made of oil.

Back on the road, I ask Charles if he'd like a cheeseburger. He agrees, and I look forward to seeing Theresa and Dean of the Hot Spot. When we pull into Five-Mile Camp hours later, the Hot Spot is boarded up for the season. In Theresa's handwriting on the marker board: *Thanks for your support. Please don't vandalize our property!*

Yukon River Ventures, the restaurant on the Yukon, is just five miles up the road. Charles doesn't dally, but we miss the 9 p.m. food service cutoff by 10 minutes. To spend the night, Charles pulls into the same campground in which Jane and I escaped the black bears a month ago. He makes dinner, boiled vegetables, for both of us. I hanker for meat, such as that being pursued by about 70 moose hunters who have left their pickups and boat trailers on the north bank of the Yukon.

After dinner, we walk down to the river, smooth and brown and quiet. Charles and I sit on rocks and watch the river migrate silently toward the Bering Sea, more than 500 miles away.

The farther south we travel, the warmer it becomes and the subtler the oranges and yellows. The foliage was peaking in the southern Brooks Range. By driving south, we get a chance to watch another blaze of color, perhaps in a week.

The air is clean on September 6, with a little bite to remind that winter lurks nearby. We roll down the windows of Charles's Ford as we reach the Elliott Highway. After 450 miles of riding on rocks, we reach smooth asphalt near Wickersham Dome, the boundary of the Fairbanks North Star Borough. We're close.

One more diversion. I ask Charles if he wants to try the best pie he's ever had. He agrees, and we stop at Hilltop, a truck stop just outside Fox. There, Charles eats a mammoth slice of Dutch apple; I devour a wedge of Fatman's. After I finish, I call Smits, ask her if she can pick me up soon. She can.

Charles drives me the few remaining miles to the Fox General Store. On the way, the anxieties and excitement of the near future charge me up. The trip is near done. At the store, Charles fills two tanks with gas while I use my remaining four dollars to buy a *Rolling Stone*. I carried $125 on the trip; thanks to the hospitality of people I met along the way, the money lasted me four months.

When Charles tops off the tank, then pays, our time together is done. He has asked me if I'd like to accompany him on a trip to Mexico this winter, but a fifth-wheel trailer is not the way for me. We swap addresses on scraps of paper, and Charles continues south, where he will stay with his cousins in Fairbanks.

I take the last steps of my journey to the nearby Howling Dog saloon, where Smits will pick me up. I lay my pack by the side of the road, use my sleeping bag for a seat, and flip through Rolling Stone. The sunshine warms my face when I look up from the magazine at the hillside in front of me. The aspens are more gold than green. My eyes lock on a formation of geese, thousands of feet above, maybe the same geese I saw in Prudhoe Bay. Each goose is a pinpoint in an arrow headed south. At this height, they won't stop at Fairbanks. They may not stop until Canada. I hear the faintest of honks. The breeze makes me shiver. Another short summer of life is over.

Printed in the USA
CPSIA information can be obtained
at www.ICGtesting.com
LVHW022038081023
760530LV00001B/20